2.00

- 11

Racing and (E)Racing Language

Racing & (E)Racing Language

Living with the Color of Our Words

Edited by Ellen J. Goldner and Safiya Henderson-Holmes

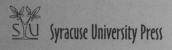

Syracuse University Press

Keith Gilyard. "A Legacy of Healing: Words, African Americans, and Power" is reprinted from *Let's Flip the Script: An African American Discourse on Language, Literature, and Learning* by Keith Gilyard by permission of Wayne State Univ. Press. Copyright © 1996 by Wayne State Univ. Press, Detroit Michigan 48202.

The paper used in this publication meets the minimum requirements of American National Standard for Information Sciences—Permanence of Paper for Printed Library Materials, ANSI Z39.48-1984.

Library of Congress Cataloging-in-Publication Data
Racing and (E)racing language : living with the color of our words / edited by Ellen J. Goldner and Safiya Henderson-Holmes — 1st ed.
    p.   cm.
  Includes bibliographical references and index.
  ISBN 0-8156-2891-9 (alk. paper) — ISBN 0-8156-2892-7 (pbk. : alk. paper)
    1. American literature—Minority authors—History and criticism. 2. English language—Social aspects—United States. 3. United States—Ethnic relations. 4. United States—Race relations. 5. Ethnic relations in literature. 6. Race relations in literature. 7. Ethnic groups in literature. 8. Racism in literature. 9. Racism in language. 10. Race in literature. I. Title: Racing and (e)racing language. II. Goldner, Ellen J. III. Henderson-Holmes, Safiya.
PS153.M56 R3 2001
810.9'920693—dc21

                                       00-047100

To the memory of Safiya Henderson-Holmes, who died as this book went to press, for her passion and labor, which fostered these conversations against racism, and all that might follow from them

Contents

Contents

Illustration. U.S. Government poster during World War II
about Japanese ancestry, 145

Contributors

Juliana Chang is an assistant professor of English at the University of Illinois, Urbana-Champaign. She is the editor of *Quiet Fire: A Historical Anthology of Asian American Poetry, 1892–1970.* She is currently working on a book-length study of Asian American poetry.

Kimberly Rae Connor holds a Ph.D. in religion and literature from the University of Virginia. She is the author of *Conversions and Visions in the Writings of African-American Women* and *Imagining Grace: Liberating Theologies in the Slave Narrative Tradition.* She teaches at St. Mary's College of California.

Kathy Engel was the founding executive director of Madre, a national women's organization working in partnership with women internationally for human rights and equality for women and children. She was cofounder of Riptide Communications, a consulting firm for social justice organizations. She is a cofounder of the Hayground School, a multicultural, progressive alternative school. Her poetry has appeared in the anthologies *And Not Surrender: American Poets on Lebanon* and *The University of Iowa Anthology of Women Writers,* as well as in numerous journals. She is the author of a book of poems, *Banish the Tentative.*

Arthur Flowers is the author of the novels *De Mojo Blues* and *Another Good Loving Blues,* and of a childrens' work, *Cleveland Lee's Beale Street Band.* He teaches M.F.A. fiction at Syracuse University, is a member of NewRen Writers Guild, and is a *babagriot* of the hoodoo way.

Keith Gilyard is a professor of English at Pennsylvania State University. He formerly served as vice president and president of the Black Caucus of the National Council of Teachers of English. He is the author of several books, including *Voices of the Self,* for which he received the American Book Award; *Let's Flip the Script: An African-American Discourse on Language, Literature, and Learning;* and *American Forty: Poems.* He is also the editor of *Spirit and Flame: An Anthology of Contemporary African-American Poetry.*

Ellen J. Goldner is an assistant professor of English at the College of

Staten Island of the City University of New York. She is the author of several articles on the politics of race, gender, and economics in American fiction, which have appeared in *Women's Studies, Arizona Quarterly, MELUS,* and *Studies in American Fiction.*

Kimiko Hahn is the author of five collections of poetry, most recently, *Mosquito and Ant* (W. W. Norton) and *Volatile* (Hanging Loose); *The Unbearable Heart* (Kaya) was awarded an American Book Award and *Earshot* (Hanging Loose) received the Theodore Roethke Memorial Poetry Prize and an Association of Asian American Studies Literature Award. In 1995 she wrote ten portraits of women for the MTV special, "Ain't Nuthin but a She-thing," for which she also recorded the voice-overs. Hahn is a professor in the English Department at Queens College, CUNY, and the mother of two daughters.

Safiya Henderson-Holmes was associate professor of English in poetry and creative writing at Syracuse University. She was the author of *Madness and a Bit of Hope,* which won the Poetry Society of America William Carlos Williams Award. Her poetry has appeared in numerous anthologies and periodicals. She was the recipient of grants from the MacDowell Fellowship for Poetry and the New York Foundation for the Arts Fellowship for Poetry.

Gale Patricia Jackson is an assistant professor on the faculty of the City University of New York. Her poetry and essays have appeared in a number of journals and anthologies, and in the collaborative work *We Stand Our Ground: Three Women Poets.* Her latest publications include *Bridge Suite: Narrative Poems Based on the Lives of African and African American Women in the Early History of These New Black Nations* and *Khoisan Tale of Beginnings and Ends: A South African Story.* She is Storyteller-in-Residence at the Hayground School.

McKay Jenkins is an assistant professor of journalism at the University of Delaware. He is the author of *The South in Black and White: Race, Sex and Literature in the 1940s* and *The White Death,* a book about avalanches, and editor of *The Peter Matthiessen Reader.*

Wendy Motooka is an assistant professor of English at Oberlin College. She is the author of *The Age of Reasons: Quixotism, Sentimentalism, and Political Economy in Eighteenth Century Britain.*

Dominique Parker holds a law degree from New York University. She has published poetry in *The Spirit and Flame: An Anthology of Contemporary*

African-American Poetry. She is currently working on a manuscript for an M.F.A. degree in the creative writing program at Syracuse University.

Ted Wilson is a writer, producer, and promoter. He was an editor with *Pride* magazine and served on the editorial board of *Liberator* magazine. He is the author of a forthcoming book of poems, *Slow Dance.* His work has also appeared in *NOBO: A Journal of African-American Dialogue, Black American Literature Forum, Callaloo, The Black Nation,* and in the anthologies *In Defense of Mumia* and *Black Fire: An Anthology of Afro-American Writing.* In addition, he is a construction contractor and developer currently working on an Arts Development Community in Newark, New Jersey.

Abbreviations

B   *Beloved.* Toni Morrison. New York: Knopf, 1987.

BE   *The Bluest Eye.* Toni Morrison. New York: Washington Square, 1972.

DN   "Dave's Neckliss." Charles W. Chesnutt. In *The Short Fiction of Charles Chesnutt*, edited by Sylvia Lyons Render, 132–41. Washington, D.C.: Howard Univ. Press, 1981.

FCD   *Fifth Chinese Daughter.* Jade Snow Wong. 1950. Reprint. Seattle: Univ. of Washington Press, 1989.

FM   *Fires in the Mirror: Crown Heights, Brooklyn, and Other Identities.* Anna Deavere Smith. New York: Anchor, 1993.

HS   *The Heroic Slave.* Frederick Douglass. In *Three African-American Novels,* edited by William L. Andrews, 23–69. New York: Mentor-Penguin, 1990.

KD   *Killers of the Dream.* Lillian Smith. 1949. Reprint. New York: W. W. Norton, 1961.

LC   *Legends from Camp.* Lawson Fusao Inada. Minneapolis: Coffee House, 1992.

MB   *My Bondage and My Freedom.* Frederick Douglass. Edited by William L. Andrews. Urbana: Univ. of Illinois Press, 1987.

MC   *The Man Who Cried I Am.* John A. Williams. 1967. Reprint. New York: Thunder's Mouth, 1985.

NA   National Archives at College Park (Archives II).

       NA a   511.903/1-2353

       NA b   511.903/3-1753

       NA c   511.903/3-2053

       NA d   511.903/3-2653

       NA e   511.903/4-253

       NA f   511.903/4-853

NL   *Narrative of the Life of Frederick Douglass, an African Slave.* In *The*

Classic Slave Narratives, edited by Henry Louis Gates Jr., 243–331. New York: Mentor-Penguin, 1987.

ON   *Our Nig: or, Sketches from the Life of a Free Black.* Harriet E. Wilson. New York: Random House, 1983.

SF   *Strange Fruit.* Lillian Smith. New York: Reynal and Hitchcock, 1944.

TL   *Twighlight: Los Angeles, 1992.* Anna Deavere Smith. New York: Anchor, 1994.

WB   "Wilshire Bus." Hisaye Yamamoto. 1950. Reprinted in *Seventeen Syllables and Other Stories.* Latham, N.Y.: Kitchen Table, 1988.

Racing and (E)Racing Language

Introduction

Safiya Henderson-Holmes and Ellen J. Goldner

Racing and (E)racing Language is a response to recent calls by Toni Morrison (1992) and others for many and much needed conversations about "race" and racism in the United States. Such conversations comprise an extensive political and cultural project that must be carried out in many locations by participants from many cultural positions. This book grew out of a series of conversations between Safiya Henderson-Holmes—an African American teacher and writer of poetry and fiction—and Ellen Goldner, a European American teacher and literary critic. In editing this volume, we claim to be neither definitive nor comprehensive. Rather, we seek to set our book in the cross-currents of other conversations, written and oral. This project grows out of our *yearning*—in bell hooks's sense of the word, our "longing for insight and strategies for change" (1990, 27)—to stimulate new ways of listening, thinking, and feeling about racism in the United States.

When we began this project, we envisioned it as a book on cross-"racial" dialogue. Yet, as we read, wrote, sifted, and talked about the pieces that comprise the book, our aim grew more complicated. We came to see that in a society that so often avoids naming racism, we had to address the language and the patterns of cultural imagery within which we speak, as well as their histories, as a major part of any early "conversations." We also came to see that our initial topic presumed too simply that dialogue across racialized groups is always what is most needed, when, indeed, there are times when what is most valuable is turning away from such dialogues for a sounding of voices within groups or within persons. As a poet and a literary critic working together, we continually reshaped our own language, sometimes seeing ourselves as engaged in casual conversation, at other times as in serious dialogue, always negotiating the space between mutual support and interrogation. The aim of this book increasingly became the unfolding process of discovering what we need to hear, see, and experience in order to begin conversations about "race" or racism.

We conceive of *Racing and (E)Racing Language* as a language experiment in how a diverse community of peoples and voices might be constructed. This anthology brings together poetry, critical essays on literature and language, personal narrative, dialogue, and political speech in order to address the question of how varied voices might come together in a community that respects cultural differences and acknowledges different positions amid racism and power. We aim to speak to multiple audiences and, in the act of addressing them, to make our book into a gathering space for intersecting communities. We treat the creation of a space of juxtaposed voices as a praxis in the resistance to racism in a collection that takes as its subject matter issues that speak to whether and how we can or cannot meet. In this anthology, the meeting place always also must be a space that breaks hegemony. As it explores the various ways in which multiple communities are at stake amid racism, the volume aims to prompt the emergence of an ever-shifting common ground that subverts the domination of one community by another.

A major premise of the anthology is that we need both to hear and to speak at many levels and in many ways in order to create multiple *kinds* of spaces for voices from a variety of positions. We theorize the space of juxtaposed of voices, genres, and identities, as a charged space—urgent, immediate, and unpredictable—and therefore as a space of radical opportunity for resistance to racism and for coming into relation amid that resistance. We see the intersection amid vernacular language, academic language, poetry, and narrative as the shifting ground where many voices, ethnic groups, and classes exercise different kinds and degrees of influence on one another, providing an opportunity for different communities to come into new relations. We mean for the sheer look of the mixed voices and genres on the pages to provoke an immediate response that throws into relief the terrain of the written word, prompting readers to ask, for example, What defines the borders or margins of an elite academic text? The placement of a dialogue or a poem before an academic essay is meant to invite those readers usually kept outside those borders to enter into the text and into a conversation with it. The juxtaposition is meant to validate the vernacular, to raise it out of its muted position, but also to energize the academic language in the essays with new urgency and audiences so that each voice adds new dimensions to the others. For example: How does reading an angry political poem before or after an academic essay legitimate or delegitimate the anger of the poem? How might a poem draw out the sensibilities in academic writing that infuse its formal interrogation of racism with a more personal one? How does an activist speech help us rethink the relations between academic language and politics? We believe that such questions bear powerfully on the meaning and efficacy of our own interventions in a racialized discourse.

This anthology is indebted to the work of many others over the past decade and a half. We acknowledge a special debt to Henry Louis Gates Jr., whose *"Race," Writing, and Difference* (1986) placed *"race"* in quotation marks, bringing a striking visibility to the discourses that have constituted "race."[1] We draw on the theoretical work of Gates's edited volume, which probes practices of hegemony in Western discourses. We also draw on Toni Morrison's *playing in the dark* (1990) and on the various studies that Morrison's theoretical work has stimulated regarding cultural constructions of "blackness" and their interdependence with constructions of "whiteness." The poems, essays, narratives, and performances in this volume also tap the recognition of the importance of multiplicity in the projects of Donald Pease and many others who have interrogated nationalism.[2] As we negotiate between two currents of language, the disjunctive and the connective, our volume juxtaposes features of Samia Mehrez's description of "radical bilingualism" which brings together in "a new literary space . . . separate systems of signification and different symbolic worlds . . . in a relation of perpetual interference, interdependence and intersignification" to undercut domination (1991, 260), with features of language highlighted in bell hooks and Cornell West's *Breaking Bread* (1991) that bridge groups that have been divided against each other.

Crosscurrents that run through multiple modes of language in *Racing and (E)Racing Language* characterize not only our (the editors') different subject positions and the joinings and disjoinings of language, but also the conceptions of history within which we explore race and racism. This col-

---

1. Following Gates's lead, we dispense with the quotation marks in future uses of *race* and *racial* with the understanding that readers recognize their implied use throughout this anthology.
2. See, for example, Pease 1994.

lection of voices treats the self in its experience of the particular confluences of time, place, and circumstance within a historical moment as the
basis of its major understanding of history at the same time that it underscores questions of access to language: Who tells whose present history?
Who writes or erases whose past? In an important sense, history *is* the
shifting common ground that we, in our differences, inhabit. At the same
time, we believe that power has a stake in repetitions that must be named
before they can be subverted. The unique combination of elements that
comprise an historical moment includes the insertion and replaying of
racialized images and assumptions that carry power because they adapt
themselves to the conditions of the moment. We believe that recognition
of recurring racialized scenarios can contribute to radical opportunities.
The political protest sparked by the 1999 killing of Amadou Diallo in New
York City is a case in point. In response to the killing, diverse communities
in New York City joined in sustained protest against racial oppression and
violence for the first time in years. Because of his particular circumstances
in a particular historical moment, Diallo became a mobilizing symbol of
those who suffer oppression and violence. Perhaps Diallo (a native of
Ghana, not New York) has been cast in the symbolic role of "the foreigner,"
bearing resonance for the many communities in New York whose ranks include recent immigrants or who themselves feel cast in the role of the Other: Hispanic Americans and Asian Americans, as well as African Americans.
At this time, after recent brutality against gays has made national news, European Americans, whose communities overlap with the gay and lesbian
communities, may find themselves at stake in hate killings. We might add
to the causes of the protest the economic gap, highly visible in New York,
between the very wealthy and people of other classes. Yet even as the features of this historical moment converge, the anger that has led people to
protest the police killing of a black man draws on the recognition that similar events have happened before: in this decade, in this century, and in
previous ones. At the beginning of a new century, a historical moment very
different from the beginning of the last century, many people nonetheless
bear in mind the earlier time when so many African American men were
hunted down and killed because people remember (differently and discon-
tinuously) the stories that have been told across that temporal expanse.

   This anthology often dwells on or breaks apart the potent American
color division at the symbolic line of black and white. Our emphasis on

the black/white division grows out of our own experiences as African American and European American women in conversation. Even more, it grows out of the symbolic power that resonates at that dividing line in a nation that first produced its preoccupation with skin color within the institution of slavery. The black/white division is so potent in our national consciousness because slavery required a durable ideology of racial superiority to sustain itself, given its reliance for more than three centuries on a "presence" of the other that continually had to be denied. In this century, the nation first witnessed the refusal of color-ridden domination in the terms of black and white, amid the televised images of black people gathering in mass demonstrations during the Civil Rights movement. The Asian American voices in this volume interrogate the symbolic division between black and white in crucial ways, as they highlight experiences of differently racialized oppressions as well as cultural affiliations and crossings that fracture expected boundaries. Some of the Asian American contributors also bring to this volume critiques of racism and identity formations set within U.S. nationalism; some undercut that nationalism by drawing on international contexts.

Racing and (E)Racing Language begins with a dialogue in which we speak as two women, African American and European American, in order to bring personal experience to bear on some of the more formal essays in the pages that follow. Through the dialogue format, we aim to invite readers to enter into the discussions of this volume and into further discussions they might stimulate. In addition, we hope that our opening dialogue highlights our sense of this book as a work in process in which we find ourselves already within the mesh of race and language that inheres in American culture, as we try to define our own "being-in" that web. We hope that the various kinds of language will light up the many levels of experience at which racism affects all of our lives: from the emotional to the rational, from the unconscious to the conscious, from the personal to the public. If, as we believe, a racialized culture infiltrates our lives, then it is likely to affect us across all of these registers and even at several points along each one. We also hope that the juxtaposition of various kinds of language will pull readers to read, feel, and think about racism differently as each piece resonates through its neighbors or interrogates its neighbors.

We have organized this volume into three sections: "Embodying Struggles," "(Un)Balancing Psyches," and "Contesting Identities." Each section focuses on a site (body, psyche, or group identity) where social constructions of race are powerfully inscribed, resisted, and contested. We have organized this volume along these sites to emphasize how pointedly and how extensively a racializing discourse can intersect with persons, shaping the meanings of the material body, forming and informing the most intimate aspects of the imagination, and entering into a person's relations with others in her cultural group. We have loosely clustered the pieces within each section to give full play to the confluences and tensions among them. Because bodies, psyches, and identities are never clearly separable, the pieces comment on one another across sections as well as within them. The poetry that weaves through the sections—written by Kathy Engel, Kimiko Hahn, Safiya Henderson-Holmes, and Ted Wilson— often highlights the interplay of bodies, psyches, and identities in personal experiences amid a racialized culture. We leave the poems to speak for themselves.

The first section of the volume, "Embodying Struggles," begins with Ellen Goldner's essay, "Allegories of Exposure: *The Heroic Slave* and the Heroic Agonistics of Frederick Douglass." She finds that a subplot of Douglass's novella allegorizes his struggle with the predominantly white audiences he addressed in his early career as a public orator. As Douglass stood before his audiences in the same role as his protagonist—the heroic fugitive from slavery—he was a highly symbolic figure: a free African American man with a newly uncolonized voice and body. Goldner argues that Douglass's novella tracks his Northern white audience's attempts to recolonize his body, as they inscribed upon it a set of racialized images complicit with the interests of slaveholders. In the subplot of *The Heroic Slave* and in the public responses to the 1841 slave revolt on which its main plot is based, Goldner finds the precursors of the postbellum discourse that sanctioned lynchings: images of African American men as thieves involved in acts of "breaking and entering" that are dangerously eroticized. The essay emphasizes the psychological strength required for Douglass's struggle over the meanings of his symbolic body.

Gale Jackson's essay on the songs of African American men who worked on the U.S. railroads in the late nineteenth century inextricably entwines bodies that perform physical labor with voices that perform cultural labor. Jackson's essay turns away from the dominant culture and the meanings it assigned to the bodies of black men. The worksongs become sites of powerful resistance because they bespeak a living and adaptive African American culture that produces its own many-sided meanings for and in the singers' labor. Jackson explores worksongs that improvise, (un)weave, and (re)weave their significance: out of threads of African culture and threads of Western culture; out of the disjunctions of the African diaspora and the mobility that attended slavery; and also out of a bone-deep awareness of the participation of African American labor in U.S. history.

Unlike the two essays that precede it, Kathy Engel's speech—given at the International Women's Day Conference in Buffalo in March 1993—does not seek links between present and past, but rather aims at a possible future. It focuses not on the experiences of men, but on the experiences of women. Perhaps the obvious place for Engel's speech would be in the section on identities in that she sets herself, as a white woman and feminist, in the position of speaking primarily to other white women about racism in the hope of unravelling racialized identities, and enabling a common feminist struggle. We have, however, placed her speech in the section on embodying struggles to call attention to her particular mode of feminist embodiment. Hers is an activist, feminist body that conducts its struggle against racism in part by defying patriarchal divisions between language and body and between the active and the passive. Engel merges thought with action, action with speech, and speaking with listening. For her, self-critical thought is political action; political speech is charged with intense desire; and speaking is contingent on the receptive posture of listening, which is itself an important political action. For Engel, language that becomes action and action that becomes language together provide the fluid medium that might enable the interconnections she seeks with other women across racialized, nationalized, and class-ified boundaries.

The essays in the second section, "(Un)Balancing Psyches," highlight the complex psychological processes and psychological pain that racism inflicts. Two of the essays suggest strategies to heal the pain. In "Metaphors of Race and Psychological Damage in the 1940s American South: The Writings of Lillian Smith," McKay Jenkins writes about Smith's *Strange Fruit* and *Killers of the Dream*. Jenkins illuminates in Smith's fiction the patterns of psychosexual development that produce patriarchal white supremacy. He adapts to relations between whites and blacks a Lacanian model of man's relation to woman as Other—as lack and as loss—through which man produces the myth of his own stable identity. Jenkins finds that for the elite white male, as Smith draws him, sexuality and physical joy are demonized and displaced under the requirement for self-mastery and then projected outward onto black characters. Smith's fiction, Jenkins argues, shows how such projections produce psychological damage to both blacks and whites because the elite white male's desire and his battle for control over it are played out on black men, on black and white women, and on children of both races. Jenkins stresses that, for Smith, the white man suffers spiritual damage as he shuts out his humanity in the struggle.

Jenkins's essay takes up, from another vantage point and at another time, some of the same features of racism raised in Goldner's essay. Both essays highlight the binary racial divide by which the United States so often identifies itself. Juliana Chang's essay, "Time, Jazz and the Racial Subject: Lawson Inada's Jazz Poetics," responds to and revises the binary description of American race relations. Chang finds that Inada's affiliation with African American jazz musicians forces us to rethink the meaning of American in "Asian American" culture.

Chang posits that jazz, with its syncopations or breaks in time, provides an alternative to standard national historical time, as well as an alternative code of legitimation by which racially subordinated subjects within the United States can form networks of affiliation with one another. Chang finds that in *Legends from Camp* Inada employs the syncopation and repetition of jazz in order to restage and redefine the traumatic displacements, disjunctions, and modes of marginalization that internment imposed on Japanese Americans during World War II. She finds that Inada draws on the African American tradition of call and response, both between performer and audience and between poet and his jazz musician predecessors, to enable speech in place of the unspeakable—the silence that the trauma of internment otherwise would impose at the intersection of nationalist politics and the psyche. Chang raises the question of whether Inada appropriates African American culture and finds that he avoids appropriation in a mode of affiliation that acknowledges and honors the centrality of African American culture for his poetry, even as he retains the difference of his own subject position.

With Kimberly Connor's essay, "Negotiating the Differences: Anna Deavere Smith and Liberation Theater," the volume returns to a black/white division, but with a difference. Connor discusses *Fires in the Mirror,*

Smith's dramatization of the 1991 conflict in the Crown Heights section of Brooklyn between African Americans and Hasidic Jewish Americans, whose customs and clothing mark them as dissimilar from most American whites. Connor describes Smith's intervention in the conflict at the intersection of the multiple differences. A major intersection for Smith is that of the theater and the psyche, with psyches in conflict at many levels: within individuals, within and between communities, and within the nation. She articulates the strategies of Smith's theater, in which the playwright interviews people on all sides of the controversy and, in a one-woman show, takes on their roles, and repeats their words. Connor identifies a provocative tension in Smith's method that aims to undermine racism doubly. Smith situates conflict in the specific words and embodied stances of many participants, undercutting the simplistic terms of opposed camps. Yet, at the same time, she desituates the conflict by placing it in the liminal space of the theater, where images and narratives about race and ethnicity—both conscious and unconscious—can be seen, heard, and examined.

The third section of the book, "Contesting Identities," presents a set of differing views on the ways historical, cultural, and racialized aspects of identity interact, and on how and where racist inscriptions on the identities of groups and persons can be revised. In "A Legacy of Healing: Words, African Americans, and Power," Keith Gilyard underscores the commonalities among different voices in African American culture in order to provide a coherent "counterstory" to the American master narrative of black racial inferiority. Gilyard's strategy consists of honoring differences and then gathering them together. He discusses the value of the African American oral tradition from rumor to rap; he honors the literary tradition from Harriet Wilson through Chesnutt, Morrison, and others, and then loosely ties together the two strands of tradition. He then adds to these strands a parallel thread in the continuous history of the African American struggle for literacy. Gilyard ends his essay with a practical discussion of language instruction in the public schools, where he calls for a respect for language diversity among African American students and a varied action agenda in the classroom, both in the service of the counterstory that values the expression of black voices.

In "'Nothing Solid': Racial Identity and Identification in *Fifth Chinese Daughter* and 'Wilshire Bus,'" Wendy Motooka works to break apart coherent narratives, dismantling both racialized stories that would define identity and coherent counterstories to them. Motooka situates Wong's novel and Yamamoto's story in the historical context of American cultural/political narratives about Chinese and Japanese identities, as well as Chinese American and Japanese American identities, during and after World War II. She places the fiction within a network of essentializing racist narratives, including those that appeared in *Time* and *Life* magazines in the early 1940s. For Motooka, racialized identities are produced and adapted in the interests of the dominant culture through a complex interplay between binary categories (us/them) and fluid features of definition that accommodate the changing needs of the dominant culture. Hence, the essentialized identities assigned to different racial groups acquire their meanings only within specific historical contexts. Motooka carefully tracks the details and relations of shifting identities, both to contextualize them and to trace the ways that essentialized categories infiltrate Asian American narratives, and to suggest that authors may use such categories to enable or disable critical responses.

Arthur Flowers's "Literary Blues and the Sacred Text" works with shifting identities differently from Motooka and gathers them differently from Gilyard. His essay is a creative meditation on the powers of a blues-based tradition in African American writing. Flowers dramatizes the shifting voices within African American cultural identity in a call and response with other blues-based writers. Stressing transformation in work set at the crossroads (at once literate and vernacular) he finds the sacred functions of blues-based literature in its care for the "tribal soul," as it invokes powers for healing and transformation that link cultural memory to the prospect of a vital future. Flowers bridges past and future not in a unified narrative but in the rhythms and diction of incantation and prophesy.

Dominique Parker provides a personal exploration of identity as fluid. Her prose poem "In the Spaces Between the Words: An Interpretation and Performance of Identity" is a personal, but not private, negotiation of multiple identities for an American, African American, African Caribbean, Haitian American life. Her negotiations of identity aim to elude the racializing language that would name, confine, or exclude her. Her piece, which dramatizes a freeing and sometimes frightening unbalancing of the psyche, should shed light on the essays of the second section of the volume. We place Parker's writing in the third section, "Contesting Identities," to emphasize the specific cultural contexts across which she shapes her senses of self and the tensions amid and between them. Parker figures some of these tensions in the various kinds of language that run through her prose poem: the language of memoir and poetry; the oral tones of languages in a Queens community; and the rational and power-invested languages of national institutions, including universities.

The volume ends with a second conversation between the editors, in which we find hope for the future, even as we raise doubts and questions that we cannot yet fully answer.

Just as it takes a village to raise a child, it has taken a community of friends, family, and colleagues to bring forth *Racing and (E)Racing Language: Living with the Color of Our Words*. The contributors were not only generous with their scholarship and their art, but also with their patience and understanding amid the process of book publishing. The contributors, who were close personal friends before the process began, are still close personal friends, and their colleagues are still there to give constructive critique and encouragement. This community nurturing has allowed the editors to take the much needed time with the text to learn not only what each contributor is saying but what they themselves are saying to each other and what the book might say to its readers.

Safiya would like to thank her daughter, Naimah, and her grandson, Dal-Jeem, for the room they continued to give her and for the joy that helped her to continue the creative process. She would also like to thank the great life-giving Spirit for giving her room and more time on this earth for work and play. She would like to thank her coeditor, Ellen Goldner, for all of her time, energy, and endurance—the sweat and tears—that kept this project moving forward.

Ellen would like to thank her husband, Stephen Rosow, for the inspiration, personal support, practical advice, and stimulating ideas he so often brought to conversations about this book. She would also like to thank Safiya Henderson-Holmes for her spirit, for her commitment, her ideas, and her friendship throughout this project.

Friendly Town, going #1

Safiya Henderson-Holmes

it's july. i'm inner
city and ten, on a bus
with fifty-two inner city tens:
blueblack, brownbeige faces as public,

as crowded as the schools
we attend. we're leaving
the city quickly. escaping in twos.
going to the country. to camp.

—where you run in grass,
sleep in trees and piss
in wind. friendly town—
the counselor says, as she counts

and taps our seats:
the bus a long yellow
and green cut in gray.
the counselor counts us

three times before we leave
the corner. after each count
she smiles pearly and perfect.
we're given bologna,

potato sticks and red apples
in white paper bags. our names
in blue marker on square,
white labels, stuck,

ends curling on our chest:
we're shirley thick black bangs
and babyblue bows; maria thin lips
long, thin black hair, jose chewing gum,

reading superman, paulette crying,
edward pointing to trucks,
debra eating the apple,
not swallowing its skin.

i smooth my name,
wonder about camp animals:
cows, goats, pigs. or did friendly
towners have regular cats

and dogs that fight, regular
birds that perch, but never fly.
jose explodes his white
lunch bag. the counselor

grabs her head. the perfect pops
—my god—, she says,—i thought
you had a gun—. jose laughs.
i close my eyes, listen to paulette's

crying, turn her tears into dog teeth,
sharp and chasing our bus.

Conversation One

Ellen J. Goldner and Safiya Henderson-Holmes

E.G. In your poem about going to Friendly Town, you imagine what it is to "piss in [the] wind." Can you say what was freeing about pissing in the wind? Does that imply a natural space or a natural moment in which you felt there was an alternative to a racialized identity?

S.H. Yes, because for a moment I think that I was conscious of not being a "colored little girl," that for a moment I was out and about on the land and as free as that. And that I didn't have to be "the little colored girl" integrating the white school or "the little colored girl" shopping in the store and being looked at. . . .

E.G. Always with the label?

S.H. Yeah. Or "the little colored girl" playing in the park with all the white kids. That I was just running on the grass, looking at the trees and shouting in the wind. That didn't last long in Friendly Town. Friendly Town was racialized. But there were moments, many moments when I could feel like that, and I could actually act like that.

E.G. And put them together for yourself? In the past, when you've talked about Friendly Town, you've mentioned a resolution about how to be.

S.H. Right, about how to be. Because just like there were moments of not feeling free or having to prove that you are, you could be conscious of those moments when you *are* free, and how powerful that felt—how powerful it felt not to prove anything. Sometimes it felt empowering to prove something to someone, but I learned that it was even more empowering when you didn't have to prove anything to anybody.

E.G. To step outside those expectations?

S.H. Yeah, and just do it.

E.G. Does this come from the part of your childhood when you lived in an integrated neighborhood?

S.H. Yeah. I was often alone. I was often alone in a setting with a majority of whites, which is not unusual for kids growing up in the city, when your parents are trying to send you to a good school, when your parents are trying to take you to other parts of the city and other parts of the world. And since my father was a socialist, I had to just be in that setting because that's where that setting was.

E.G. You began speaking in the poem about events in your childhood. What is the importance to you of those early years, of childhood for those revelations or those feelings of constraint?

S.H. Those are your first sightings of yourself and of "others." And those first sightings are very impressionistic. Some first sightings are very familiar, and *that* forms a big impression. Some first sightings are very foreign, and *that* forms a big impression too. So when you start from that first moment, realizing how someone's looking at you, you carry that with you to the next sighting. How you look at them, and remembering, and how they look at you, and remembering. Then you just have this bag of stuff of how you are approached or how you're not approached.

E.G. And you use that later in your life.

S.H. Yeah. Like what's attraction? What's social? What's emotional? What's political? And those are from your first sightings. I'm always interested in how little babies who have never seen a person of color before look at me or look at anything that's not within their initial frame. If you have a little baby who's never seen a person of color, they're, like, wowed. They're totally amazed. So the adult person of color can enter that new space and feel the amazement. Not the fear, not the horror, not the distrust or the trust or the love, but just sheer wonderment, like "This is something new."

I remember when I was teaching this course "What's Love Got to Do with It?" We were talking about race. And you know, it's so easy to dismiss how everyone and everything in a racialized society is racialized. That racism and race issues are not the sole interest (problematic or otherwise) of the people that, supposedly, the formula is written against, like me. It's so easy for us to talk about, "Well, people of color or black people *this* or black people *that,*" but to be racialized as a white person is as horrific to me as the other way, and that doesn't get the discussion it deserves. I remember Baldwin saying one time—he was speaking to a large audience about this—he says, "As long as you continue to be white, I'll continue to be black." And so what does that mean in the scheme and landscape of things? What does that mean to be "a white person"? What does that mean anyway? I'm not talking about pigmentation here.

E.G. You mean socially?

S.H. We're talking about the social construction of a person. What does it mean to be "a black person"? I'm not talking about their pigmentation either. The social construction of a person. Social construction is given from culture to culture, from generation to generation, as if it is some congenital thing.

E.G. Yes. That's so important. As I think about how much it mattered to you to piss with the wind against your thighs—to find an unracialized space—I think that as a white child, as a white girl, I often needed to learn the inverse of that: that parts of my identity *were* racialized. And inside the frame of a racist culture, it always took the presence of somebody who wasn't white to make me see those parts of my identity. If I think of those early years of strong impressions that you carry with you all your life—and I include both childhood and adolescence here—my experience in some ways meets your experience, but from the other side of some of the same processes. I grew up in New Haven. New Haven approached its problem of segregated life by trying to integrate the schools, and they did it by busing white kids to black schools. So that as white children, we entered into what in some ways was an African American place. It's different from your experience, though, because I didn't feel alone. A lot of white children were bused to that school. Looking back, I can see that this mode of busing had its problems. In many ways it was an intrusion, in which white kids took over places and things that had belonged to black kids.

When I think about junior high school and high school, I remember many moments when I was taken aback . . . surprised . . . baffled . . . bewildered by a sudden glimpse of parts of my identity that I never knew were there. And those moments mattered tremendously even though I couldn't understand them at the time, or *because* I couldn't understand them at the time. Now I can look back and comprehend the source of the pain, of the frustration, in response, say, to the young man in the black separatist movement after race riots in my high school, who told me, very pointedly, that I could never understand him. At the age of fifteen, I didn't know why that was so or what that meant. But his resistance made me sense what this social, racialized world was that I lived in and that made up part of my identity. Although I didn't fully comprehend it, he made me *feel* that network of relations that was part of my childhood. That network of relations that had taught me, at a young age, that the black woman who cleaned the house and the white man who cut the lawn were the only adults outside of family or close family friends who I could call by their first names. These were networks of race and class.

S.H. Right.

E.G. In high school, those networks were also was very much part of a friendship—a close friendship, but always in some ways a frustrated and troubled friendship—with a young black woman. I remember a moment when I asked my friend to spend the evening at my house, and she said, "No, I have to go home and wash my hair." I said, "Wash it here."

S.H. (Laughter.)

E.G. And she said, "You really don't know what I have to do when I wash my hair." This gap in my knowledge of a powerfully racialized part of her life strikes me as a less-urgent version of an issue you brought up the other day: about black women with cancer—black women who have no insurance—whose lives remain invisible in the dominant culture.

S.H. Same thing. Your story reminds me of the time I went to this camp, and there was this girl there, a Jewish girl. She wanted to know how I kept my hair so straight. She had very, very curly hair, and after a few days her hair was frizzing up.

E.G. That's what mine does.

S.H. It was getting to look like nappy hair, and so one day when all the kids were away in the other part of the camp, I took her, and I parted her hair like I part mine. I put my grease in my hair. Posner's Bergamot. This blue grease. And I put it on her hair like it was a little black girl's hair. It was acting like every little black girl's hair that I knew of. And I put it on little sponge rollers, curlers that I used, and tied it up in a scarf. And she walked around like that all day. I said, "When you go in the shower, you have to put your shower cap on. Don't let it get wet." And she did. When she came out, her hair was straightened again. And she was my best friend throughout camp, because she said, *"I didn't know you could do this!"* That was such a bonding moment because we were so, so different, but so, so the same at the very same time.

E.G. Those were the moments that my friend and I always missed. We circled them—met at them—but were never quite able to break through and touch, despite all the social static between us.

S.H. Right.

E.G. You asked about gender the other day, and for me that's the place where gender comes in—looking back at early relations. They weren't as early as yours because I grew up in a white neighborhood. When I was in grade school, there was one African American family in the neighborhood. The Wilsons. I remember their name because they were the only black family. But with junior high school and high school, I have a real basic sense of something missed and lost because there were always moments when something stopped short. And it's in relations to African American women that I feel that loss. . . . I notice we've been dwelling on childhood here.

S.H. Yeah. Maybe that's because these *are* first sightings, for all the adults I've known. Yes, we've grown and matured, and can call ourselves other names now, but what we first thought of who we are or who "they" were is still kind of in our guts. Not that we're going to stay within that way of thinking.

E.G. Yes. It matters so much to me now, as an adult, to know what a discourse is because it was always what was naturalized. My identity was naturalized, as opposed to being racialized, within the discourse, which is why it is always hard for me to explain what it might mean to be racialized as white. The moments that come to mind are when I was racialized as Jewish. Though there *is* one incident in which I guess I did suddenly sense I was white, and that it had a tangled and painful meaning. This is very hard to talk about. It's a very, very powerful early memory about living in a racialized world, that somehow I was implicated in.

S.H. I remember asking my class of graduate students when and where was the time and the feeling that they first recognized themselves as white. And they all looked like, "What do you mean?"

E.G. Yeah. I don't know if I recognized myself as "white." I recognized for a moment that I was living within and being a part of something horrifying, connected with racism, when I was eight or nine, and I didn't understand the meaning of it at all. It is really hard to talk about this. I was playing a game with a friend who was a year older than me, and that year's difference carried a lot of power. We were playing a game she called "Truth or Consequences." And what you had to do, if you didn't answer a question right, was something you weren't supposed to do. One thing we did as a "consequence" was jump over the neighbors' bushes onto their lawn. We weren't supposed to do that. This friend also had a neighbor next door who was not a very pretty woman. She was an older, spinster woman. One "consequence" was that I had to tell her that she was "looking very pretty today," and I did that. The next "consequence" I was given was to go touch the pocketbook of the lady at the bus stop. The lady at the bus stop was African American. And when I did it, she screamed in rage, "You white spit!" I guess this *is* a recognition of being "white." And we ran and hid. I recognized that I had done something absolutely terrible. But it was as if the world had ignited and exploded, and I barely, barely understood why, even though I was sure, at nine years old, that that woman was at the bus stop in a white neighborhood because she cleaned houses here. That moment is just engraved in my memory.

S.H. Right.

E.G. That was the most explosive moment. But always, always those times of learning about being "white" for me were accompanied by bewilderment—surprise—because my identity had been so naturalized in a racist culture. I was "natural," "the norm," while you were always aware that you were "the little black girl."

S.H. Yeah. Now I have a question for each of us. As we became familiar with difference in color as something that was a conscious sighting, what were we imagining or thinking or feeling when we did see that difference, like when you said you were playing "Truth or Consequences"? You touched the pocketbook of this black woman, and she turned around and cursed you. And that was so horrific, so shattering, but you knew you had done something wrong. Why?

E.G. Because she cursed me for being part of something that I recognized in my gut as racism. Now, in my memory, it's jumbled up with TV images of Selma, Alabama, of Georgia, the loosing of police dogs on people and of things my rabbi said, but I think some of those images came later. The rabbi had been jailed on marches in the South. He gave sermons on how, as Jews who had been stereotyped and persecuted, we needed to commit ourselves to ending racism in this country. But what the rabbi said and what many people in the congregation believed were not necessarily the same thing.

S.H. What were you seeing? What were you feeling? What was being suggested to you from the rabbi, from your own imagination, from the television that gave you some kind of visceral image to then say, "I recognize this person?" The black woman who cursed you identified you with this curse. How did *you* identify *her?*

E.G. There was no question in my mind that she must have been a domestic worker.

S.H. Why were you so sure of that? You saw a domestic worker. She could have been the cousin of the one black family that you mentioned lived in the community or an in-law, but because of the image you were given of the black woman in your community, she was the domestic worker. How is that image of her *yours?*

E.G. I mentioned before that the woman who cleaned our house was one of the only adults I called by their first names. That signals a strange relation that was different from my relation to other adults.

S.H. The people that you called by their first names were children and black adults.

E.G. Yes, though it was a little more complicated than that. The racialized image crosses with class. The person who cut the lawn was a white man, who I also called by his first name.

S.H. That's a good point. That it does cross with class. The black woman who cleaned your house you called by her first name, and the white man who cut your lawn you called by his first name. But the other adults in your immediate place you dared not. You knew not to.

E.G. Yes. That's clearly how I identified that woman. And she, in important ways, turned the tables when she named me and cursed me. When she cursed me, she opened up the contradictions of my world. The rabbi spoke about one thing, about respect, but something different often went on in daily life in the community. And in some gut-level way, I recognized or felt that I was embroiled in something that I had thought was distant from me.

S.H. For me, when we moved into the Soundview projects in the Bronx, around the same time, '59, '58, I was four or five, and the place was integrated. These were new housing projects in the tip of the Bronx. We moved into an integrated building. My neighbors across the hall were Hispanic. The neighbor down the hall was black. It was very integrated. There were Asian Americans. The whole population. And across the street from these projects were these small army barracks. We called them the "little green houses." My public school was right across the street from my house. Integrated. Junior high school was up the hill. Integrated. The co-op apartments were integrated. One of my mother's best friends was part of an interracial couple, and their children were interracial. We all went to the same church, with our white minister in the integrated church. My godmother was a white woman, Mrs. Faulkner, and was married to a black man. So I grew up in this integrated thing. My father was a socialist. The racism that I knew of, that I was committed to be involved with and talk about, was immediately a political situation because of the meetings in my house—demonstrations that my father was in. White girls for me were the girls that I played with, with the long hair. And if I wished to have long hair, then I wanted to have long hair like Anna. But I didn't want to be white. I just wanted to have long hair. I had a black woman come to my house, too, to help clean. Mama Thomas.

E.G. And you didn't call her by her first name.

S.H. No. It was "Mama Thomas." She helped iron, cook, clean, and everything when my mother and father were working. When my mother and father separated, we moved to Bed-Stuy in Brooklyn, which is a predominantly black neighborhood. And for me, that was a cultural shock because in the integrated, interracial, predominantly mixed place, I knew who I was as a black girl, even though "colored." When I moved to a predominantly black neighborhood in Bed-Stuy, I was "colored" and had to prove myself to be "black."

E.G. So you were named from both sides.

S.H. Yes. So then I went to a school that was black. I remember entering the ninth grade—all these black students and a very hostile-looking white teacher. It was completely new to me. And there was one "other" in the class. "Other" meaning that she looked as different as me. I was different not because I was colored different. I was different because my feeling and seeing was different. Also, I think my clothing was because I came to school with my blouse tucked in and my socks up to my knees. I was different because I came from another neighborhood. I needed a partner, an ally, and the only ally that I felt I could have was the only white girl in the classroom, Anna Muller. I looked at her, and I knew she was going to be my friend.

E.G. You came originally from a much more cosmopolitan background early in childhood than I did.

S.H. Yeah. What I was going to say about Anna was that she was blond, blue-eyed, the whole nine yards, and we became best friends because of that—because I needed an ally in the difference.

E.G. I was never in the middle of difference in that way. I was in the middle of something confusing, but it was an ideology. I think, for me, watching how a discourse works or watching how social relations work is so important because some of those early sightings were about that. And I had no words in my vocabulary at all to put around them. As I think back to the woman at the bus stop who cursed me, or to calling the woman who came to help clean the house by her first name, or to school integration as it was spoken of in New Haven, an assumption of inequality ran through all these things. There was a continuity between calling the woman who helped to clean by her first name and feeling that the schools had to be integrated because whites had something "to give" to blacks. I think one of the hallmarks of a potent ideology is that its assumptions are often not directly stated. So I was in the middle of confusion in an ideology that was often contradicted by what was directly spoken, whereas you were directly confronted with the politics of differences and of being named.

S.H. Yeah. When I was eight or nine, when we lived in Bed-Stuy, I did by that time recognize that the racial tension, particularly between whites and blacks in New York City, was very strong and pervasive, and was included in my household, however integrated the former household was. But when I saw Anna, I recognized her as different from me, but also as someone who'd be my ally because I was different in a political sense, but not different from the racial problem that encircled all of us. And I realized that neither was Anna. And it's interesting to me to think about Brooklyn and Bed-Stuy because it has these many, many layers, because it does include a white neighborhood, a Jewish population, where blacks come to clean houses and an Italian population. And what it also has is this layering of these different places to go and how you end up there. I knew that when I looked at Anna, I saw my friend, but as I got older, I met the other kids from the other neighborhood, who may have just seen me or people who look like me as folks who just swept the streets or cleaned their homes, did their laundry or were unemployed. When it came to junior high school and high school, and I was sitting next to them, then the structures all changed. Someone would sit next to me and say stuff like, "I didn't know you could read."

E.G. Really?

S.H. I'd be amazed. "How could you not know I could read? What are you thinking about? Doesn't everyone read? Where I come from, everyone I know reads." What I'm looking for is the "I." After the ideology or the media gives us something, how far do we then carry that? When you left your neighborhood and saw the black woman doing *x*, was she still the domestic worker? When I left my neighborhood and saw white women who were not my friends, like Anna, what happened? To Anna? Did I then come back and see Anna differently? Sometimes I did. So when Anna—who is a German/Scandinavian mix, so she's very blond—so when Anna and I would walk down the street in a black neighborhood, what kind of tensions did we bring to that neighborhood, and what kind of tension did we put on ourselves? And how did we deal with it? Sometimes it was very uncomfortable. We felt unfriendly toward each other, and we couldn't figure out—at what time did that happen? What street did we cross?

E.G. It was very geographical?

S.H. It was geographical. It was political. It was a change in not only a physical space but a psychological space. So when you touched that woman's pocketbook, you were crossing that street, too. When she spit those words at you, she was crossing that street.

E.G. Absolutely.

S.H. So how did you carry that into junior high school?

E.G. I carried it as my part in or my contribution to the tense social distance between white students and African American students. Not in a conscious way. Not in a simple way. But I did not become friends with the people I sat next to in classes. My friendships didn't cross the racial line in junior high school—not until high school. I certainly didn't see the people I sat next to, say, in math class, as potential domestic workers. That's far too simple. But I have no doubt I carried with me that more pervasive, indirectly expressed view that there was something "not quite equal" in the lives of African American kids. Now, sometimes that "not quite equal" that I carried in my mind might have been simply addressed to money, and *that* did not make someone less worthy than me. It simply meant that she had less money. But the sense of the "not quite equal" was slippery. And I'm sure that at other times I applied it to say, the street smarts of some African American students. Here, of course, the racism is mixed with class issues again. Once, when a black girl I didn't know threatened me in the hall, I'm sure I compensated for my fear—and I was afraid—by thinking that her way of dealing with things was not quite equal to mine. And, I was barely aware that I carried that sense of "the not quite equal" with me. I was certainly not aware of how that idea slid around in my half-conscious sense of others.

On the other hand, junior high school was the first place that I had African American teachers. Their visible role of authority clearly countered the image of African American adults as people I called by their first names. So I carried to junior high school the traces of racism inside of me, and black and white students met across an uneasy distance. But there were also other influences that began to clear away some of the racism of earlier sightings, though always in a tangled way. None of it was easy.

S.H. What about black men? Did you have any thoughts about black men when you would see them?

E.G. When I think about gender categories, I don't recall sorting out African American men as a category. But of course I'm sure I did because in high school people dated, and only with very rare exceptions did black and white students date each other. The category of African American men was taboo or cordoned off ahead of time. I don't remember thinking about it much. Very few people challenged that taboo.

S.H. What did you see or think about when you looked at a black man?

E.G. I knew many young black men in high school, whom I saw as different from each other. I can't retrieve an easy category.

S.H. You knew them to talk to?

E.G. Sure. The line was drawn at dating, not socializing in school.

S.H. When you go back and feel this memory and think of black men, you think of them in relation to something that could not happen.

E.G. Yeah, though it wasn't very conscious at the time.

S.H. What did you sense, feel, think about, if anything? Was there a feeling of their being different than white men? For me, white men were *really* different. They walked different. They talked different. I found them unattractive. When I saw a group of white men I didn't know on the street, I was afraid of them. I had heard stories about the Klan, about white men who'd rape you, about the violence of white men. What did you think when you saw a group of black men, older men who you didn't know?

E.G. You know, I hardly ever saw a group of grown black men on the street. That was part of the cordoning off of black men as a category— ahead of time. From the time I was old enough to take a bus, I was told to avoid dangerous neighborhoods, poor neighborhoods, and I didn't go to them. As race crossed with class, at a time and in a place where the African American middle class was very small, I didn't much see groups of grown black men. I think the association of African American men with danger was powerfully in the background of all the taboos, and yet it was erased from my sight. And I didn't inquire. That seems very important to me.

With the riots in '68 the news media began to draw on images of black men and violence. And I know that I absorbed some of those images, but I think I absorbed them later. When I think back to high school, I don't feel a sense of danger attached to young men I knew. But there's an important interplay between what was visible and what was not visible. Years later, I wrote a piece of fiction—fifteen years ago or so—that I couldn't finish. It involved a young black man with a gun, and the main character, a white woman, was convinced that somehow the problem was *hers*. I think I was trying to work out my role in that image. I didn't succeed fifteen years ago. I never finished that piece of fiction. In my essay on Frederick Douglass, I'm still working on that issue.

S.H. I'd like to talk about adult life and how I see some of my adult students, and how we still "color" ourselves. There was a student taking one of my courses because she thought she could learn how African Americans think. I said, "We're going to be reading ten books by ten African American women. Reading books by ten women will not teach you how African Americans think." So how much of this racialized coloring continues in our adult circles, conversations, and workplaces? One day I had on a Guatemalan shirt, and my hair, which was in dreadlocks, was not in a ponytail, and a faculty member approached me with what he considered a compliment. He said, "Boy, you look very ethnic today!" In my mental retort, I wanted to ask, "Do I look African? Guatamalen? Carribean? 'Other' than American?" And he doesn't even realize what he's saying or why he's saying that. Should I then retort, "Well, you look ethnic every day. You always look like a white man to me."

E.G. Right. He's "natural."

S.H. Exactly.

E.G. Fifteen years or twenty years ago, I had no language for seeing myself inside a discourse of racism or for navigating it. Now, as an adult and a teacher, I see that as my task, especially when I'm challenged by my students. For example, some of my African American students come into the classroom with a lot of anger, and it's part of my job to know what produced that anger. To know that the personal is political is also to know that the hostility I see isn't purely personal. It's not helpful to respond as if it were simply directed against me. It's my job to know that this is directed against something I live within. And I'm still in the classroom testing how and how well I respond to that anger, so that this classroom might be an opportunity for something different from what produced all that anger—for all of us.

S.H. Sure. And I'm in the classroom working every day to show that I am capable of enlightening my students' world—of enriching it, of making it broader, not narrower. That this is not an example of what isn't available to you. My standing before you is an example of all that *is* available to you. You're not getting less because I'm standing up in front of you.

E.G. Right. What you're talking about now ties back into what you began speaking about, the sense in the dominant culture that the issue of what is racialized is really only *your* concern and not the concern of white adults, white students.

S.H. This is a concern. And until we start realizing as a *whole* body that this whole body is affected, we will get nowhere with it. It will be the same thing generation after generation. Nothing will change—maybe a little bit of fluff here, a little bit of fluff there—but nothing will change because we still think it's this problem that this other group has. "We have to help them. We have to now respect them. We have to apologize to them. And that will make it all better."

E.G. "Let's perform the right ritual, and it will all be better."

S.H. Exactly. "It will all be better. And we, who have been untouched, unmoved by this whole thing are just helping." Oh, it's so crazy.

E.G. Can we say a little about how all we've been talking about is connected to language? As I think of my experience with racialized identities and spaces, I'm very aware that there were some things I had names for and some things I did not. And the things I did not have names for all dovetailed very easily with racism. I did not have names for social/political relationships because this individualist culture encourages me to define myself as if there are none. I did not have names for what this thing was between me and my friend—the friend who had to wash her hair. It was as if space was curved. Each of us tried to say things to the other, and the language twisted in the discourse between us and often ended up meaning what we hadn't intended. As an adult, now, I'm very aware that I had no language with which to know that space between us. How are the experiences you've talked about here related to language for you?

S.H. I remember when I was trying to figure out what people were saying when they were talking about "niggers" or "colored people" or "black people." Not only what they meant, but how they said those words, and at what given moment were they thrown out. And why. I think the language of racism is very much formed to establish hate and tension.

E.G. You're talking about being named—by those who treat you as other.

S.H. Yeah. Being named. Being called "a black bitch." How does that happen? What does that mean? Or just talking about your color all the time. I think that's when I started listening. When black people had this range of colors: "You're light-skinned," and "You're dark-skinned," or "You have good hair," or "You have bad hair." When those words started conjuring images—when I had to find out by touch and seeing—What did "good hair" mean? What did someone "fair-skinned" or "light-skinned" look like?

E.G. And who did you hear these words from?

S.H. Black people, and white people who were around black people. White people who were not around black people just threw us all in the box.

E.G. Right. Made no distinctions of any kind.

S.H. So, I think language started for me there, when I was being described or when I was trying to describe another. "Well, you know she has blond hair," or "she's white." Well, what do you mean, she's white? "She's white, and she has blond hair." You couldn't go much further with "white." But with black people . . .

E.G. There were endless gradations.

S.H. Exactly.

E.G. So you want to work and rework the language you heard that carries racism, and I want to work and rework the language I didn't hear that carries racism.

S.H. It sounds like we're both coming to the same point in the road from different paths, looking at ourselves and how we've become what we are amid language.

Part One. Embodying Struggles

Allegories of Exposure

The Heroic Slave and the Heroic Agonistics of Frederick Douglass

Ellen J. Goldner

> *Speaking of marks, traces, possibles and probabilities, we come before our readers.*
> Frederick Douglass, The Heroic Slave

Frederick Douglass opens his only work of fiction, *The Heroic Slave,* as a dialogue with his readers, but a dialogue whose discursive field is painfully troubled. The introduction of *The Heroic Slave* is framed in the rational expectations of Douglass's republican oratory. The opening paragraph contrasts the fame of Thomas Jefferson and Patrick Henry with the obscurity of the novella's hero, who is known only in chattel records, offering a reasoned argument that turns on irony.[1] The rational opening anticipates the introduction's closing image of Douglass as a speaking subject who directly faces his audience, as he "come[s] before [his] readers" (*HS,* 26). Yet, between the opening paragraph and the final image, Douglass introduces gothicism that sets "howling tempests" and "angry lightning" between the reader and the heroic fugitive—a figure that designates not only the novella's protagonist, Madison Washington, but, as Sundquist notes, also its author, Douglass (1991, 123): "He is brought into view only by a few transient incidents, and these afford but partial satisfaction. Like a guiding star on a stormy night, he is seen through the parted clouds and the howling tempests; or, like the gray peak of a menacing rock on a perilous coast, he is seen by the quivering flash of angry lightning, and he again disappears covered with mystery" (*HS,* 26).

The gothic weather that charges the atmosphere introduces a subtext

---

1. For an important discussion of Douglass's highly conscious uses of irony and of reversals of dominant cultural meanings, see Gates 1991, 89.

of *The Heroic Slave* that alters the meanings of rational public debate. The electrical storm, with its unpredictable bolts of lightning, figures the political discourse as a field across which power plays erratically and erotically as it veils and unveils the heroic slave. The inadequate "marks and traces" of the hero indicate their invisible counterparts: the often irrational resistance of white audiences to rightly seeing a heroic African American man. Like those marks and traces, the subtext of *The Heroic Slave* indicates the all but invisible conditions of the discourse within which Douglass himself so often stood, as he addressed predominantly white audiences in the role of masculine fugitive slave.[2]

When Douglass published *The Heroic Slave* in 1853, he had already established an international reputation as an orator and an author. He often spoke to packed halls at a time when oratory was converging with the emergent culture of celebrity that attended a mass press.[3] By the 1850s, Douglass was "an international celebrity in the English speaking world" (Andrews 1991, 135). In the mid–nineteenth century, the growing audience of celebrity began to make new kinds of nonrational claims on public figures. Wheras earlier audiences of republican oratory often listened to a speaker to be roused to his cause, the audience of celebrity increasingly focused attention on the celebrity figure himself, fetishizing the celebrity's body (Newbury 1994, 168–69) and far more often projecting onto him or her its desires, anxieties and aggression.[4] Newbury finds that cultural un-

2. My inquiry concerns the problematics of Douglass's address to white audiences, first, because in the decade before writing *The Heroic Slave,* when he was sponsored by the Garrisonians, Douglass addressed primarily white audiences; second, because the character Mr. Listwell, as a white abolitionist, carries a racism connected with his dominant position; and finally, because my own position as a white woman reading Douglass's novella leads me to focus on the dynamics of that interaction. During the course of the 1850s, Douglass increasingly addressed the concerns of African American audiences (Martin 1984, 56, 59). The exploration in *The Heroic Slave* of the troubling relation with his white abolitionist audience comprises part of Douglass's movement toward an increasing solidarity with other African Americans. See Sekora for a discussion of Douglass's increasing sense of community with African Americans as shown in his 1856 *My Bondage and My Freedom* (1994, 620–25).

3. See Reynolds's *Walt Whitman's America* for a discussion of the development of the mass press and its connection with sensationalism by the 1840s (1996, 81, 86). Also, see Newbury for a discussion of the commercial literary market, as it first produced celebrities in the 1850s (1994, 55–60).

4. Both Newbury and Coombe discuss the projection of desire onto the celebrity figure (Newbury 1994, 161, 165; Coombe 1992, 63). Coombe also addresses the way that celebrity images dramatize social anxieties (1992, 61). Gabler treats gossip about celebrity figures as a mode of aggression rooted in envy and resentment (1995, xiii).

derstandings of celebrity in the late antebellum United States drew heavily on slave narratives and antislavery fiction, as these popular genres brought fame to authors such as Harriet Beecher Stowe. He argues that as celebrity emerged alongside accounts of slavery, and as audiences clamored for a glimpse of the celebrity's body, the culture began to imagine the body of the celebrity, like the body of the slave in popular narratives, to be irrationally desired, possessed, attacked, and sacrificed by the audience (1994, 161, 165). As a former slave who became one of the most well-known orators of his time, Frederick Douglass was a symbolic personality who united the two desired and attacked bodies. The Garrisonians, for example, did not hesitate to reinscribe the image of the slave on Douglass's body when they introduced him to crowds by describing the whip marks on his back (*MB*, 219). Although such introductions marked his early career, Douglass continued to call attention to both the introductions and the whip marks when he was famous, protesting against them, even as he enlisted in his cause the powerful iconography of the celebrity's/slave's body.[5]

The symbolic figure of Douglass could function for his white audiences in complex and even contradictory ways. Coombe defines the celebrity image as "a cultural lode of . . . meanings mined (by the audience) for its symbolic resources and simultaneously a floating signifier invested with libidinal energies, social longing and political aspirations" (1992, 59). On the one hand, the self-elevated Douglass embodied the "Representative American Man," onto whom all of his audiences might project their desires for achievement and their admiration for a man who had risen from the most difficult of circumstances (Andrews 1991, 140). On the other hand, as Douglass acknowledged in later years when he embraced the persona of the "Representative Colored Man of the United States," he stood before his European American audience as a representative of his people.[6] In this role, Douglass was a symbolic site onto which white audiences

5. See, for example, "Men and Brothers," delivered in May 1850 (Blassingame 1982, 238). In *My Bondage and My Freedom* (1856), Douglass protests his early abolitionist sponsors' attempts to limit his speech (*MB*, 220) and highlights John Collins's introduction of him as a man *"with (his) diploma written on (his) back"* [my emphasis](*MB*, 219). Douglass does not, however, comment on Collins's introduction as he calls it to mind for his readers.

6. Walker calls attention to the title as Douglass embraced it. He also notes Douglass's highly conscious recognition of himself in the role as representative of his people in his later years (1978, 210). For a discussion of the ways that Douglass historically filled this role for his African American audiences and readers, see Martin 1991 and 1984, 55.

could project the floating signifier of race, a signifier that, as Morrison demonstrates in *playing in the dark,* carries dangerous libidinal charges from white society (1990, 78–79).

In the 1850s, Douglass's persona as antislavery advocate resonated with his audiences' hopes and fears about the ending of slavery. Hence, Douglass often stood amid the conflicted energies of a white audience that could favor abolition even as it feared violence from former slaves and the costs to white society that emancipation entailed. In paradoxical sentiments that Takaki describes as simultaneously antislavery and antiblack (1979, 112), between the 1830s and the 1850s, many European American groups expressed open hostility toward African Americans amid fears that black labor would discredit or displace white labor. The Wilmot Proviso of 1846 illustrates the issue. It prohibited slavery in territories newly acquired from Mexico, but it did so in the interest of white labor. Wilmot, the Pennsylvania representative who introduced his proviso, said: "I plead the cause and rights of white freemen. I would preserve to free white labor a fair country, a rich inheritance, where . . . [men] of my own race and color, can live without the disgrace which association with negro slavery brings upon free labor" (qtd. in Takaki 1979, 112). The same sense of white entitlement kept free African Americans out of skilled labor in the North and fueled antiblack riots in several Northern cities. If, as Coombe argues, celebrity is "an icon of the significance of the individual . . . embodying the possibility of upward mobility for the masses" (1992, 66), and if for many whites in the 1850s "the masses" meant the pool of white labor, then for much of Douglass's audience, the celebrated African American man who had risen from slavery stood in the place of the aspiring white man.

Douglass's speeches entailed a struggle with his white audience because currents within that audience sought to shape his public persona into manageable images of their own, often at points where white men feared a black man might displace them. After Douglass broke with Garrison in 1847 and began publishing his own newspaper to compete with the Garrisonian *Liberator,* the *Liberator* tapped the emergent power of widely circulating gossip that arose with celebrity as it tried to taint Douglass's image. The *Liberator* responded to Julia Griffiths's—that is, a British white female abolitionist's—financial backing of Douglass's newspaper by exploiting the dominant culture's most resonant and most irrational racist fear, miscegenation: the embodied and libidinally charged symbol of "racial" mixings of all kinds. *The Liberator* described Griffiths as a "Jezebel" who had undue influence over Douglass (W. Martin 1990, 45), and insinuated that she and Douglass were engaged in a sexual liaison, commenting that she "had caused much unhappiness in his . . . household" (Foner qtd. in Franchot 1990, 147).[7] The *Liberator* was not alone in circulating gossip that fed on racist fears of white men's displacement. After Douglass had appeared in public with Julia Griffiths and her sister, a woodcut circulated through Boston that depicted the Griffiths sisters vying for the romantic attentions of "Nigger Douglass" (W. Martin 1984, 43).

In the context of the dominant culture's irrationally charged discourse of race, especially as Douglass encountered it in crowded lecture halls, the subtext of *The Heroic Slave* becomes crucial, for it does its work at the points where reason breaks. I do not mean to slight the importance of reason for Douglass. On the contrary, as many critics note, Douglass modeled much of his own rhetorical work on the "Dialogue Between a Slave and a Master" in the *Columbian Orator,* in which a slave convinces his master to free him through the sheer force of reason. Fisher Fishkin and Peterson argue cogently that the "Dialogue Between a Slave and a Master" tropes both Douglass's insistence on equality with his predominantly white audience and his rhetorical interventions in the racism of the dominant discourse. They find that Douglass employs the premise of the *Columbian Orator* dialogue, in which the slave construes the mere fact that the master speaks to him as a recognition of his status as a man to construct himself as an equal, speaking subject who directly faces his white audience and overturns their racist categories (1990, 190–92). Ziolkowski also highlights the "Dialogue Between a Slave and a Master," calling its liberating speech act set within the dominant discourse "a kind of dream-text for Douglass" that informs his entire literary career (1991, 163).

The subtext of *The Heroic Slave* is important precisely because reason matters so much to Douglass. The subtext guards the rational terms of the *Columbian Orator* by supplementing them: it works in the gaps of the "dream-text," alert to the moves of a racist discourse infused with irrational force. The subtext of *The Heroic Slave* allegorizes an emotional strug-

---

7. Sundquist builds his interpretation of *The Heroic Slave* on its connection to Douglass's break with the Garrisonians and the *Liberator.* The novella was published as part of *Autographs for Freedom,* a volume compiled to raise money for Douglass's paper (1991, 123).

gle between Douglass and his white audience. Whereas currents within that audience seek to "expose" Douglass (both *to* its attacks and *through* its attacks), the subtext exposes or tracks the strategies of racism. Even as the subtext registers pain and frustration in the repeated task of confronting racism, it prepares Douglass to cast off some of the terms of the white audience's gaze.

In the broad lines of character and plot, *The Heroic Slave* presents an idealized dialogue between idealized characters: the heroic slave, Madison Washington, and the attentive, Northern white listener, Mr. Listwell. The terms of their dialogue are set in their first encounter in the Virginia forest, which Robert Stepto calls "a ritual ground . . . for symbolic encounters between slaves and abolitionists," "a sylvan glen" in which both Washington and Listwell dedicate themselves to the task of freeing slaves (1991, 113). Here, Washington first adopts the role of eloquent speaker and Listwell the role of silent listener, as the slave gives an account of himself and his humanity, which, like the dream-text in the *Columbian Orator,* convinces his listener that he should be free.

In its subtext, however, Douglass's novella recognizes that even idyllic settings such as the Virginia forest cannot shield the encounter between the representative African American hero and its representative of the Northern white audience from the irrational dynamics that join racism to celebrity. Unlike the parties in the *Columbian Orator* who "face each other directly" (Fisher Fishkin and Petersson 1990, 191) and use only the force of logic, Washington and Listwell leave a tense and guarded space between themselves. Despite Listwell's silence, that space is shot through with traces of the white listener's racism and hegemony. Even as Stepto calls the Virginia forest scene idyllic, he finds troubling the soliloquy through which Madison Washington converts Listwell to abolitionism; he asks us to "[dismiss] the florid soliloquies which unfortunately besmirch" Douglass's novella. (1991, 111). Elsewhere, he describes Madison Washington's soliloquies as "overwrought" (1986, 144–45). I would suggest that the soliloquy is "overwrought" because, as Madison Washington stands in for Douglass, the orator, it registers Douglass's anxieties about his relation with his (pre)dominant audience. Douglass can disrupt and revise the currents of racism in his audience only by standing in their path. Hence, he must prepare both himself and his speeches to confront the white audience.

Washington's soliloquy seems overwrought chiefly because it reads like a prepared public speech even though the novella insists it is the spontaneous language of a man talking to himself: "What then is life to me? It is aimless and worthless and worse than worthless. Those birds, perched on yon swinging boughs . . . sounding forth their merry notes in seeming worship of the rising sun, though liable to the sportsman's fowling-piece, are still my superiors. They *live free*" (*HS*, 28). As the African American speaker describes his life as "aimless and worthless and worse than worthless," his soliloquy, like poetry, repeats and varies sound in order to affect the ear of an audience. The "florid" description of "birds, perched on . . . swinging boughs . . . in worship of the rising sun" sets a highly visual, if stock, image before a listening audience. The soliloquy ends with sentences whose parallel structure dramatizes Washington's growing resolve: "If I am caught, I shall only be a slave. If I am shot, I shall only lose a life" (*HS*, 27). The tension between the soliloquy's formal rhetoric and the plot's claim that it is private speech redefines fiction as theater and requires the representative African American orator, even in his most private moments, to be engaged in theatrical performance. The tension highlights a powerful anxiety about being overheard that runs through *The Heroic Slave*.

To be overheard is to be caught unprepared by the audience that Listwell represents. And to be unprepared for such an audience is to be in danger. By the early 1850s, Douglass had repeatedly intervened in Northern whites' discourse. He had lectured his Northern audience not only on their immoral complicity with slavery in the Fugitive Slave Act but also on the immorality of their religion, which sanctioned the pro-slavery churches of the South.[8] Whenever Douglass stood before a white audience, he had to be prepared to suffer and to meet the backlash his interventions provoked. In *The Heroic Slave*, Douglass places his double, the fictional Madison Washington, amid the same political and cultural forces that impinged on himself. Here, Douglass sketches his perception of an audience that exacts psychological pain from the African American heroic speaker for every intervention he makes.

In the Virginia forest scene, the male African American hero and

8. For Douglass's attacks on Northern complicity with slavery in the Compromise of 1850, see his 1850 address, "An Anti-Slavery Tocsin" (Blassingame 1982, 269–70), and his 1851 address "Slavery's Northern Bulwarks" (Blassingame 1982, 279–91). For examples of Douglass's attacks on pro-slavery religion, see the appendix of his 1845 *Narrative* (*NL*, 326–31) and his 1849 address, "Too Much Religion, Too Little Humanity" (Blassingame 1982, 177–79).

speaker finds himself symbolically violated both mentally and physically by an audience that places him in the position of the subordinated other, the position that a patriarchy attempts to cast as passive and "feminine" in order to know him and to possess him, as it interweaves cultural images of three kinds of bodies that can be placed on display: the celebrity body, the slave body, and the female body. Although recent critics such as Franchot and Yarborough have taken Douglass to task for accepting the terms of European American patriarchy, I wish to illuminate here the painful context in which Douglass accepts them.[9] The scene in the Virginia forest, idyllic though it may seem, is structured like a rape that dramatizes a struggle between the symbolic African American male speaker and his European American audience. The scene is shot through with images of arousal, aggression, and penetration. When Listwell first hears Madison Washington's voice, Washington occupies the "feminine" position in which he, like the male slave, as Gates finds him in slave narratives, is troped as "the dark lady of romance" (Gates 1991, 83). Washington stands alone "in the dark pine forest," while Listwell "stealthily draws near . . . and conceal[s] himself" (*HS*, 26) because "he has *long desired* to sound the *mysterious depths* of the thoughts and feelings of a slave" (*HS*, 28) (emphasis added). In a "dangerous intrusion," Listwell overhears Washington's secret desire and catches "a full view of the unsuspecting speaker" (*HS*, 28). In the erotically charged field of power, Washington, like Douglas at the podium, must present himself not only to be heard but also to be viewed by an audience who finds him fascinating, body and soul: "Madison [is] of manly form. Tall, symmetrical, round and strong." "His face [is] 'black, yet comely,'" (*HS*, 28). Despite his "manly form," the description of Washington as "black but comely," from the description of the bride in the Song of Songs, underscores his feminized position. Listwell, as the emblem of the desiring Northern audience, repeats the act of the slaveholder, taking pleasure in his intrusion into the fugitive slave's body and personhood. Listwell's excessive curiosity breaks the boundary of Washington's sylvan retreat as Listwell presumes the right to "know" him erotically.

9. Newbury's discussion of the cultural view of celebrity in the 1850s, which fused the celebrity body with the slave body, probes the discomfort publicity produced for women authors because it violated the norms of middle-class women's privacy (1994, 169–70). Douglass must cope with a differently inflected confluence of the three bodies, as a former slave and celebrity whom the dominant culture attempted to treat as the passive and eroticized Other. For Franchot's critique of Douglass, see note 13. Also see Yarborough 1990, 176.

Unable to alter the violent eroticism that defines the terms of meeting, the Virginia forest scene gradually inverts the positions of aggressor and victim. Once the heroic fugitive "stand[s] erect," revealing his "Herculean strength," it is Listwell who trembles. By the time Washington finishes his soliloquy, Listwell is "feminized" and passive, "fastened to the spot," and "half in fear" of Washington (*HS*, 29). In Listwell's conversion to abolitionism, the text cannot distinguish between his acceptance of slave's cause and the erotic violence of penetration: "The speech of Madison rung through the chambers of [Listwell's] soul, and vibrated through his entire frame" (*HS*, 29–30). Because Douglass's political interventions must occur within a highly charged social arena, Douglass has no choice but to participate in the eroticized field of power in which he and his character find themselves, even when that power undermines the idealized dialogue between heroic slave and listener.

The Heroic Slave stages three other scenes of overhearing that link the covert, symbolic violence of Listwell's attack on the fugitive slave's body with the overt physical violence of attacks on the slave's body in the South. Although anxiety-provoking acts of overhearing mark a racist society's violation of the African American man as other, they also dramatize what I shall call a heroism of exposure: they force into visibility around endangered characters the dynamics of racist discourses in both the South and the North so that those discourses might be known. Thus, the characters, much like Douglass at the podium, bear violence actively in order to transform its meaning, as the novella performs the hard work necessary for Douglass's own increasingly alert subversions of American racism. In scenes of overhearing, *The Heroic Slave* tracks a resilient racism that preempts the direct dialogue of the *Columbian Orator* and defies that journal's Enlightenment categories as it works through means at once subtle and brutal, and intertwines eroticized violence with reason.

Douglass sets the most overt attack on an African American body in a scene of overhearing amid slavery in the South. The scene comments ironically on the seemingly idyllic initial encounter between Listwell and Washington, for it too is set in a Virginia wood, and it too places its hopes for freedom in a direct bond between speaker and listener. During his escape from slavery, Madison Washington hides in a tree, from where he overhears an old slave's prayer for deliverance, which echoes his own earlier soliloquy in the forest: "'O God, deliver me from the chains and manifold hardships of slavery!'" (*HS*, 41). Recognizing another slave who shares his most passionate longings, Washington reveals himself and speaks to the old man. He comes down from his hidden position above the speaker, and standing on level ground with him, he exchanges narratives with the old slave in a dialogue between equals that fulfills some of the basic requirements of the *Columbian Orator.* Yet their direct and equal dialogue proves inadequate to produce freedom because it is penetrated and waylaid by the powerful discourse of slavery.

Washington, who must remain in hiding, gives the old man his last dollar and asks him to buy some food for him. The old slave returns, however, not with food for Washington, but with fourteen angry white men in his wake, who have come to hunt Washington down. Washington's dollar has set in motion around it the entire ideological apparatus of the slave system that yokes the blood lust of the manhunt to the relentless logic of slavery. The dollar is an intervention into the economy of the local slave system because it is a token of power that a slave is not supposed to have. Washington explains that "it is so unusual for slaves in the country to have money, that fact, doubtless, excited suspicion, and gave rise to inquiry" (*HS*, 42). The slave with a dollar disrupts the ideology that insists a slave cannot have money. Money, as we know from Douglass's 1845 *Narrative,* can confer powers on a slave. If exchanged for a slave's labor (as when Douglass was hired out to the Baltimore shipyard), money registers the value of his labor. It also sets a distance between slave and master because the slave with money need not fully depend on her or his master for the necessities of life. In addition, money in its exchange value renders equal not only commodities, but also theoretically (if not actually) those who trade because it establishes the basis for equivalent exchanges.

As soon as the local slave system registers the dollar as an intervention in its terms, its ideology functions automatically to entrap and attack the slave associated with the token of power. Hence, the angry white men immediately search for the fugitive, whose escape signifies a second threat to their hegemony. Unable to locate the fugitive, the white men turn their rage on the old slave who carried the dollar. They label the old man a liar and a thief, and beat him brutally. Here, the fourteen white men vent the irrational blood lust of the man hunt that cares not who its victim is so long as it finds a convenient outlet.

Although the rage of the white men is irrational, it nonetheless follows the logic of the slave system and enforces its rationale. The old slave is singled out for an unjust beating by the slaveholders' discourse, which combines the arbitrary associations of language with the relentless logic of its ideology. In the absence of the actual violator of the law, the old man, who is already associated with the dollar, is arbitrarily made to represent the violator. He suffers great pain and humiliation because floating symbolic meaning is projected onto him by the white crowd. The unpredictable, irrational attack on the African American body is also linked with the certainty of the rules that enforce the system. When the white men justify their brutality with their unjust accusation that the old man is a thief, they unconsciously enact the abstract logic of their ideology: if the local version of slavery prohibits slaves from earning money and discourages whites from giving them money, then it follows that any slave with a dollar must be a thief. The beating itself demonstrates the rule that for every intervention into the slave system, a black man will be punished. Although it is certain that a black man will pay for the breach of the rules, which black man will pay is arbitrary. Random, violent, and irrational retaliation is itself the logic that enforces the slave system: it forces each slave to live in constant fear that he might be beaten and defines any slave who intervenes in the system as the cause of pain to other slaves.

In the few paragraphs that narrate the old slave's beating, Douglass's novella maps power within the slave system that mixes reason and unreason, everywhere frustrating the direct dialogue of the rational dream-text. The old slave can have no dialogue with white men who see only their own projection of him as thief and who refuse to hear his words. At its most pernicious, the ideology intervenes even in the dialogue of equals that Washington tries to establish with the old slave. When the two slaves exchange narratives and embrace each other, Washington's desire for mutual trust is thwarted by a power first figured in his own intrusion into the old man's privacy: the moment of the old man's exposure as Washington overhears his prayer for deliverance. Washington intervenes in the slave system, intending to break its hold on him as he escapes and sustains himself as a fugitive. Yet in the scene of the old man's beating, slavery wrests from the fugitive the meaning of intervention and redefines it as a brutal violation of the body and person of the slave with whom he would establish common cause.

The discourse of slavery that overtly penetrates both the dialogue between equals and the old slave's body resonates with Douglass's uneasiness about his role as orator in the North and converges with the novella's subtextual distrust of Listwell. The scene of the old slave's beating troubles over the dangers of being overheard and of being made to bear the symbolic projections of a crowd of whites. It also meditates on Douglass's own position as orator/hero who is held above other African Americans and on the dynamics of racism that might retaliate for Douglass's interventions into slavery in a backlash against the slaves whose cause he aims to serve. From amidst these concerns, the scene exposes the convoluted dynamics of the discourse of slavery.

Listwell, the Northern abolitionist, is metonymically associated with the discourse of the South through the two trips he makes to Virginia. In the first, he overhears Washington's soliloquy; in the second, he overhears through a tavern wall the conversation of drunken Southern whites. In the broad lines of the plot, Listwell's overhearing of the Southern whites is a subversive act that penetrates their perspective and violates their interests. The conversation warns Listwell that he should hide his identity as Northern abolitionist from the whites he overhears. It thereby enables his greatest service to Madison Washington when he slips Washington the files with which he will free himself and his fellow slaves aboard the *Creole*. Nonetheless, a complicated subtext shadows the scene of Listwell's overhearing in the Virginia tavern. The conversation Listwell hears through the wall includes a debate about his own identity. The scene thus turns the act of overhearing back on itself, dramatizing a complex relation between performer and audience as the celebrated performer and subject of gossip surveys his spectators. From his room in the tavern, Listwell becomes the unseen audience of characters who act as an audience to him, much as Douglass might secretly become a careful auditor of his own audience, figured in Mr. Listwell. *The Heroic Slave* engages in the complex activity of listening to Mr. Listwell as it turns from the overt exposure of Southern slavery to the covert exposure of Northern racism in a subtext that casts suspicion on Listwell despite his helpful role in the main plotline.

The debate about his idenity that Listwell overhears in the Virginia tavern includes discussion of his business in the South, a discussion prompted by a character named Wilkes, who insists that Listwell is a slave buyer. Although the gossipers in the bar are clearly unreliable judges of character, their dispute is charged with the text's own anxieties about the

Northern abolitionist—anxieties manifest by unaccountable repetition and unexplained actions. Wilkes repeats his identification of Listwell as slave buyer three times in the space of two pages (*HS*, 50–52). Wilkes believes Listwell to be a wealthy man, from whom he hopes to receive tips in exchange for small favors, but the expected tips hardly seem adequate motivation for him to repeat so often and so adamantly his charge that Listwell is a slave trader who won't reveal his true identity: "'Well,' said Wilkes, 'I am willing to bet any man in the company that *that* gentleman is a nigger-buyer. He didn't tell me so right down, but I reckon I knows enough about men to give a pretty clean guess as to what they are arter.' The dispute as to *who* Mr. Listwell was, what was his business, where was he going, etc., was kept up with much animation for some time, and more than once threatened a serious disturbance of the peace" (*HS*, 52).

Even though *The Heroic Slave* satirizes Wilkes and his drinking companions, their questions threaten a serious disturbance of the narrative's peace. The drinkers at the Virginia tavern are not alone in their ignorance of Mr. Listwell's primary business in the South. Neither Douglass's text nor his readers know what that business is. Listwell travels to Virginia twice in the course of this brief novella, but his business with the South is never clarified. Three years after the passage of the Fugitive Slave Act that rendered the North complicit with the South, as Douglass so often charged, Listwell's business with the South is highly suspect.

Key elements of the Southern racism that led to the violent attack on the old slave recur in a symbolic form in the Northern discourse that is linked with Listwell. When Madison Washington first enters the North and approaches Listwell's Ohio farm, the gothic atmosphere, emblem of the disturbed Northern discourse, treats his approach as a provocative violation and a threat to property, the "place" of wealthy, white male privilege. The Listwells' windows clatter in the wind, and their "trusty watchdog" growls (*HS*, 31). It seems that once a fugitive slave successfully arrives in the free state of Ohio, he no longer needs a dollar to signal his power or resistance because the discourse in the North registers his very presence there as violation. Like their watchdog, the Listwells are immediately aroused to danger: "[T]here are certain seasons when the slightest sound sends a jar through all the subtle chambers of the mind; and such a season was this. The [Listwells] started up, as if some sudden danger had come upon them" (*HS*, 31). Mr. Listwell unthinkingly defines the stranger as a violator of property rights. As Listwell dismisses the noise as nothing but the wind, he says, "[f]riends would not be likely to come out . . . on such a night; and thieves are too lazy and self-indulgent to expose themselves to this biting frost" (*HS*, 32). Even though he denies there is danger, he constructs all visitors who are not friends as thieves. Because the fugitive is not, in the usual sense of the word, a friend but rather a stranger in the North, he falls into the the same category as the old slave who was beaten in Virginia: the category of thief.[10]

Listwell's very first response to Washington is aligned with the Fugitive Slave Act, which required Northerners to identify fugitives as stolen property to be returned to their Southern owners. The watch dog that polices the Listwells' property figures the automatic functioning of a Northern discourse that supports slavery and attacks the fugitive slave before he can intervene in its terms. The Listwells' watchdog, which "growl[s] and bark[s] furiously" (*HS*, 32), presents yet another variation on being (over)-heard. Here, unlike the scene of Washington's soliloquy, the hero is not heard giving a speech that might be unprepared for an audience; he is heard before he can speak at all. The encounter with the keen-eared watchdog figures the dangers and difficulties of penetrating a racist discourse that is always already in place, threatened and ready to attack. The problem is so vexing that Douglass's novella can solve it only through chance. The Listwells' dog suddenly shows his "true instinct" to recognize Washington as a friend, and Listwell breaks his tendency to define the fugitive as a thief because, five years earlier, he overheard the very man who now appears at his door in that eloquent soliloquy in the Virginia forest.

The coincidence that allows Washington to have already spoken (five years) before the watch dog barks elides the difficulties of intervening in an always already functioning system of racism, though the solution remains troubled by the problematic act of overhearing that enables it. When Listwell greets the fugitive at his door, saying, "'I have seen your face and heard your voice before. . . . *I know all*,'" Washington is understandably "disconcerted and disquieted" (*HS*, 33). Although Listwell's wel-

10. Douglass was aware that the fugitive in the North might well belong to the category of stranger. He addressed the danger of that category and redesignated thievery as a characteristic of Northern whites in an 1853 speech on the Fugitive Slave Act, which, he argued, led Northern whites "to rob every black stranger who ventures among them" of body and soul (Blassingame 1982, 431).

come circumvents the problems of intervening in a racist discourse that is always already in process, Douglass implies the problem everywhere elsewhere through his choice of subjects: the historical Madison Washington and the revolt he led aboard the slave ship *Creole* in 1841.

The revolt aboard the *Creole* and the national responses to it cast the Fugitive Slave Act as only the most recent and most blatant act of Northern complicity with slavery. The national debates that reacted to the revolt led by Madison Washington show in the collective psyche of the dominant American culture, in the North as well as the South, a repertoire of images of African American men that derived from the interests of slaveholders. *The Heroic Slave* exposes the content of the American repertoire of racist imagery when the old slave in Virginia is labeled a thief and then stripped and beaten, when Madison Washington is confronted by the watchdog that guards the Listwells' property, and when the novella taps the contentious atmosphere associated with the *Creole* revolt. Elements of the dominant culture in both the South and the North responded to the *Creole* incident by linking the charge of violated property to tropes of sexual violation.

In 1841, Madison Washington led the revolt aboard the *Creole* as it carried slaves from Virginia to New Orleans. Washington and eighteen other slaves took control of the ship and steered it to the port of Nassau, where the British government declared the slaves on board free. The revolt was not a very bloody one—only two men, one black and one white, were killed. Nevertheless, it was met with outrage in the Southern press and with anger in the United States Congress (Jones 1975, 30–31). When the slaves on board the *Creole* revolted in an act that proclaimed their humanity, *their very presence as persons* was registered in the United States as a violation of the whites' property rights. The Senate documents record a verbal battle between the U.S. consul and the British governor of Nassau. The U.S. consul "contended 'that the slaves were as much a portion of the cargo as the tobacco, and entitled to the same protection from loss to the owners.' [The British governor] at the same time insisted the slaves were and could only be treated as passengers" (U.S. Senate 1842, 4). It is not surprising that Southern interests moved rapidly to deny the former slaves' disruptive personhood. Those interests, however, were relayed through the U.S. Congress. When the *Creole* reached New Orleans, the company that had insured the slaves sought financial reparation from the U.S. Congress, which in turn requested reparation from the federal government (Jones 1975, 33). These actions reaffirmed the definition of the *Creole* rebels as a mode of property—stolen property—and, by implication, the now free African Americans who removed that "property" as thieves. Secretary of State Daniel Webster (the prominent statesman from Massachusetts) accepted the Southern view that protection of U.S. property rights was the paramount issue in the affair (Jones 1975, 39, 42).

The rhetoric of violation that surrounded The *Creole* affair was fraught with images of breaking and entering that fueled vigilance over property in both the South and the North. The Senate hearings on the revolt included a description of the rebels taking "complete possession of the vessel, [and] breaking open and robbing the trunks of the passengers" (U.S. Senate 1842, 17), as well as a repeated report that whites feared "the cabin of the *Creole* would be sacked and robbed" by Bahaman blacks who came in their boats to aide the newly freed slaves (U.S. Senate 1842, 43). In addition, the hearings provided a vivid representation of blacks *entering* into U.S. politics in order to *break* slavery. When the *Creole* landed at Nassau, the American consul requested that the British government there send a guard to prevent the slaves from escaping. In response, the British government "sent twenty-four negro soldiers, with loaded muskets and bayonets . . . commanded by [one] white officer . . . [who] took possession of the vessel and all the slaves" (U.S. Senate 1842, 42).

Frederick Douglass clearly appreciated the powerful representation of black soldiers boarding the vessel of American slavery. When he recounted the incident in an 1849 speech, he laced the narrative with humor and provoked laughter form his audience (Blassingame 1982, 156). *The Heroic Slave,* however, shows that Douglass was also keenly aware that his audience could appropriate such racialized images of intervention. Whites could view African Americans as symbols of the violation of American property, much as the Listwells and their watchdog do when Madison Washington first approaches their farm.

The *Creole* controversy of 1842 entwined images of black intervention with outcries against violated honor (violated national honor). The company that insured the *Creole* argued that because the *Creole* had been en route from Virginia to New Orleans, the British government had unlawfully intervened in U.S. internal trade and that the U.S. government should rebuke

Britain. The *Creole* revolt thus became part of a larger dispute with England over its interference with U.S. ships at sea, as the British enforced their ban on the African slave trade. The British claimed that they had to board ships flying the U.S. flag because the flag was not proof enough that a ship was indeed American. Many in the United States treated such boardings as assaults on national honor (Jones 1975, 35–36). Hence Daniel Webster introduced the testimony of the *Creole* affair with a protest against "the indignity offered the American Flag" (U.S. Senate 1842, 1).

As the debate about the *Creole* revolt combined images of black intervention with the rhetoric of violated honor in 1841 and 1842, it already bore the seeds of the emergent racist discourse that after the Civil War would provocatively sexualize images of violation associated with the potential empowerment of African American men. The testimony in the Creole affair was rife with the precursors of that discourse. Alongside the primary narrative that documented white fear of violence from the Bahamans, a secondary sexualized narrative emerged as the American vessel, repeatedly troped as feminine, was faced with threat of being boarded by yet more black and foreign men. "I . . . was informed that the moment the troops should be withdrawn an attempt would be made to board her by force" (U.S. Senate 1842, 6). The Senate documents refer more than a dozen times to fears that the American vessel would be forcibly boarded by the black Bahamans in the boats (1842, 1–12). In addition, the testimony gave vivid representation of the boarding of the *Creole* by the black crew of the pilot's boat (all men) and by various white British officials (also men), at times to the exclusion of white men sent by the U.S. consul (1842, 11, 42).

Douglass's heroism of exposure responds to the troubling question *The Heroic Slave* raises as Washington approaches Listwell's house: How does one intervene in a racist discourse that is always already in motion and that relies on a shifting but potent repertoire of symbolic images, which it might tap differently at different historical moments to reinvigorate itself? In *The Heroic Slave,* the former slave, Madison Washington, does not elude the North's symbolic violence as he does the physical violence of the South when the old slave is beaten. Instead, the speaker-hero must stand in the midst of the painful and complex symbolic violence of Northern racism and track it from within.

As the public forum became the increasingly eroticized space of celebrity, Douglass—the symbolic figure who, for many whites in his audience, stood in a place reserved for a white man—had to endure his white audience's sexual and bestial projections. Morrison argues that the dominant culture in nineteenth-century America treated African American bodies as objects for its "meditations on terror" (1990, 37), not the least of which was its terror of forbidden sexuality.[11] Douglass, as master of reason and verbal eloquence, clearly intervened in the European-American fixation on black bodies and in the emerging terms of "scientific" racism that placed African Americans in the category of animals.[12] Yet Douglass could not intercept racism without agonistically bearing on his body and in his words the pressure of backlash from his Northern white audience.[13] We see this most clearly in the Boston woodcut of Douglass and the Griffiths sisters, and in the hecklers who hooted and howled like animals during a speech Douglass gave in New York in 1850.[14]

The speaker-hero, as Douglass fashioned him in his own persona and in his character Madison Washington, has to marshall the courage not simply to bear exposure to his audience, but to bear it repeatedly in arduous work, at once psychological and political, that grapples with a complex dynamic of supplementation. In an essay that features Douglass, Gregory S. Jay argues that supplementation can open moments for subversion. He writes: "[Ideology] cannot reproduce itself without agents, and this dependence creates a supplementary relation of ideology to agency that opens up the space for a [subversive] difference" (1990, 228–29). Although Douglass clearly exploited supplementation for such subversions,

11. See Morrison's discussion of fetishization (1992, 68). Gilman argues that nineteenth-century European culture used African bodies to sexualize itself, even as it excoriated sexuality (1985, 228, 232).

12. Gould gives a full discussion of "scientific" racism in the eighteenth and nineteenth centuries. See especially chapter 2 (1981). Spillers traces the European view of captive Africans as bestial to the early slave trade in the fifteenth century (1987, 68).

13. I am indebted to Jenny Franchot for my understanding of the importance of the eroticized, violating gaze of Douglass's audiences. Whereas Franchot emphasizes Douglass's adept management of his audience's gaze, arguing that Douglass averted attacks on the black man's body by displacing them onto slave women (1990, 144–46), I would argue that Douglass's novella emphasizes the moments in which the masculine, heroic speaker cannot fully control the sexually charged discourse amid which he finds himself.

14. While Douglas was giving an address in New York in May 1850, a group of white men ran onto the platform, "hooting, groaning [and] hissing," then one of them "attempted to prove that blacks were descended from monkeys" (Blassingame 1982, 237–38).

the novella complicates the issue by registering the ways that the dominant discourse could itself manipulate supplementation.

In the Virginia forest scene of *The Heroic Slave*, Madison Washington experiences his white audience's sexualized projections as meanings that supplement his will. The subtext of his soliloquy enacts the African American masculine speaker's painful struggle to name and to cast off the supplemental racist meanings that have worked their way into his voice and onto his body. The image of the snake in particular signals a subtext in which Douglass's surrogate must cast off the terror of the bestial:

> "How mean a thing am I. That accursed and crawling snake, that miserable reptile, that has just glided into its slimy home, is freer and better off than I. He escaped my blow and is safe. But here am I, a man,—yes a *man!*—with thoughts and wishes, with powers and faculties as far as angel's flight above that hated reptile,—yet he is my superior, and scorns to own me as his master, or to stop to take my blows. When he saw my uplifted arm, he darted beyond my reach, and turned to give me battle. I dare not do as much as that." (*HS*, 27)

The figurative resonances of the snake signal a barely suppressed panic within Washington's soliloquy. Washington designates the snake as the "crawling" and "accursed" snake of Genesis: the lowest of beasts and the damned. At the same time, the image is sexualized as the snake "glides into its slimy home." When linked with the other sexualized imagery of the scene, like Listwell's "dangerous intrusion" and Washington's "standing erect," the hero's battle with the snake enacts his struggle to free himself from the sexualized animalist imagery that appears upon Listwell's stealthy approach and amid Listwell's desire "to sound the mysterious depths" of the slave (*HS*, 28). The attempt to fend off such imagery becomes evident when Douglass adds to the snake "the raging bull." Washington asks about the bull: "Did I not keep [it] at bay. . . ?" (*HS*, 27).

Washington keeps the bull at bay, but he cannot fully distance himself from the snake, whose coils figure entrapment. What can it mean when the hero says, "he scorns to *own me as his master*" (emphasis added)? The circular language inextricably enmeshes and confuses who is owned with who is master, even as the snake calls to mind the whip and the chain of slavery.[15] The supplementary meanings of the snake imagery, laced with an

---

15. The imagery also echoes Douglass's description of the overseer, Covey, in his fight with him in the 1845 *Narrative*, where Douglass vanquishes the snake in less problematic terms.

eroticized power, augment the image's ability repeatedly to entrap Washington as they overlap and circle back on themselves to challenge his identity as a man. Although Washington goes on to assert his identity, his entanglement with the snake that "dart[s] beyond [his] reach" is not yet fully resolved.

The Heroic Slave registers an audience that seeks to enforce its inscription of the bestial on the body of the African American masculine speaker through tactics of surveillance that also manipulate the meanings of supplementation. Douglass's novella illuminates the cultural surveillance that aims to keep the African American speaker "in his place," where, in Foucauldian fashion, he is repeatedly to be judged by his audience. The audience's disciplinary gaze requires unstinting perseverance in the speaker exposed to it, for its tactics demand seemingly endless repetition of the narrative that figures his transformation from a slave who was used as a brute to a free man. In the Virginia forest scene, Listwell's surveillance accompanies his desire to probe the thoughts of a slave who is contemplating escape. Listwell thus reinscribes the disciplinary demand of Douglass's old master, Hugh Auld. When Auld feared Douglass was unfitting himself for slavery by learning to read, he tried to keep Douglass in plain view; when he could not, he would call on Douglass "to give an account of [him]self" (*NL,* 277).

Madison Washington's soliloquy makes visible the demand that Washington give an account of himself by reiterating the format of the slave narrative, beginning with its introduction: "I am a slave,—born a slave" (*HS,* 27). In addition, the plot of *The Heroic Slave* repeats the story of escape no less than three times. Washington's first attempt at escape fails when he loses his way and finds himself back on the plantation where he began. His second attempt succeeds, taking him to Canada, but in a futile attempt to rescue his wife he again returns to the plantation where he began. Here, he is recaptured and must escape yet a third time. Although Douglass clearly engages in subversive tactics of his own, expanding Washington's heroism with each escape, the need to escape so often marks his own frustration as his text wrestles with his white audience's surveillance.

The audience pressure that led Douglass to write his 1845 *Narrative* sheds light on the repeated demand that the African American masculine speaker account for himself. Douglass wrote the *Narrative* to placate an audience who did not believe that the articulate Douglass had actually been a slave (*MB*, 221). Although the disbelief shows that Douglass's eloquence impressed audience members, it also casts suspicion on their motives for reading his narrative. Whereas Douglass sought to prove he was a man, his audience wanted proof that he had been a slave. The white audience thus emphasized his initial debased position as slave. As the popularity of slave narratives that featured brutal beatings suggests, even his debased position as a slave fascinated elements within Douglass's audience. Winks describes slave narratives that featured brutality as "the pious pornography of their day, replete with horrific tales of whippings [and] sexual assault" (Winks 1969, vi). Because the demand that Douglass give an account of himself entangled the proof of his identity as a man with the proof of his identity as a slave, elements of his white audience could, consciously or unconsciously, fetishize his position as slave, using Douglass's symbolic persona as "African American man in transition" to prevent him from ever arriving at a position they would consider equal. To ask the heroic fugitive to give his account yet again was to ask him to start once more where he first began: in slavery.

Douglass called direct attention to the problem in his 1852 address, "What to the Slave is the Fourth of July?" The address expressed his frustration that—no matter how many narratives he told, and no matter how many human categories he provided for African Americans, supplemental to that of slave—his white audience did not acknowledge them.

> For the present, it is enough to affirm the equal manhood of the negro race. Is it not astonishing that, while we are ploughing, planting and reaping, . . . erecting houses, constructing bridges, building ships . . . ; that while we are . . . acting as clerks, merchants and secretaries, having among us lawyers, doctors, ministers, poets, authors, editors, orators and teachers; that, while we are . . . living in families as husbands, wives and children . . . we are called upon to prove that we are men! (Blassingame 1982, 2: 370).

Here, Douglass chastises an audience that treats his narrative task as though its completion were endlessly deferrable and hence in need of continual supplementation by additional accounts and by the audience's judgment. In the Virginia forest, Listwell gives the ideal response to the end of Washington's soliloquy. He declares, "I have seen enough and heard enough" (*HS*, 30). Quite clearly, however, Douglass sensed that his white audience could never hear enough of the fugitive slave's account(s) of himself to count him a man.

Repetition in *The Heroic Slave* shows that Douglass's heroism of exposure requires work that is difficult in yet another respect. Because the speaker-activist works from a position thoroughly situated in the political field, she or he labors without a privileged and reassuring vantage from which to measure the results of the work. In 1853, *The Heroic Slave* did not fully subvert the meanings the dominant culture projected onto the body and voice of the African American masculine speaker. In its repetition, the novella reveals a racist discourse that supplements Douglass's meanings, even as it marks the places where his own text cannot quite supplement the meanings of the dominant culture.

From the constructed vantage of hindsight, I find that as Douglass's novella repeatedly registers the tactics of racism, it brings them toward consciousness and visibility, doing important work that is necessary before those tactics can be confronted. I find that the subtext of *The Heroic Slave* prepares the way for Douglass's 1856 narrative, *My Bondage and My Freedom,* which, as critics have argued, recasts the meanings of slavery and freedom in light of Northern racism (Andrews 1987, xv) and casts off the framing gaze of a white audience, exchanging William Lloyd Garrison's introduction for an introduction by the African American activist, James M'Cune Smith (Sekora 1994, 614). And Smith's introduction, as Andrews argues, locates the meaning of Douglass's life in his abolitionist activity and consequent position as national figure, not in his role as slave (1987). Yet in 1853, Frederick Douglass could not have constructed a position of hindsight; he could not have known that the troubling work of his novella's subtext was also productive work. The hero of extended exposure must await the results of his labor with patience, albeit an anxious and impatient patience.

As the broad lines of the plot of *The Heroic Slave* announce Madison Washington's unquestioned heroism and a relation of mutual respect between him and Listwell, the novella is disturbed by its repetition and its subtext. Together, they call attention to those tactics of power that disrupt both the straightforward movement of the plot and the direct relation between Douglass and his white audience. Repetition and subtext confront the problem that Douglass's novella raises in its opening pages, as the African American narrator comes before the dominant cultural audience.

Under the cover of a confident narrative, the subtext of *The Heroic Slave* assumes the novella's riskiest work. It highlights instances of racism and begins to track the dynamics of the electrified cultural field that comprises that racism, the field within which the heroic fugitive can appear to his white audience only in marks and traces.

In probing the troubling subtext in Douglass's novella, I, like Mr. Listwell, engage in an act of overhearing. I explore a strand of *The Heroic Slave* of which Douglass may not have been fully conscious. And if he was conscious of it, he very likely did not intend the subtext that dramatizes the heroic fugitive's anxieties for the ears of his European American audience, of which I am a member. In his autobiographies, which collectively Walker calls "a carefully painted portrait that Douglass intended to fix as part of the public record" (1978, 212), Douglass does not long dwell on his anxieties. When he mentions them, he is usually careful to link them to adverse social conditions and moral failures in American society. My work, like Listwell's actions, includes the exposure of the heroic African American speaker in his anxiety and his pain. Yet I hope it follows the direction of Douglass's own work, illuminating through the heroism of his exposure the tactics of racism that become audible whenever the writer or character perceives resistance to his claims for equality. Douglass's subtext might then enable me and other European American readers to overhear something of ourselves in the American cultural legacy of racism. With Douglass's perception of his audience before us, we might turn back on ourselves and become conscious of a racist discourse that often functions best when unacknowledged. In the act of listening to ourselves in the discourse of racism, we might produce a difference between ourselves and that racism.

Perhaps it seems strange to ask twenty-first century readers to turn to a text almost 150 years old to view or hear *our* American racism, but many of the features of racism underscored in Douglass's novella are still powerfully with us. I do not mean to dismiss the important historical differences between the United States of mid–nineteenth century and the United States of the beginning of the twenty-first century, but rather to suggest that different historical moments in American history tap differently the same reservoir of racist imagery. Douglass's novella is very much a text of the 1850s, a decade of national tension and, for African Americans, as

Blight notes, a decade of disappointment and even despair after the passage of the Fugitive Slave Act (1989, 3). Douglass's repeated acts of facing, subverting, and exposing the racism of his European American audience clearly responded to the heightened anxieties of the decade. Surely Douglass's work helped to animate the tensions that led to the Civil War. Yet, when *The Heroic Slave* dwells on the repeated insistence that the African American hero give an account of himself, it highlights features of racism that are not only of one historical moment. Instead, they recede and return within the dominant cultural psyche to be tapped, though perhaps differently, today.

In contemporary American culture, so thoroughly permeated by visual images and by practices of celebrity that invite audience projections, the symbolic violence of racism may be more intricately woven into our daily lives than it was during Douglass's life. Our political discourse, relayed through the news media, taps the same repertoire of symbolism exposed in *The Heroic Slave* when it produces image after image of African American men as thieves and violators of white persons and their property, and turns them into symbols of national ills. We need only recall the use of Willie Horton in George Bush Sr.'s 1988 presidential campaign or the entire nation's transfixed gaze on the trials of O. J. Simpson to see our contemporary discourse revive the images of bestial violation that began to gather around the *Creole* revolt.[16]

Current media attention to African American gangs is enmeshed in a complex deployment of strategies that draw on the repertoire of symbolic racism that so frustrated Frederick Douglass. In an economy in which well-paid working-class jobs have suffered severe erosion, institutional racism has blocked for many poor African American men the avenues to dominant cultural constructions of "manhood," such as the role of "breadwinner." When, in response, gangs posit alternate and threatening definitions of "manhood," the news media is often quick to frame its images of gangs not in analyses of the economic, social, and cultural conditions that would

16. During the 1988 presidential contest, the Bush campaign used the image of Horton to discredit Michael Dukakis as soft on crime. Horton, a prisoner in Massachusetts who had been convicted of murder but was on furlough, broke into the home of a white couple and raped the woman. The image of Horton flashed across the media and quickly become a powerful and nationally recognizable racist symbol. Jim Ross, a journalism professor at Northeastern University, summed up the issue when he accused the newspaper that first reported the story as "pandering to . . . a lynch mob mentality" (qtd. in Burkholder 1989, 15).

contextualize them, but in the old frame that justified slavery: the frame of the bestial that treats poor African American men as brutes whose humanity is in doubt.[17]

The subtext of Douglass's *Heroic Slave* points to a dominant audience that plays an active role in the circulation of symbolic racist meanings. Douglass's subtext presses beyond the Enlightenment terms of the *Columbian Orator* to notice and to track a cultural discourse that is by no means rational, though it clearly has a rationale, and by no means comprehensible in simple static categories. As active participants in U.S. culture at the beginning of the twenty-first century, amid imagery that is so much denser and so much more rapidly circulated than that of Douglass's time, we must work to make audible and visible not only the repertoire of racist language and imagery but also the transpersonal dynamics of cultural discourse unavailable to ideologies of individualism. In 1853, Douglass began to probe the activity of a cultural discourse despite his predilection for Enlightenment republican oratory and his own embracing of individualism. Yet at the beginning of the twenty-first century, hegemonic discussions of politics in the United States often fail to acknowledge political relations between people that are rooted in the culture rather than simply in the separate acts of individuals. Often our political discussions fail to acknowledge connections of any kind between past and present. When the subtext of *The Heroic Slave* implicates Mr. Listwell—the declared abolitionist—in the racism of the slaveholder, it implies that simple categories—such as those that isolate the individual, the region, and perhaps even the present historical moment—supply us with the ideological blinders that enable us to deny American racism. Only with the recognition of the cultural dynamics that we help to circulate and to vary according to the pressures of our time, can we see how we participate in, and thus how we might refuse to participate in, an American racialized discourse that is historically and powerfully ingrained.

17. For an exception in the mainstream press, see William Julius Wilson, who in the *New York Times Magazine* calls attention to the lack of work as a major factor in producing crime and drug addiction in inner-city areas (1996, 27–28). For recent discussions of the persistence of dominant cultural images of African American men as bestial and violent, see Earl Ofari Hutchinson's *The Assassination of the Black Male Image* (1994) and John Hoberman's *Darwin's Athlete* (1997).

Friendly Town, being #15

Safiya Henderson-Holmes

dear daddy;
no one ever
told me that
white men
were shaped
like black men.

today, in celebration
of a double bingo hit
almost dad and sons
wore their birthday
suits in the rain.

almost mom
giggled and covered
my eyes. i peeked
through her laughter:
not one extra arm or leg.

not one less.
a father and his sons
skipping toward a barn.
their pale skin not glowing,
only wet by rain.

daddy, what is all
the marching for?

"If He Asks You Was I Running You Tell Him I Was Flying, If He Asks You Was I Laughing You Tell Him I Was Crying"

Reading John Henry as American History 1870

Gale Patricia Jackson

> *"In a little time after, amongst the poor chained men, I found some of my own nation, which in a small degree gave ease to my mind. I inquired of these what was to be done with us. They gave me to understand we were to be carried to these white people's country to work for them. I was then a little revived, and I thought if it were no worse than working, my situation was not so desperate."*
> Olaudah Equiano, *The Interesting Narrative of the Life of Olaudah Equiano*

> *"I am a God sent man. All the education I got, it was out in the fields. That was my fountain pen and pencil. The blade of my hoe was my pen, and my slate was the ground."*
> Works Progress Administration informant, Fisk University,
> *Unwritten History of Slavery*

> *"Trouble in mind I'm blue / but I won't be blue always / cause the sun's gonna shine / in my back door someday / I'm gonna lay my head / on a lonesome railroad line / Let the 2:19 train ease my troubled mind"*[1]
> *(blues traditional)*

The story goes like this: In 1870, the Chesapeake and Ohio Railroad began laying tracks in West Virginia. The work gang was a group of black men.[2] While they worked, they sang. Weren't no new thing. African Americans have a deep work history in this country and, until late in the twentieth century, a tradition of worksongs—of working and singing. Africans came

---

1. The widely known early-twentieth-century blues song "Trouble in Mind" is derived, inspired, or related to the old spiritual "I am Troubled in Mind" and was published in 1926 by the Leeds Music Corporation in New York. Reprinted in Silverman 1968, 101.

2. The narrative of the "historical" John Henry that I have adapted here is based on the

to this continent working, moved south to north and east to west working, and told the tale while setting the pace, getting the groove, and making the rhythm of synchronized labors with their songs. In 1870, laying railroad lines was all done by hand, and in the South it was black men's muscle and voice that moved the industry.

> Big bell call you, little bell warn you / If you don't come now, I'm gonna break in on you / Ain't you going boys ain't you going.[3]

Shack rousters knocked on the box cars or company shacks of the railroad construction crew to wake the workers up with what they called "field hollers," refit for these new fields of steel. "Big bell call you," they sang, or:

> Wake up buddy / and sit on a rock / It ain't quite day / But its four o'clock / Rat-tat-tat / Hey buddy / It hard but it fair / If you had a good home you wouldn't stay here.[4]

Then, not far behind the shack rousters were the voices of the *mule skinners* who plied the right of way and carried water up and down the line. They might be singing:

> Well it's good morning captain good morning shine / Yes it's good morning captain and it good morning shine / Do you need another mule skinner on your new railroad line?

> Well I like to work I'm rolling all the time / Yes I like to work, I'm rolling all the time / I can carve my initials on a mule's behind.

> Working on the railroad making a dollar and a dime a day / Working on the railroad making a dollar and a dime a day / Give my woman the dollar and throw the dime away. (Silverman 1958, 32)

From the first tie and the first sigh on southern railroad lines, black railroad gangs laid down polyrhythmic works of vocalizing and sweated the same way they had picked and planted, cleared and carried since their great-grands arrived in this place, in working traditions wrought from a new gathering of the African continent bound together in a fabric woven in call and response.[5]

---

only two extensive studies done while contemporaries of the incident at the Big Bend were still alive. See Johnson 1929 and Chappell 1933.

3. "Shack rouster" song from Lomax 1960, 254.

4. "Shack rouster" song from Parrish 1965, 246.

5. For discussion of the African roots and African American practice of worksong, see Courlander 1963, Landeck 1961, and Scarborough 1925.

When I was young and in my prime (hah!) / Sunk my ax deep every time (hah!) / Now I'm old and my heart's growing cold (hah!) / Can't swing my ax to save my soul (hah!) / Come on mister tree you almost down (hah!) / Come on mister tree want to see you hit the ground (hah!)[6]

What worked in the field worked one hundred years later on the railroad. A *steel caller* would synchronize the movements of a gang of men unloading two ton rails and swinging them into buckets with a series of physical and vocal responses. *Tie toters* sang as they carried railroad ties on their shoulders, and in the course of the day a *gang leader* lined out song after song as men laid rails, poured gravel, and then "lined the track": putting crowbars to the *johnny head* (joint ahead) on the downbeat to pull, push, and lift the rails into place. All along, they recorded their lives and their work with their songs.[7]

When I get to Illinois / I'm gonna spread the word about the Florida boys / Shove it over! / Hey Hey can't you line it? / Can't you move it? Hey! Hey? /Can't you try? / Ah-shack-a-lack-a-lack-a-lack-a-lack-a-lack / Me and my buddy going across the field / I heard a train when it left Mobile / Shove it over . . . /I heard a mighty noise around the river bend / Must be the Southern crossing the L & N. / Tell you what the hobo said to the bum—If you get any corn bread save me some . . . / A nickel's worth of bacon and a dime's worth of lard / I would buy more but the time's too hard.[8]

So it was in 1870, in the West Virginia mountains, as they lay tracks on the Chesapeake and Ohio Railroad line, that the work gang hit a wall of stone along the Potomac River at a place called Big Bend and had to call on a powerful steel-driving team to clear the way for them, to make a way through the mountain. People say it was the biggest job yet attempted by North American railroad men, and some thought it was too big for any human. Work stopped. Bosses brought in a new machine, a steam drill, which was purported to outhammer any man, any steel-driving team. Men

6. Antebellum "ax" tune recorded in Lomax 1960, 514.

7. I've learned more about how the work of these men was performed from gathering their songs than from any particular technical source. The simulated "performances" of work and song by retired railroad men in the film *Gandy Dancers* (1995) brought it home for me. The descriptions in Lomax 1960 and the photographs from Frederic Ramsey 1960 were helpful illustrations for this city kid.

8. From track workers' lining song; recorded in Florida and reprinted from Hurston 1935. "This song is common to the railroad camps. It is suited to the 'lining' rhythm. That is, it fits the straining of men at the lining bars as the rail is placed in position to be spiked down" (270).

stepped back and they brought forward the machine. That's where John Henry comes in.[9]

> John Henry said to his captain / A man ain't nothing but a man / but before I let that steam drill beat me down / I'll die with the hammer in my hand / Lord Lord / Die with the hammer in my hand. (Lomax 1960, 107)

John Henry was a *steel driver*, a lead man in the two-man shaker/driver team who tunneled through solid rock with axes, hammers, and hands. Those two men worked face to face, five to six feet apart, stripped down to rags in a mountain's dark sweltering pits, where the walls were as dense as a forest and, when they gave, as stone dangerous. The shaker would hold a drill or a piece of steel in place, and the driver would "drive" it home into rock face. Although railroad work was *the* moneymaker for black men then, driving steel was the highest paying. You had to be strong, you had to be fearless, and you had to have God-sent luck. The best steel drivers were considered "charmed" men.

> I got a rainbow / Rainbow round my shoulder / I got a rainbow / rainbow round my shoulder / Ain't gonna rain / Lord Lord ain't gonna rain.[10]

Legend carried word around in those days, and legend had it that John Henry was bad—as in really good. Word was that he could drive steel better and faster, that he had a "rainbow round his shoulder," and that he was, of course, exceptionally treasured by men and women for the manner in which he was endowed. A contest was proposed: John Henry against the steam-powered drill that would in time replace the labor of men's arms. He accepted. There was the question of "a man's" dignity—a question of humanity. You know the story. When the day of the contest arrived, John Henry drove steel with a hammer in each hand and drove farther and faster than the machine. Then he died the way he had lived

9. See Johnson 1929 and Chappell 1933 for historical background and especially Johnson 1929 for compilations of railroad worker records.

10. A well-known worksong stanza in the southern United States cited as a nineteenth-century predecessor to the twentieth-century John Henry ballad, this stanza appears in a number of the John Henry worksongs and is assumed to be a part of the pool of worksongs/ditties that were gathered together in the making of the ballad. Hurston cites it as a verse of "Mule on the Mount," which she notes is "the most widely distributed and best known of all Negro worksongs": "Since folksongs grow by incremental repetition the diversified subject matter that it accumulates as it ages is one of the evidences of its distribution and usage. This has everything of folk life in it" (1935, 275–76). See also Southern 1971 on the growth of black song styles.

and as had been foretold. Some say he dropped dead on the spot from a "busted" heart. Some say that he died later, after returning home to the woman (women) in his life. All the same, it's about heart—about needing to have "heart" to live and die a black man.

> This old hammer / Rings like silver / This old hammer / Rings like silver / This old hammer / Rings like silver / Shines like gold, boys / Shines like gold
>
> Ain't no hammer / In these mountains / Ain't no hammer / In these mountains / Ain't no hammer / In these mountains / Rings like mine, boys / Rings like mine
>
> Take this hammer / To the captain / Take this hammer / To the captain / Take this hammer / To the captain / Tell him I'm gone, boys / Tell him I'm gone.[11]

There is the echo of John Henry's hammer haunting the mountains—like they say, "laughing, crying, running, flying"—where hundreds of others died laying the lines, buried under the collapsed walls of stone that created a United States. Railroad working men say that they've been singing his song since John Henry's partner took up the refrain when John Henry fell to the ground, and those men carried that living history, which holds within it their own, across the land from that moment into the twentieth century.[12]

> Take this hammer—huh! / And carry it to the captain—huh! / You tell him I'm gone—huh! / Tell him I'm gone—huh! / If he asks you—huh! / Was I running—huh! / You tell him I was flying—huh! / Tell him I was flying—huh! / If he asks you—huh! / Was I laughing—huh! / You tell him I was crying—huh! / You tell him I was crying—huh! (Hughes and Bontemps 1958, 399)

11. This is a hammer song recorded in West Virginia among the workers at the Big Bend Tunnel of John Henry fame in 1927. According to the workmen, this is the song John Henry himself sang when he drove steel. There is evidence that the song is rooted in antebellum ax songs that predate the 1872 contest between John Henry and the steam drill, supporting Hurston's contention about "aging" a folk song. See Lomax 1960, 515–53; Johnson 1929, 68–83; Chappell 1933; Odum and Johnson 1926.

12. This footnote is actually a chapter elsewhere but to sum it up quickly: In search of an appropriate methodology for "decoding" the history within African American song, I have attempted to develop an interdisciplinary approach. I have borrowed heavily from the work of literary theorists such as Melvin Dixon in Dixon 1987 and Henry Lewis Gates Jr., particularly in Gates 1988 where he utilizes Yoruba divination as a model for literary explication centering the deity Legba and Legba's cultural function in the development of a system for "reading" the layers of meaning in African American texts. I am also shamelessly utilizing the signal paradigms that Robert Farris Thompson has developed in African and African American art history (1974, 1980, 1983). (I cite Thompson profusely.) Clearly, too, I jump off from the important ground laid by both Lawrence Levine in Levine 1977 and Sterling Stuckey in Stuckey 1987.

John Henry is about the railroad as a symbol: one "track" of African American entrance into a "free" and industrializing America. John Henry is about the black male contest for human recognition and a truly radical proposal for social reconstruction.[13] After the "emancipation," African American laborers continued to clear, to plough, to harvest, to pile the levees, to load the steamboats, and to screw bales of cotton into the holds of ships. After the emancipation, as before but increasingly, the muscle of black labor, primarily male, laid the roads east to west and south to north that would take black life spiraling out from the old locations of enslavement and across the nation into the "mainstream" of American life (Greene 1930).

> This old hammer / Killed John Henry / But it won't kill me / It won't kill me. (Work 1940, 233)

Then there's Big Bend and the symbolic watershed of the 1870s. After the 1870s, though certainly beginning before and continuing after, the internal social relations of production changed. The constructions of identity, of race, of work, of American society, of the mode and relations of production were shifting. How that was, how that moved—the dialectical motion of people and production and what that meant to African Americans—is told in the ballad/story of John Henry. That's why the brother won *and* died and became a "mythical" figure. Contemporaries and their African American descendants did very well (thank you) without this, but for modern readers who have lost their place it may be necessary to do some "spelling out" of the time the song is talking about when they sing:

> If I could hammer / Like John Henry / If I could hammer / Like John Henry / Lord I'd be a man / Lord I'd be a man.[14]

Call: Africans to African Americans Worksongs to Blues

> Listen to my story / Tis a story true / Bout a mighty man John Henry was his name / And John Henry was a steel driver too / Lord Lord / John Henry was a steel driver too.[15]

---

13. For general discussions of African American laborers and the "making" of America, see Philip Foner *The Black Worker* (1978–85); Lorenzo Greene *The Negro Wage Earner* (1930); Morgan 1975; Wood 1974; Quarles 1964. For discussion of the ideologies of work and blackness, see Jordan 1968.

14. The best gathering of thought on this subject is done, again, in literary theory, notably Carby 1985 and 1987; see also Giddings 1984.

15. Leon Harris of Moline, Illinois, gave a version of the John Henry song to Guy Johnson.

This story begins with the memory of Africans transplanted into the Americas.[16] Within and framing that memory is a *new* African construction of meaning and society through culture—specifically, here, in performance or song. It is part of the narrative of a history continuously unfolding as Africans become Americans. The children of those many thousands of diverse peoples (many who were themselves children) who had been taken from their native lands and enslaved become women and men forging a new "black" identity in this country.[17] So the story begins with memory, memory contextualized by experience and location in history.

> do ba-na co-ba, ge-ne me, ge ne me!
> do ba-na co-ba, ge-ne me, ge ne me
> ben d' nu-li, nu-li, ben d' le

W. E. B. DuBois, in *The Souls of Black Folks,* his 1903 volume on African American culture, recalls learning this song as a child. According to family lore, the song had been passed down generation to generation from his grandfather's grandmother, who had been seized from her African home and enslaved by Dutch traders. Now that song had inside it at least one forgotten and two remembered things. DuBois did not know what the words "meant" or even what language they were in, but the memory, the structure and the function, of the song remained. DuBois recognized it as a place to begin talking about what he called "the sorrow songs" and about what it meant to be black at the turn of the century. The song had been passed to him, and he knew to pass it on. The structure of the music tells of an African beginning, of a way of life, an epistemology, a way of understanding (DuBois 1969, 268).

Harris writes, "I have been a 'Rambler' all my life. Ever since I ran away from the 'white folks' when I was twelve years old—and I have worked with my people in railroad grading camps from the Great Lakes to Florida and from the Atlantic to the Missouri River, and, wherever I have worked, I have always found someone who could and would sing of John Henry" (Johnson 1929, 90–95).

16. I will, with the support of critical sources, speak alternately of a generalized "African" culture and of specific ethnic or language-based African cultural groupings. The former is based on the work which has been done both on precolonial "pan-African" cultural similarities (see Mbiti 1975) and on the idea of an "incubated" African American identity arising out of the experience of slavery (see Bastide 1971 and Stuckey 1987). For the latter, specifically structuring my discussions around Bantu (central African) and West African (Niger Congo and Sudanese) cultural practices, I follow the lead of linguist Turner (1949) and anthropologists such as Bastide, who developed some language-group-based paradigms for discussing Africanisms in America.

17. Two early sources on the historical performance of seventeenth-century Africans and jump-off points for looking at their continuities in the practice of African Americans are Equiano 1987 (original 1814) and Park 1800.

That three-line stanza with its "call and response" speaks to the way identity is wrought from a performance of community—how, in this place, philosophically, creativity arises in dialogue, from people calling back and forth, and how such a multilayered dialogue that a community of people makes is a place of transformation, a place not unlike any diaspora "church." Here, in an older performance of cultural identity, music is not separate from how people will speak, the telling of stories, the recording of history, the clapping of hands, the moving of feet, or, in DuBois mother's case, the swaying of baby in arms. These polyrhythmic musics, inseparable from dance or voice or work, speak to a social construction without strict genre or Western time distinction, which brings us nicely to a song's use. The songs were and remain dialogues within a liminal space. Parents sing them to children, generation to generation, to soothe, to remember, to teach (DuBois 1969, 269).[18] DuBois's song is a story that comes down from a woman and is given again and again to generations of children, perhaps by women, perhaps as a lullaby until DuBois, in his fragmented time, "remembers" it to speak of "the souls of Black folks."[19]

> Told my captain my hands were cold / God damn your hands boy let the wheeling roll / Told my captain my feet were cold / God damn your feet boy let the wheeling roll. / Captain Captain you must be blind / Look at your watch it's past quitting time / Captain Captain how can it be / Whistle done blow you still working me? / Raised my hand to wipe the sweat off my head / Damned old captain shot my buddy dead / If you don't believe my buddy's dead / Just look at that hole in my buddy's head / Asked the captain to give me time / Damned old captain wouldn't pay me no mind. / If I had my weight in lime / Would have whupped that captain till he went stone blind / Captain walking up and down / Buddy's lying on

18. African musics and the "African" musical practices of Africans in the Americas have a number of features in common that are distinctively different from Western music at the turn of the century. Those African musical forms have, according to musicologist Beatrice Landeck, a distinctive degree of "rhythmic complexity and syncopation," "an indeterminate pitch of single tones in melody and dissonances in harmony," predominating "contrapuntal and antiphonal form *in a dialogue*" [my emphasis] between a leader's call and a group/choral response and an "improvisational treatment of all music" and hence musical composition (Landeck 1961, 13–15). Those "technical" elements are, in turn, distinctive aspects of both the execution and the philosophy of those forms that we call worksongs and the blues.

19. See Green 1983 for some discussion of the relationship between music and day-to-day life in West African society. See also the discussion of African musical practice in the early chapters of Southern 1971 and Oliver 1970 for a wider-ranging discussion of musical practice in the African interior and East Africa and of their specific relation to our study.

the burning ground / Buzzards circling 'round the sky / Buzzards sure know captain's gonna die.[20]

All cultural performance is historical text. You just have to know how to read it. Those complex rhythms of African performed "texts" are music or song in "dialogue" with storytelling, dance, sacred ceremony, and social activities—from childbirth celebrations to the harvesting of rice—*across* time. That's how the worksong is working. It's about work, but it's also about history, thought, and feeling, and about how that doesn't have to be written to have profound meaning for its generations. A leader and a chorus or an individual "dances" with or against a task and in response to particular situations.[21] As the blues and jazz players would say, people "play out the changes." Oral or performed history is a living text built to sing from a gathering of story. So let's gather.

Response: Lord, Lord

Some say he's from Georgia / Some say he's from Alabam / But it's written on the rock at the Big Bend Tunnel / John Henry's a East Virginia man / John Henry's a East Virginia man. (Hughes and Bontemps 1958, 345)

John Henry, according to legend, was a first-generation African American, the massive "pure"-blooded son of an African. Any man. Every man. Those who have tried to find the "real man" behind the mythology come to a dead end following the "paper trail" of a steel driver named John Hardy, who landed in the gallows at Welch, West Virginia, in 1894 (a nineteenth-century death row). Those papers say that Hardy was accused

---

20. "Blues as Worksong, Worksong as Blues" (Silverman 1958).

21. Thompson (1974) analyzes this question of the formal structure of dance performance in a way that raises exciting points about the "zeitgeist" of African cultural articulation, particularly when juxtaposed to studies in what we understand to be other areas of expression, such as Melvin Dixon's study of place and performance in African American literatures in Dixon 1987. Studies of African and African American dance, for instance, present us with the same general and distinctive traits: multiple meter, the dominance of percussion, call and response, dancing apart, and the role of social commentary. See Thompson 1980.

The practice and study of African American verbal arts bring yet another dimension in which the same formal structures are at work. Here, I refer to a whole range of "signifying" performances from girls' games to language plays such as "toasts," early examples of which can be found in Abrahams 1983. Contemporary examples can be found in Hughes and Bontemps 1958, Gates 1988, and Levine 1977. There is also a significant body of writing on black English and its Africanisms, its grammatical systems, which arise from Turner 1949 and have been explored in Dillard 1972, and Holloway and Vass 1993.

of having killed a man while working in the coal mines following a stint as a driver with the Chesapeake and Ohio. The research road forks at the divide between John Henry, well recalled in oral history, and the white folks' records of John Hardy jailed and hanged.[22] Most agree that Hardy ain't Henry, but even the mix-up is an important part of the story. See, later, it's in the penitentiary that these worksongs survive and are, in the 1940s and 1950s, written down, just as throughout the late twentieth century, American popular culture fed on the jailhouse "style" of young incarcerated males.

> John Henry told his captain / Bury me under the sills of the floor. So when they get to playing good old Georgy skin / Bet them fifty to a dollar more / Fifty to a dollar more.[23]

As in all oral traditions, a lot is in the naming. *John, John Doe,* the prostitute's customer, any man, is a signal name in the vast conception of oral historical recollection.[24] *John* is certainly a signal name in the African American oral text. *Jon* is the Mandingo word for someone who is owned by someone else and variations on this enslaved "everyman" appear regularly throughout the African diaspora as a major player in stories, songs, and sacred and secular performance for as far back as we have memories and recordings.[25] There's both history and magic in the continuum to John Henry's time. The railroad crossing is a liminal place, and John Henry pulls from a spectrum of deeply "buried" conjuring.

> John Henry was a little boy / Sitting on his mammy's knee / Said "the big Bend Tunnel on the C. and O. Road / Is going to be the death of me / Going to be the death of me." (Johnson 1929, 100)

22. See "John Henry and John Hardy" in Johnson 1929.

23. Unless otherwise indicated, all the stanzas used from here on are from the chapter in Johnson 1929 entitled "John Henry Ballads."

24. Thanks to the writer and essayist Charles Fredrick for pointing out, as he has done in so many of his works and in our lifelong conversation, these so obvious and forgotten "vernacular" roots of *John*.

25. Meaning taken from Hollaway and Vass: "Mandingo jon, slave, person owned by someone else. An average man, esp. one who can be exploited or easily taken in; a male lover, a prostitute's client. Also used in black American folklore as in John Henry, name of slave hero frequently in conflict with 'massa.' The term massa provides a convenient convergence of English master and Mandingo 'massa,' chief. That Mandingo speakers in U.S. were conscious of this convergence is suggested by the cycle of black American tales involving John-versus-Massa, which corresponds to a similar genre of Mandingo tales in West Africa involving jon, the slave, versus massa, the chief" (1993, 143). Good reference sources on African folklore include, but are

The name *John* is, in fact, a trope in African American oral and performed histories, appearing again and again in syncratic, "creole" gatherings that propose a cumulative depth of meaning. *John* is metaphorical, metaphysical, and metamorphosis. In the early tales of the North American South, there's John the trickster slave, who, like the spider and the rabbit of African and African American folklore, manages to use his wits to survive his disadvantaged position. There's also a later John, "the Conquer," in North American lore, whose characteristics suggest that he is the "spirit" twin of the earth-bound enslaved John. This "John the Conquer" is like the deities "Old Joaquim" and "Old John," who arise as new ancestors among the Brazilian *candombles* of enslaved Africans.[26] There are also the "Jonkonnu" male-masking (root *Jon*) performance processions of the English-speaking Caribbean, which date back to an eighteenth-century creolizing of the circular rituals of Central and West Africans. Then, back in North America and following on the war and the railroad-borne journeys of black folks' northern and western migrations, up (pardon the pun) comes *Johnson*, who remains a signal term for the male sexual organ. Of course, etymologically speaking, most folks figure, if they think about these things, that the ancestor of *Johnson* can be found in the "jazz," "jisms" and Bakongo-inspired "conjuring" of New Orleans. Which brings us nicely back to a number of things.

> John Henry went up on the mountain / Come down on the other side / Mountain so tall and John Henry so small/ He throwed down his hammer and he cried. (Lomax 1960, 561)

Zora Neale Hurston called John the Conquer, old-time hero of the African American folkloric pantheon, "a spirit" and "a longing" among the first generation of transplanted Africans, reminding us of the connotations of magic in the name *John* (1958, 93). Hurston's description calls us back to the interconnections of ancestor worship, historical method, and spirit possession among the West and Central African peoples, the diverse practices that coalesce in the construction of what becomes African American.

---

not limited to, Abrahams 1983 and Courlander 1963. Bascom 1969 is a good source for discussion of African folktale types.

26. Bastide 1971, discussing the transference in Afro-Brazilian religious possession from the familial African "lineages" to their neo-African formations, names "Old John" and "Joaquim" among "creole" African ancestors.

Interestingly enough, in many of the healing traditions of these African "root" regions, the plant African Americans call High John the Conqueror was considered powerful medicine in both the physical and metaphysical senses. High John the Conqueror root was something that the Africans immediately recognized and used, and that came to be known, like the black cat's bone, as a conjurer's item. What we might call an example of syncretization and creolization drawing strongly on Bakongo (Congo/Zaire) tradition is something, in John Henry's time, most people would *simply* have known.[27]

> John Henry was on the mountain / The mountain was so high / He called to his pretty little wife / Said I can almost touch the sky / Said I can almost touch the sky. (Hughes and Bontemps, 1958, 346)

The Bakongo bring a number of concepts to the American lexicon that were *simply*, vernacularly "known" in many locations, among them rituals of transformation (conjure) and performances of liminality that cross the line between the living and the dead into discrete, ritually potent and potentially regenerative moments in time, like John Henry on the mountain. In addition to grave markers, bottle trees, the ritual markers for the four moments of the sun, and all manner of magical wonders still drawn on in the "metaphysical traditions" of black Americans, there is the Bakongo *nkisi,* or healing art.[28] (*Nkisi* is linguistically related to *jizz,* which is derived from the Ki-Kongo verb *dinza,* to discharge one's semen, and is a root word for the performances that blend the ideas of sex, potency, and music like *jizz,"* *jism,* and "jazz, which bring us back to *Johnson, jizz's* linguistic son.) *Nkisi* objects appeared in the Americas as early and as far flung as Barbados, New Orleans, and seventeenth-century Salem, Massachusetts, where, in 1691, a black girl named Candy was accused of witchcraft and a *nkisi* object was used as evidence.

27. Hurston 1983, Deren 1953, and Thompson 1983 are my major sources for information on Vodun in Haiti as well as on the more general question of syncretic African American religious performances in the diaspora. In addition to Thompson's wide-ranging synthesis of the literature, I draw from Bastide's numerous observations on cultural fusion and "association" (1971), particularly on his theories about the creole reconstruction of "African" nations in the Americas and about the "double levels" of cultural fusion (wherein somewhere such as Louisiana might have Dahomean religion, Vodun, and a Bantu folklore tradition).

28. See Bastide 1971 on this marriage question from an anthropological turn and Thompson 1983 for a view on the gathering with an art historical spin.

Captain got a mule, mule on the Mount called Jerry / Captain got a mule, mule on the Mount called Jerry / I can ride, Lawd, Lawd, I can ride.[29]

The High John the Conquer root was considered a *nkisi* object (a juju, a conjure, a mojo). Its shape is just right. In the Bakongo belief its gnarled and twisted roots are power incarnate. High John the Conquer root was (and still is) used as a charm for love and against evil fate but also as a vehicle for centralizing power. Contemporary art historians have described *nkisi* figures, made from decorating actual plants or in modern sculptural forms, as "power sculpture." Another strong symbolic connection between the John Henry story and older African philosophical systems is the fact that traditional practitioners incorporated and continue to incorporate railroad nails into these "power sculptures."

John Henry took his little boy / Held him in the palm of his hand / And the last word he said to that child was / I want you to be a steel driving man / I want you to be a steel driving man. (101)

You go on and ask anybody in the diaspora religions what John Henry's doing before that mountain. Mountains. Valleys. Wilderness. All symbolic locations well known in the texts of oral traditions. All tropes in African American articulations. Drawing on the past to move from a time that's ending as it's beginning, John Henry is to the urbanizing African American of 1872 as Joonkanoo was to the primarily African-born rural slave populations of the seventeenth and eighteenth centuries; as John the trickster slave was to broken up black families of the nineteenth century; and as John the Conqueror is to black possibility. He is a container of history, and he is a charm, a marker of a place, and a sign for moving. In fact, in the motion of history, they appear to me to be one.[30]

The steam drill was on the right hand side / John Henry was on the left / Say before I let this steam drill beat me down / I'll hammer myself to death / I'll hammer myself to death. (Hughes and Bontemps 1958, 346)

---

29. From "Mule on the Mount" in Hughes and Bontemps 1958, 401. Zora Neale Hurston calls this "the oldest" of worksongs (1935, 275).

30. This discussion formally brings together much that is discussed in Thompson 1983, taken up in tandem with studies of African American language origins including Turner 1949, Hollaway and Vass 1993, and Major 1970.

John Henry also plays off, or signifies on, the stories of "Janqua" or John Crow, the buzzard, the vulture. In much of the traditional religion brought together in the African diaspora, the vulture is a symbol of power, maleness, and death. "Taking off" from the early King Buzzard tales of native Africans, there are the Janqua, John Crow, and High John the Conqueror stories of an American generation who had given new meaning to the question of the wandering soul, a meaning particularly resonant in the historically composed identity of the black man. Whereas the King Buzzard tales tell of a hopelessly wandering soul without proper funeral rites and, hence, with no place for eternity, the reality of the second generation was the need to re-create "home" in that place of wandering and the challenge of turning that image around. John Henry "flying" when the law considers him "running," John the conqueror literally walking across the performance of African American reconstruction, and Jon the slave before them—trapped physically but not spiritually by the slave system—form a line of signification that poses the questions, not of the "mainstream" discourse but of the African American worker's imagination.

> Some say he came from England / Some say he came from Spain / But its no such thing he was an East Virginia man / And he died with his hammer in his hand / And he died with his hammer in his hand. (121)

John Henry the roustabout, the man of metal, the railroad worker, takes off from the mountain crossroads toward ancestry, and in this way he's also related to Ogun, the Yoruba God of metal workers and, particularly in the Americas, of iron, weapons and fugitive slaves. Yet in North America at the turn of the century, they were singing him as a man from Virginia, where, in the eyes of black workers, black labor transformed everything. Same thing. Put a black man on a mountain, and it pulses with meaning. Make that the mountains of Virginia and it gets even thicker. Virginia, where the first enslaved Africans landed; Virginia, notable in the eighteenth century as the North American colony with the most dense population of native Africans, Virginia of the founding (white) fathers was also, by 1778—the date of the legal end of slave trading, the home of an essentially American-born black population. The Sally Hemmings story was, no doubt, as familiar to all of black America a century later as it was an anathema to the white supremist conception of the nation's birth. But there is actually an older history of Africans in Virginia that should call our attention.

John Henry went to the tunnel / And they put him in lead to drive / The rock was so tall and John Henry so small / That he laid down his hammer and he cried. (Hughes and Bontemps 345)

The mountainous, forested, or swampy regions of North Carolina, South Carolina, Virginia, Louisiana, Florida, Georgia, and Mississippi were locations, between 1672 and 1864, of North America's few "maroon communities" (Aptheker 1973). In fact, one of the most noted of those communities, with a population of more than two thousand self-emancipated men and women, was located in a place called the Dismal Swamp between Virginia and North Carolina. Virginia as a location gathers together the story of black labor, black enslavement, and national freedom as well as a tradition of subversive black nation building and black nationalism arising from the amalgamation of African nations. Virginia signaled all of those things to African Americans in 1870. Virginia "meant" (and in some places continues to mean) Gabriel's rebellion in 1800 and Nat Turner's rebellion in 1832 and the final surrender at Appomattox, which ended the Civil War. We know for sure that the former two used conjure and the groupings of African nations in order to build a secret society of black revolution. This is where John Henry was coming from: where Guinea culture was revolutionary; where slave labor supported the revolution of the American colonies and made necessary the war that rendered the nation asunder.[31]

Refrain: A Man Ain't Nothing but a Man

Old John Henry / Got to find a job / Old John Henry / Got to find a job / That steam driller here / Here a good man to rob. . . . Boss man listen / Listen to my plea / Boss man listen / Listen to my plea / I'll work half the night / If you just let me be. / Got a wife and children / Waiting for me at the fire. / I Got a wife and children / Waiting for me at the fire. / If I don't work / Ain't no way they can smile.(73)

Right behind the armies, right after the jubilees, black people were moving, hundreds, thousands, looking for loved ones, looking to build "homes," and looking to strike a balance between food on the table and freedom—between "the system" and living. Debt peonage. Black codes. Ku Klux Klan. Jim Crow. Lynching. The question from 1870 into the twentieth century was the color line and how a man could walk it. How he could

---

31. Morgan 1975 is an apt treatment of the relationship between the founding colony and African slavery.

move it. How he could aim to be a man in this place where a black man could never be at home, but where he must, of necessity, make a home. Where the buzzard, if you will, could land. Literally, "between a rock and a hard place," folk cultures engaged in gathering wisdom. There was no linear proposal here but rather a series of spirals. John Henry the hero dies from a busted heart, with a tear-stained laugh.

> John Henry he had a woman/ Her name was Mary Magdalene / She would go to the tunnel and sing for John / Just to hear John Henry's hammer ring / Just to hear John Henry's hammer ring. (108)

> Who's going to shoe your pretty little feet? / And who's going to glove you hand? . . . Who's going to be your man? (Lomax 1960, 560)

> John Henry had a little woman / she come all dressed in blue / This what she said when she found him dead/ John Henry I been true to you / John Henry I been true to you. (108–9)

> John Henry had a little woman / The dress she wore was red / Says I'm going down the track / And she never looked back. / I'm going where John Henry fell dead. / Going where John Henry fell dead. (109)

Black women weren't, by and large, waiting by the fires, but there was enough struggling for position to cause a major fall in national production when, right after the emancipation, black women decided en mass that they weren't picking cotton. Having been worked like beasts, systematically raped or castrated and hung for entertainment at picnics, regular black folks *had* to struggle with the quagmire of race and sex and dominance within the social construct. John Henry plays on a number of tropes to represent black men and women, pithing the conceptual memory of communal identity—kinships that are not rape—against the contest of patriarchies and its brutalities. Between black men and women, you got all the contradictions of the times, and they too are present in the song—there is a woman and a love longing from a Scots ballad, and there's a woman who "drives steel like a man"—yet in this telling of the story the relation between the sexes is about history.

> I got my shoes from a railroad man / My dress from a man in the mine / My dress from a man in the mine. (Lomax 1960, 156)

> John Henry had a little woman / Her name was Polly Ann / She could pick up a jack and lay down a track / And hammer like a natural man / And hammer like a natural man. (104)

John Henry had a pretty little woman / Her name was Julie Ann / She walked through the land with a hammer in her hand / Saying "I drive steel like a man." (109)

John Henry's woman Lucy / Dress she wore was blue / Eyes like stars and teeth like marble stone / And John Henry named his hammer Lucy too / John Henry named his hammer Lucy too. (92)

Lucy, Polly, Julie Ann are all complicated images of black women. Strong. Little. Big. Loyal. Competitive. Challenging. Writing themselves, playing the changes against an image that was not their own, against the society's vicious images of black women. John Henry sings the thick and deep of black family life against a contorted racist collapsing of attack on African American work (lazy negroes/welfare cheats) African American women (breeder/Jezebel/whore/welfare mother), and African American family structure. There's even a nod, in some versions, to the old story about the red cloth that, folklore says, Europeans used to trick Africans onto the slave ships. Mostly John Henry ballads present the "little woman," the "pretty woman," as a working equal to the man just as black feminists at that time tried to propose a womanhood "good" as white women, strong as any man and replete with all our society's contradictions.

John Henry he could hammer / He could whistle, he could sing / He went to the mountain early in the morning / To hear his hammer ring / To hear his hammer ring. (Hughes and Bontemps 1958, 345)

John Henry went to the section boss / Says the section boss what can you do / Says I can line a track, I can heist a jack / I can pick and shovel too / I can pick and shovel too. (Hughes and Bontemps 1958, 345)

John Henry told his captain / When you go to town / Please bring me a nine pound hammer / And I'll drive your steel on down / And I'll drive your steel on down. (119)

In John Henry ballads are older beliefs in love charms and male figuration mixed in with contemporary ideas about power, sex, and work. To be a man here is to be able to work and to be able to sing. It is an aesthetic thing—to be beautiful working, to sing your own praise song in a world of equally strong women and men. The songs call on the problem of "fitting" strong black women and men into the prevailing patriarchal conception of home. In the world of black railroad working men, a "man's job" is one of creation in a place of destruction. To be a man means to beat the machine.

What then? To be a man means to die as you win. How resonant in the face of the reality of lynching. How resonant in the hard times of decreasing employment, of riots in the industrial work places, of competition with white men.

> John Henry said to his shaker / Shaker why don't you sing a few more rounds / And before the setting sun goes down / You're going to hear this hammer of mine sound / You're going to hear this hammer of mine sound.
>
> John Henry told his shaker / "Shaker you better pray / If I miss this piece of steel / Tomorrow be your burying day / tomorrow be your burying day. (107)

There's a male tale here. At the heart of the song is relationship between black men—between coworkers and between generations, between the living and the dead and those not yet born. Those relationships probably have many old names lost in the amalgamation of becoming African Americans but remembered in the call and response and in the danced performance of lead and chorus. The practices of ancient male societies and peer groups also came over on the slave ships and remained mostly hidden except for in moments of social crisis and reconstruction. (I think of Nat Turner's rebellion and of the incredibly complex gathering of the recent march of a "Million" black men.) Yet those relationships were evident in the force and power of those old worksongs.

> Me and my captain don't agree but he don't know cause he don't ask me. / He don't know he don't know my mind. When he sees me laughing just laughing to keep from crying. / Oh my lord what's the matter now / Me and my captain can't make it no how . . . / Captain cusses but I just smile / I'll be gone in a little while. / Got one mind for the captain to see. / Another for what I know is me . . . / One of these days and it won't be long / He'll call my name and I'll be gone. (Morgan 1975, 61–62)

According to the story, it's the shaker who carries on John Henry's song, which says a great deal about the role of a man in this moment of the African American imagination. As in the relationship between the Caribbean Jonkonoo and the older West and central African, male masked dances, these performances of communally generative identity say that to know this man you must circle his community, his history. They say that part of the generative role of maleness is "historative." That "Johnson" is a historical, ritual, vessel. Within this ritual performance of work and the circle of life, the black man can love other men as he loves himself. Here, within the prevailing constructs of patriarchy and before them, men may laugh and cry and "know" and carry each other's name. Here, men call *on* each other and are transformed.

Captain ask John Henry / What's that storm I hear?

He says

Captain that ain't no storm / Tain't nothing but my hammer in the air / Nothing but my hammer in the air. (119)

Oh the captain said to John Henry / I believe this mountain's sinking in / John Henry said to the captain oh my / It ain't nothing but my hammer sucking wind / Ain't nothing but my hammer sucking wind. (Hughes and Bontemps 1958, 346)

The question of black male identity is a formidable one, and the metaphor of the mountain, with all its layers of meaning, is a real one. Sure, there are other stories of work and heroes in the African American pantheon, but John Henry has lived long as a sign. Symbolically connected to the crossroads, to history and healing, to gods of steel and iron, to the weapons of woodsmen, hunters, fugitives and maroons, accidents and transportation, John Henry is one example of how the circle of African culture is a wide one that sprawls throughout the lexicon of oral history and makes for recognition and continuity wherever those symbols are found.

John Henry took his little boy / Sit him on his knee / Said the Big Bend Tunnel / Going to be the death of me. / Going to be the death of me. (100)

Like Osiris and the Nubian corn gods before him, John Henry dies only to return, to be resurrected. Maybe in the old men. Maybe in the blue steel of the smoke stack of a time come and left, but not ever really gone. Probably in the "rock." Probably in the young ones. John's sons. Definitely in the songs where death, ever present in the mines, is continually "played" against the immortality of history in the performance of work and song. John Henry dies in a blaze because die you must; then there's the death of a way of life, and the death of the worksong itself, but . . . but . . .

They took John Henry to the white house / And laid him in the sand / When people came around you would hear them say / He sure was a steel driving man / He sure was a steel driving man (130)

It is a circular tale about fate, work, prophecy, memory, and continuity, and whether John Henry is buried along the railroad tracks or in the white house, he's calling his self a piece of history.

John Henry, Oh , John Henry / Sing it if you can / High and Low and everywhere you go / He died with his hammer in his hand / Lawd Lawd / He died with his hammer in his hand.

Buddy, where you come from / To this railroad job / If you want to be a steel driving man / Put your trust in your hammer and your God / Lawd Lawd / Put your trust in your hammer and your God. (95)

Laissez-faire

Ted Wilson

Is there madness in my thinking
Is there madness in my perception
Of   the world
The world in which I live   this society

Is my perception out of kilter
When some agent of the state calls me
up and asks for my cooperation to help him
coffin me

Behind an attempt to destroy my means of living
eradicating any chance—in his mind—of my ever
putting food on my table   again
starving my parents
crippling my children   driving my wife
to a near breakdown   along with those
once in my employ

Is there illness in my head   when
I react to this cool calm Marshall Dillon
who responds in a sympathetic tone
An attempt to equalize my situation with
a story about his miss kitty getting hives
because he had to work the day after
the day they took the turkey
from the Native American

Cause he said she thought
he didn't care about her

as I react in an excited tone   verbally
he perceives me as hostile

Am I dense   so dense
I don't understand why
he doesn't understand that
I don't understand why
he says he knows nothing
about that which I speak
thinks it is horrible
knows how I feel
and why   don't I believe
he really cares and
that makes him upset

Is my brain gnarled like
the hands of an arthritic relative
this little company helped to support
now seeking relief from wherever and whatever

Explain to me the lunacy of willful suffering
do I look like I was born in the middle of
the week looking both ways for Sunday?

he says he
wants to bring this case to closure
he says he
wants to come to my office
to check records he spent six weeks recording
two years ago   that he   distorted
to remove me from the level playing field
   ——new buzz phrase—level playing field
they call that keeping it real

I scream   madly   doubting my sanity
stomp my feet on the floor
to examine reality

do I not speak understandably   audibly
non—dialectically clear   enough english?
You destroyed my business
that means no office   not even a table
to put food upon

He says
then maybe you want to come to my office
I snarl
questioning his need for my assistance
to place me underground march peacefully and willingly
to the cemetery
I say
tell your bosses   those assholes in Albany
I know the   deal   from where
this is coming   tell them
madness in appearance   is not idiocy
and all the snow   in Buffalo
cannot cover the politician's sword

Now I ask you   tell me   please   tell me
am I insane as I speak
with a wry smile   a cold heart
contritely replying

You can rely on my complete cooperation
        SIR!!!

Revolutions

Kimiko Hahn

Forbidden to learn Chinese
the women wrote in the language
of their islands
and so Japanese
became the currency of high aesthetics
for centuries
as did the female persona: the pine
the longing. This is the truth.

(We can rise above those needles.)

The red silk from my grandmother
amazes me. Think of the peasant
immigrating from rice fields
to black volcanic soil. The black beaches.
The children black
in this sunlight
against the parents' will or aspirations.

(Anywhere else
girls of mixed marriages would be prostitutes or courtesans.)

I want those words
that gave women de facto power,
those religious evocations: dreams so potent
'she became pregnant' or 'men killed'
or 'the mistress died in pain.'
I connect to that century

as after breath is knocked out
we suck it back in.

The words the men stole after all
to write about a daughter's death
or their own (soft) thigh
belongs to us—to me—
though translation is a border
we look over or into;
sometimes a familiar noise
('elegant confusion'). But can *meaning*
travel
the way capital moves
like oil in the Alaskan pipeline
or in tankers in the Straits of Hormuz?
Can those sounds move like that?
Yes. But we don't understand.

But we don't know
what it means to speak freely
even to ourselves. Patricia,
fertility is not the antithesis of virility.
I can't help it.

If I could translate the culture
women cultivate
I would admit to plum
and plumb.

I always begin with a season.
Like: snow and plums in the wooden bowl
make me love him. How
I warm one in my fist
then lick it until the skin
grows so tender it bursts
beneath my breathing.

The yellow is brilliant.
The snow is warm.

Some of our lessons issue from song
because there are never enough
older sisters
especially from the South via Detroit
where we look for a model
with the desperation of a root—
where a bride is a state—
where *heat lightning* is pronounced:
lie down on my breast
so your tongue and teeth reach my tit
and I can—
where *yes*—

I didn't learn poetic diction from the Classics,
rather, transistor radios. Confidence
in my body also. After years—
the confidence that gives and gives
and is not afraid to take either.
Exploring the words means plunging down
not skimming across
or watching whitecaps however lovely.
Not balking at fear either:
the walls are filled with sounds,
the windows, with sorrow.

Revolution for example is the soft
exact
orbit of planet, moon, seed.
Also seizing the means of production
for our class.
Where does that come from?
It all begins with women, she said.

Like the warp and woof of cloth.

And how there's no 'free verse' so we'll search
for the subtle structures: the poetic closure,
the seven kinds of ambiguity, etc.

Not tonight, dear.

How it's not so sad really
for a husband or wife
to come alone.

Komachi's reputation came from legend:
the 99th time a lover visited her door
(the night before she would let him enter)
he died.

That's the breaks.

In a patriarchy is such cruelty cruelty
or survival? Is the father to blame
for ugly daughters, too? for the unruly ones?

Come sit by the radiator and open window.
When the baby hiccoughed inside her
her whole body shook.

Afterbirth is not a time or reform
it belongs to a separation we turn towards.

Toward an Antiracist Feminism

Kathy Engel

I delivered the following speech at the International Women's Day Conference at the State University of New York–Buffalo in 1993, soon after the death of Audre Lorde. My speech grew out of my particular experiences and perspectives working day to day, year after year, to build multiracial, antiracist, cross-class organizations. It takes into account the kinds of decisions I have felt I needed to make as a white (Jewish American) woman working to build multiracial alliances and the kind of persistence necessary for the task. The speech doesn't presume to deliver the final word on the women's movement or on the nature of racial justice work, but attempts to zero in on some of the challenges and resistances, particularly as we experienced them in those ten years or so leading up to 1993.

So much has been accomplished since that time in terms of a broader, deeper, more fully respectful feminism. I want to pay tribute to all the women who have worked throughout the history of the women's movement toward a feminism rooted in an active class and race analysis. Too many names, but I salute and thank them all.

> [Y]ou must understand that in the attempt to correct so many generations of bad faith and cruelty, when it is operating not only in the classroom but in society; you will meet the most fantastic, the most brutal, and the most determined resistance.
> James Baldwin, The Price of the Ticket

I am deeply honored to have been invited here tonight to be with you. I believe we are gathered here to discuss the most important subject in our lives. As women, as political and progressive women and men artists, intellectuals, activists, we are driven to pierce the truth, which means to dismantle the racism in our midst and uncover a woman's identity and politics whose substance is the needs and rights of *each* and *every* woman with the force those needs command.

I dedicate my words tonight to Audre Lorde, African American feminist lesbian poet warrior woman, and in doing so, rededicate myself to the path she lit to strike down the barriers that keep us apart and unequal. And to Companera Nora Astorga, Nicaraguan leader and heroine. And to Donald Walter Woods, proud black gay man poet.

Because of the nature of our subject, because of the roots and constancy of suffering, I feel particularly humble in offering my thoughts to you. What I have to say is by definition directed toward white women because as a white woman, that is my responsibility and experience, and it must be named. Naming is the essential ingredient in this journey toward an antiracist feminism or toward all antiracism. And I'm still hoping that something of what I have experienced will be inclusive.

Because we have a full program tonight, I will share some key points and then develop them further in our workshop tomorrow.

Perhaps it will not be possible to turn feminism as we think of it into something antiracist. Can we turn something with a character and legacy into something anti–something else? Historically, movements that have originated as predominantly white, defined from white middle-class needs and values, have not been able to become truly inclusive, affirmative-action driven, devoid of racist and classist traces. Some organizations have made real attempts and broken ground, but they are still viewed as predominantly white organizations that have undergone affirmative-action programs. And by and large, if you don't start out inclusive, you will never fully be.

And of course being antiracist is more than being inclusive. Let us search for a way to describe our feminist antiracism that speaks for the needs and rights of *all* women and embodies the fully intentional abandonment of all forms and manifestations and implications of the disease we know as racism. Let us create something, call it something that doesn't require a qualification, that is by definition, at the core, antiracist. And let that antiracism be founded on a philosophy and activism committed to women of all nations, that does not separate women within our borders from our sisters throughout the world.

And it should be cautious when judging or attempting to define the stages of women's liberation in other countries, in other struggles, just as no one community can ever presume to decide the most authentic and pressing issues for another community. For some, for example, water is a feminist issue, as I have often been reminded by sisters from developing countries.

Our new feminism or postfeminism—whatever we name it and however we create it, perhaps Audre Lordism or Woman Warriorism—will by definition in heart and soul never negotiate with racism in its crude and subtle forms.

I think there are two fundamental issues for white people to confront. One is the truth, relentlessly, painfully, vigilantly attempting to tell the truth about racism, and thereby to face it and to obliterate it. The other is what one is willing to give up, because racism is about power relations just like sexism. I've seen white women in their quest to end racism who attempted to take on the identity of women of color. This is one more culture robbery.

For me, as a white Jewish American woman, there are three lines of work in fighting racism. One is the responsibility to call on other white people to face and fight racism. Another is to face it and try to counter it in every aspect of my life. The third is working to create multiracial, antiracist institutions and movements, and challenging institutional racism.

On the question of every aspect of my life. Sometimes you fail and don't see it and don't see your own participation in a historical interaction or don't know what to do. And there are contradictions, when your ideals bang up against your life, your children, your convenience, like choosing schools or where to live or shop or eat or what kind of child care, in the face of history. But it starts with asking the questions. Always asking: Are there racist implications?

I have finally learned that I cannot be the completely perfectly antiracist white person. The goal is to face the truth and commit oneself to act in the face of it—to act on heart and guts and principle and politics. And there's no place for guilt. It prevents action. White liberals are famous for expensive guilt. You can wallow in your feelings and the person next to you might be getting beaten up by a cop at the same time, or being called a name, or something much less obvious.

White people shouldn't throw the responsibility of teaching about racism to people of color or wait for a person of color to bring up the issue—in a meeting, at a dinner party, at school, at work. Or address any question about race or color to the person of color in the room and then nod in vehement agreement. Or say anything in any setting that you wouldn't say in front of a person from any background or identity. I'm not advocating censorship, but consciousness.

It's not enough to believe the right things and support the right policies and work for the right organizations if you don't scrutinize every racist particle, visible or hidden. I ask us: white women, take this on. I challenge us. The hardest part, I believe, for white people in America who don't view themselves as racist is to call it what it is and implicate ourselves. But once you make that choice, you have crossed a precipice. And then what do you look like, to yourself? What is other to you, and what does other look like?

A friend of mine, the organizer of the conference on racism in the postmodern era, an African American clergyman, told me that white people aren't interested in hearing about racism anymore and that I should drop that tack. We need to focus on problem solving, he said, like in Crown Heights. And *we are* doing that together. We are working to create a model mechanism for conflictive parties to talk to each other—called practical discourse.

But I believe we must work on all fronts. And I am not willing to stop talking to white people about racism, just as I'm not willing to stop talking to men about who takes care of the kids more or whose time is more valuable or what is battering. And that means not letting things go.

How do we build multiracial institutions that are truly antiracist and not just multicultural in the euphemistic sense that has become so popular that for example a perfect multicultural lineup was trotted out to get rid of New York Chancellor of Schools Fernandez? The only way is every step of the way.

Let's think about where we hold meetings, who makes up the meetings. "I tried but couldn't get anyone" isn't good enough, and it never rings true. If the meeting's not representative, cancel it. If you don't want lung cancer, you stop smoking; if you don't want racism, stop participating in it. Like when I am invited to a meeting of Women for Clinton as I was last fall, and I walk into the room and see it is white women for Clinton. As much as I want to get rid of Bush, I must call attention to the misnomer, and if it cannot be changed, I must find another way to work to get a new president.

Make special efforts to connect. Move the location if you need to, go to someone else's workplace or neighborhood.

Let's think about who has what kind of child care; who has what kind of health care; who goes or went to what school if any; who has what kind of help in her life; whose kids are where, when, and facing the day-to-day danger in a racist city or town where schools have become prisons and weapons are the mode of communication.

Let's think about how we form staff and boards of directors. What do we mean by affirmative action? No compromise. A commitment to training. A commitment to reconsidering location, time, place. Let's think about leadership. If you are a white woman in a leadership position, do you truly support the leadership of women of color? Will you step aside if necessary?

Let's think about what coalitions and activities we participate in, and if there is any trace of implied racism, or if they are affirmative-action driven or how, and if they can be moved.

Let's think about points of reference. When we name cultural or political figures—singers, writers, leaders—do we draw from the full wealth of our historic legacies? We know Barbie's not the only doll in town, but do we call up all our cultural icons?

Take on explicitly antiracial campaigns *and* integrate antiracism into all aspects of your program. Build affirmative action into every aspect of your work. Don't hold standards that are setups for persons who have not had the cultural and economic advantages that their white or economically privileged counterparts have had.

As the director of a multiracial national women's organization, I was sometimes criticized for not demanding as much of the women of color as of the white women for fear of being called racist. Perhaps there were times when I let things go that I shouldn't have. But looking at it historically, I wanted to be sure I wasn't making assumptions and demands based on my background. *Equal is only equal if it's equal.* A young Puerto Rican single mother who grew up poor is in a very different situation than a middle- or upper-middle-class white woman in the same job, in terms of needs and access. I'm not suggesting standards be revised. But if affirmative action doesn't take into account the full conditions and ramifications of difference and doesn't offer training and support, then it's designed for failure. It's the right idea but without the carry-through to make it a step forward. Sort of like integrated education: when students of color are not given their full culture, history, dignity, in integrated schools, they are losing something they had at least in segregated schools. It's the gap that happens in change. You take a step forward, but what is entailed in fulfilling that step has not been learned or applied fully because of the systemic nature of the problem and the profound institutional resistance. So you hang in an in-between place that is in some ways harder and less—like working mothers and what is now known as the second shift. Although this is only true for middle-class mothers. Poor working mothers have been doing double duty forever without choice.

So, when we talk about feminist goals—like equal pay, access, like child care, health rights, like no sexual harassment or discrimination, no bloody noses or broken skulls in the home—we know exactly what and who we're talking about protecting. And if it's not all of us, it's not okay.

And our work doesn't progress smoothly and evenly, but in fits and starts. Tomorrow I'd like to talk more about some problems I've encountered, which I'll just outline now: a beautiful rainbow presentation to the public that is behind the scenes riddled with racial and class tension; the drive to bring up anti-Semitism in the same vein and light as racism when the problems don't seem to be racially derived.

We need to be careful not to get into hierarchy of oppression. To work against oppression I don't have to be able to claim to have experienced the same oppression as you; I have to be able to see it.

Finally, I believe it is essential—if we are to move forward together in anyway, shape or form—for us to on one hand acknowledge, respect, and stare into the past, the legacy, and the current manifestations with all their harshness, with all the blame, and then at the same time, understand that history and interaction. Be able to say, "Okay, here's where we are now. How can we move forward together? Can we move forward together?" I believe we must work together to make any qualitative change.

What I have learned most about working to end racism is the necessity of listening. The discipline of listening. The humility of listening. As a white, privileged woman I must listen intently and keenly to my sisters of color, in this country and throughout the world—the sounds, the tastes, the nuances, the subtleties. To remember the issues of class that are always present when we talk about race and how our economic system thrives on keeping us apart.

What I have learned and continue to learn from my African, Central American, Caribbean, indigenous, Asian, Middle Eastern sisters has transformed my existence and understanding of the possibilities of us in this world together. And what stunning possibilities we, women of many colors and many nations and legacies, have to share and offer one another. What magnificence we can surely imagine together if we do truly create what we are here to name. And I would never accept this journey separate from all of who make up what is *us* in the fullest most far-reaching definition that *us* or *we* can speak for.

As a child in elementary school, I saw a young black girl's head smashed against a cement wall by a white gym teacher. I went home and told my mother, but felt I should have stopped it. As an adult, after an adult lifetime of working against racism, I listened to and saw a crazy woman spew out *"nigger"* at my closest friend and godmother of my daughter. "Forget it," I said. "She's crazy," knowing that some enemies you don't waste your energy on. But racism *is* crazy. It's *all* crazy. *And* it's systemic, conscious, programmed. I don't know what I should have done. Perhaps taken my friend's hand in a silent act. Perhaps scream at the lunatic. What I do know is it has to teach me something about fighting our way out of this. And you can never do nothing in the face of it; the struggle is minute by minute *and* lifetimes, crazy *and* rational, individual *and* institutional, tactical *and* instinctive, hard cash *and* hard feelings, national *and* international, family *and* community.

No, I don't think everything's okay if we smile and work together and get along okay and call each other "sisters." Yes, I believe the truth of calling it and saying it and chasing after it with fury and passion. And the intense desire for wholeness and justice will bring us closer toward what we are here tonight trying to name and to create. No, I will not be intimidated by the lack of meaning. I am an antiracist feminist until we rename it.

In El Salvador, we said water is a feminist issue. My South African friends said housing is a feminist issue. In Puerto Rico, independence. I sat with Palestinian women in a refugee camp wildly discussing the question of what are the feminist priorities for women in a liberation struggle.

"We're all related," my friend Lex said at the Walker Memorial Baptist Church. "We just don't act like it."

Digna said that Antonia Pantoja said we must tell the stories of our work, of our hearts, of our struggles, how we join together as women, break through barriers, how hard it is and how joyful it is. What we envision for our children, what we dream. If we don't write it down, if we don't tell it, they won't know. Digna had tears in her eyes when she told me. "We have to write it down, Kathy," she said.

So this is my letter. To my mother, to my sisters. To my daughter Ella: Ruby Hill was your godmother's grammy. When she died, a piece of us went into the ground. Lex read from Ecclesiastes. Your Dad was a pall bearer. Ruby Hill was a teacher in North Carolina. When she was young, she learned cotton- and peanut-picking. In New York, she couldn't get a job teaching. She had to work in white women's homes. She taught Sunday school.

She was a black woman in America. She was a teacher. She was a religious woman. She was your godmother's grammy. She was part of you.

West Bank, Palestine, 1990.

Dear Mom: We asked the Jewish settler on the West Bank where the Arabs live. "I don't know." Do they live in refugee camps? "I think so." So the mothers like living with their children with no water. "I think so." What was here before? we asked her. "Nothing."

Remember a young white school teacher or shop owner, just a young white girl in Mississippi or Virginia. Remember what she said in that hyp-notized voice with that glazed look. Remember. She said: "They like to live like that. And we have to protect ourselves." Remember New York City. Buffalo. Today.

This letter comes from inside the body and doesn't stop and doesn't start.

And in the indomitable spirit of Audre Lorde, just as Cornel West and bell hooks talk about the force of self-love and love of blackness binding to-gether the black woman and the black man, I would venture to say that the fire of our potential self love and love of other—women of the world—can burn out the infection of male dominance, just as it must burn out the tyranny of the dollar, which means that potential love, that fire, can build something because burning without building is lost. Not a wishy-washy love, not a euphemistic love, not a polite or even multicultural love, but a fighting, intransigent passion for justice and our womanhood and the children we bring into this world, and a vision of mutual respect and forti-tude and dignity, and the imagination to be whole with other and whole with self, one to one, community to community, nation to nation.

Friendly Town, being #2

Safiya Henderson-Holmes

it's the third day. sun:
a hot-water bottle on our heads.

our heads ache from pig, cow.
cricket, bird, barn. we want the bron:

fordham road, huntspoint, pelham bay, soundview.
maria and i know of another

colored girl in this town.
we saw her in the church without a cross:

our names taken from our chest,
put into a bucket, called like lost shoes.

after each name, a hand
took us by the shoulder, a second hand

carried suitcases, led us through eyes,
from church into night, into a car,

or a truck. barbra's her name.
she went into an old yellow school bus.

words: brown's sunday school
on its dented side. crickets louder

then motor. maria and i went into a ford wagon.
two sleeping boys and a dog in wagon's bottom.

maria and i sat behind their parents: bald head
waxing car's ceiling, brown hair sweeping

my bermudas. they knew the driver
of school bus, said they'd see him soon.

but days aren't soon in the country,
stay forever in sky and grass

as nothing else exists.
on the first day, maria and i tried following

grass 'til its end, our breath slowed.
grass went on for miles. we let it go.

today, the setting out for barbra's different.
we're homesick. illness pushing us, tireless.

alone on the porch: sons at club meeting,
parents in town with their hay.

maria and i pack cold cuts and milk,
jackets tied around our waist, triple socks

against bugs. we walk toward end of grass,
this time we turn at first break in green.

blacktop with two lanes, long
as a friendly town night.

we drink milk, eat cheese. air passes us
we're saving our last slice of ham.

see a gas station. old blue chevy
pickup at pump. i flatten an ant, walk to chevy.

a white man at wheel, crates of milk
on floor. homesickness braces me.

i ask if he knows, brown's sunday school
he laughs. no teeth: gummy tunnel to his throat.

says, —you sure outta your way to pray.
that old bus 'more 'an ten miles,

outside walton. ain't givin' no ride,
got goods deliberin' 'fore supa.

now yous git on back where you belong.—
he tips his eyes, wipes his mouth,

drives. i look at maria, on stacked tires,
fanning flies. —que dice— she asks. her spanish

flipping air. i lie to keep it spinning.
—he said i know that sunday school good,

said a colored gal been askin 'bout a colored
gal too.

maria laughs,—bueno. see i told you.
barbra esta aqui.—

the return's sweaty. the last slice
of ham to the ants. our sneakers eat tar.

maria picks daisies.
i untie my jacket,

drag it like a pair of broken wings,
wonder if jose and edward

have gone this way:
into the green, into the blue.

Part Two. (Un)Balancing Psyches

Metaphors of Race and Psychological Damage in the 1940s American South

The Writings of Lillian Smith

McKay Jenkins

In April 1939, Billie Holiday recorded a song about lynching. Written by Lewis Allen,[1] the song was haunting, visceral, violent; some club owners and radio executives feared its graphic lyrics—"Black bodies swaying in the summer breeze"—would offend listeners, particularly in the South, where lynching had in fact slowed considerably since the 1920s. Several jazz critics wrote that the lyrics were "too political" and failed artistically. But the song and its performance by a singer at the peak of her career did more than offend. "Strange Fruit" became not only the signature piece of one of the country's most popular singers, it became emblematic of a generation's struggle and obsession with race.

> Southern trees bear a strange fruit
> Blood on the leaves, and blood at the root,
> Black bodies swinging in the Southern breeze,
> Strange fruit hanging from the poplar trees.
>
> Pastoral scene of the gallant South
> The bulging eyes and the twisted mouth,
> Scent of magnolias, sweet and fresh,
> Then the sudden smell of burning flesh.
>
> Here is a fruit for the crows to pluck
> For the rain to gather, and the wind to suck,
> For the sun to rot and the trees to drop.
> Here is a strange and bitter crop.

1. "Lewis Allen" was the pen name of Abel Meerpol, who also wrote "The House I Live In," a plea for racial and religious tolerance sung by Frank Sinatra in a 1945 movie short of the same name. Meerpol and his wife adopted the sons of Julius and Ethel Rosenberg after they were executed in 1953 for allegedly passing atomic secrets to the Soviet Union (White 1987, 50).

The song also had a particular resonance for Holiday, whose father, two years previously, had died of pneumonia after being denied admission to numerous segregated Dallas hospitals. "It wasn't the pneumonia that killed him, it was Dallas, Texas," she said (Maddox 1979).

Five years after the recording of "Strange Fruit," Lillian Smith published a novel by the same name, centered around a small Georgia town and a forbidden love affair between a wealthy white boy and a college-educated black maid. As central and controversial as the song was to the career of Holiday and to the heart of a culture in turmoil, so, too, was the novel. *Strange Fruit* was banned by booksellers—for lewdness, ironically, not for violence or racial provocation—in Boston and Detroit, and by the U.S. Postal Service as well; it took an intervention by President Roosevelt, acting on a request from his wife Eleanor, to have the ban lifted (Loveland 1986, 71).[2] In part owing to this controversy, the novel sold 140,000 copies in its first two months and took over the top spot on the best-seller list of the *New York Times Book Review*,[3] where it was favorably reviewed by W. E. B. DuBois; he praised "its explicit depiction of the tragedy of the South. . . . On each page the reader sees how both elements (white and black) in Maxwell are caught in a skein (economic, ethnic, emotional) that only evolution can untangle or revolution break" (1944, 1, 20). Diana Trilling wrote that *Strange Fruit* "is so wide in its human understanding that its Negro tragedy becomes the tragedy of anyone who lives in a world in which minorities suffer; when it ends in a lynching, we are as sorry and frightened for the lynchers as for the victim. Indeed, we are terrified, for ourselves, at the realization that this is what we have made of our human possibility" (1944, 342).

Although the novel *Strange Fruit* does indeed reach its climax with a lynching, Smith's use of the title was subtly and provocatively different.

2. Holiday's recording had been banned by the BBC, but not in the United States. The use of the word *fuckin'* (twice) got it outlawed in Boston and created a "dirty book" aura that helped sales. Bernard DeVoto, who bought a copy from Abraham Isenstadt in the presence of two police officers, challenged the Boston ban. DeVoto was found not guilty, but Isenstadt was fined one hundred dollars, the judgment was upheld on appeal, and because the appeal was never brought to the U.S. Supreme Court, the book is still technically banned in Boston (Blackwell and Clay 1971, 38). The book sold openly in Atlanta and Birmingham. *Strange Fruit* has since sold upward of three million copies and been translated into sixteen languages.

3. A theatrical version of *Strange Fruit*, directed by Jose Ferrer and starring Walter White's daughter Jane in the lead role, opened in Montreal, then Toronto, Boston, Philadelphia, and finally on Broadway on 29 November, 1945.

She had originally used the phrase in a column entitled "Two Men and a Bargain," written for the magazine *South Today,* which she published along with Paula Snelling. The column, which she later expanded into a chapter for her 1949 book *Killers of the Dream,* was a parable about the relationship between rich and poor whites and the specter of an emerging black work-force. "Mr. Rich White," lamenting the breakdown of his bargain with "Mr. Poor White," dreads the time when the latter will begin "filling his unions with niggers, keep right on filling them, making them bigger and stronger, and first thing you know he may not even *care* whether he's bet-ter than niggers."

> Something whispers not to worry. "Long as you have segregation none of these things can happen!" it says. "Just keep saying *nothing can change it. Nothing!*" When Mr. Rich White complains that everybody's against him, Something reassures him. "I'm for you, I'm for the guy who wants to be first, I'm for the guy who loves his own image, I'm for the guy who rides the front seat, always the front seat and won't let others ride with him." "Who are you?" asks Mr. Rich White. "You know me," Something replies. "Every man from the womb knows me until death stops the knowledge. But some won't make me a bargain. You did. . . . Who am I? Listen, I'll tell you. I'm that which splits a mind from its reason, a soul from its con-science, a heart from its loving, a people from humanity. I'm the seed of hate and fear and guilt. You are its strange fruit which I feed on." (Smith 1943, 7)[4]

In a weekly column for the Chicago *Defender*—for which she wrote for forty-three weeks in 1948–49, sharing the space with Walter White, Langston Hughes, and Mary McLeod Bethune—Smith wrote that the "strange fruit" she wrote of

> was not lynching or miscegenation (a word I hate) but the white man himself and his children and his Tobacco Roads and his own wasted life; the "strange fruit" was man dehumanized by a culture that is not good for the growth of either white or colored children. I do not believe it is possi-ble to understand the white man in America and his strange paranoid no-tions about his "superiority" without considering his equally strange childhood and the training he received before he was six-years-old, the

4. The title for *Killers* came to Smith while she was writing the novel *Julia;* in it, she wrote about the suicide note of a preacher, who used the phrase "I have killed my dream." She realized "the killers of the dream are ourselves as well as 'the others' and we kill our dreams on so many levels of being" (qtd. In Loveland 1986, 97).

heavy guilt laid on heart and body while both were so young and weak, and finally the strange fruit which this has borne, not only of White Supremacy but of mental illness, alcoholism, child delinquency, exploitation, and war-making. (qtd. in Blackwell and Clay 1971, 41–42)

In Smith's hands, then, "strange fruit" refers not to black bodies swaying in the summer breeze, although that image adds an acute dramatic weight, but to the damaged, "split," primarily *white* people raised in a culture of deep racial, sexual, and class-based taboos and conflict. For Smith, racism worked as an ambient, often disembodied, but vicious and relentless pressure on a culture, both white and black, all too frequently too weak to fight it. Her writing focuses primarily on the psychosexual damage the discourse of racism does to whites, and to white women particularly, and less on the psychological and physical damage whites in turn do to blacks; this was throughout her literary career a stated purpose. But more important for her was the *cycle* of damage, the ways racist discourse fueled itself and tore holes in the psyches of *all* members of a community. As she wrote in a letter to the publisher of *Strange Fruit,* Frank Taylor,

> I think it is first a love story of special tenderness, but I think it is also a racial fable that applies not only to the South but to the white race in its relationships the world over: the ambivalences, the conflicts, the love, the hate, the anger, the frustration, the terrible humiliations of the dark man's spirit . . . the gradual wearing away of the white man's civilized and humane feelings. (Gladney 1993, 72)

In this context, the "humiliations of the dark man's spirit" can refer either to the humiliation of the black man's spirit or to the humiliation of the dark spirit of the white man; in Smith's writing, the two are always linked. Read in racial terms, whiteness is inextricably tied to definitions of blackness; the discourse of race is always bound up in and used to mask struggles for political, economic, and sexual power. To pull apart these threads, Smith throughout her work explored the psychological damage, the "splitting," that is done when racist discourse overpowers compassion or empathy or tenderness. The "something" that speaks to Mr. Rich White is precisely the discourse that Smith saw tearing the midcentury South asunder, ultimately creating the strange fruit of a bifurcated culture. "In trying to shut the Negro race away from us, we have shut ourselves away from the good, the creative, the human in life," she wrote.

The warping, distorted frame we have put around every Negro child from birth is around every white child from birth also. Each is on a different side of the frame, but each is there. As in its twisting distorted form it shapes the life and personality of one, it is shaping and crippling the life and personality of the other. It would be difficult to decide which character is maimed the more—the white or the Negro—after living a life in the Southern framework of segregation. (Smith 1943, 9)

If this discursive "frame" could have come right out of Foucault, Smith's acknowledgment of the ways races and identities leak into each other could have come from any number of postmodern critics; Stuart Hall, like DuBois and others before him, has written about the endless slippage between cultural, political, and psychological influences on identity formation; identity, subjectivity, is meaningless except in relation to the myriad cultural and psychological relationships surrounding it. He writes: "It is not possible for the self to reflect and know completely his own identity since it is formed not only in the line of the practice of other structures and discourses, but also in a complex relationship with unconscious life" (1991, 10–11). Perhaps nothing was of such interest to Smith as the unconscious life of southern whites and the way this life was critically bound up in images of race. Her notion that whites, too, are damaged by the discourse of racism is something I explore further on, but it is interesting to note here the link with what whites are "shut away from" when they are kept apart from blacks: "the good, the creative, the human in life." The idea that blacks somehow represent something that is denied to whites, "the human," speaks to the ambient repressions felt by its white voices. If other white writers are less subtle in their use of black bodies to express physical cravings—W. J. Cash's fascination with lynching, for example, or William Alexander Percy's yearning for his black nanny—Smith often builds on race an architecture of both cultural and psychological mourning. The connections among sexuality, riotous animalism, and self-mastery were especially acute in a region where race offered an easy vessel in which to pour sexual anxieties, and Smith was well aware of the easy manner in which the cultural mainstream maneuvered these anxieties to oppress those it considered deviant, for not only was she a racial liberal in the conservative South, she was a lesbian in a culture obsessed with maintaining traditional images of sexual conduct. Her sense of herself as an alienated outsider certainly contributed to her understanding of the damage done by discourses of power and intolerance. In *Killers of the Dream,* she despairs of her girlhood exposure to

> the edgy blackness and whiteness of things . . . the breathing symbols we made of the blackness and the whiteness . . . the metaphors we created and watched ourselves turning into . . . the shaky myths we leaned on even as we changed them into weapons to defend us against external events. Now, suddenly, shoving our pleasures and games and stinging questions come the TERRORS: the Ku Klux Klan and the lynchings I did not see but recreated from whispers of grownups . . . the gentle back-door cruelties of "nice people" which scared me more than the cross burnings . . . and the singsong voices of politicians who preached their demonic suggestions to us as if elected by Satan to do so: telling us lies about skin color and a culture they were callously ignorant of—lies made of their own fantasies, of their secret deviations—forcing decayed pieces of theirs and the region's obscenities into the minds of the young and leaving them there to fester (*KD*, 12–13).

The ambient white voices that took images of race, twisted them to fit their own "secret deviations," and then fed them to the South's children not only fired Smith's imagination, but led her to draw heavily on her own experiences in her writing. She wrote that *Strange Fruit* reflected the "splits and estrangements" in her own life, that "every tension was an echo of a tension in my own life" (qtd. in Loveland 1986, 64). In *Killers of the Dream,* she explains that

> The mother who taught me what I know of tenderness and love and compassion taught me also the bleak rituals of keeping the Negroes in their "place." The father who rebuked me for an air of superiority toward schoolmates from the mill and rounded out his rebuke by gravely reminding me that "all men are brothers," trained me in the steel-rigid decorums that I must demand of every colored male. They who so gravely taught me to split my body from my mind and both from my "soul," taught me also to split my conscience from my acts and Christianity from southern tradition. (*KD*, 27)

Smith's literary influences were broad, her tastes reflecting a passion for the kind of politically engaged writing that she herself practiced. She read Hemingway, Proust, Joyce, and Woolf, whom she liked "only temperately"; she disliked Faulkner and, later in her career, would spar with him over the speed with which the South was becoming integrated.[5] She large-

5. Faulkner published "A Letter to the North" in *Life* magazine in March 1956, in which he

ly objected to modernist writers, considering them too self-involved and removed from the political tumult of their time. "What has Albee given us? Genet? Sartre? Mailer? Self-absorbed, most cannot tear their eyes from their own small depravities. So they are giving us fragmented sketches of sick people; they hold before us in play and story a never-ending bleak view of miserable, lost, lonely schizophrenics" (Cliff 1978, 162).

Smith was also a devoted reader of psychoanalytic texts; she studied Freud, Sandor Ferenczi, Otto Rank, Carl Jung, Alfred Adler, and Karl Menninger, whose *Love Against Hate* was published in 1942, two years before *Strange Fruit*. It was her investment in psychology that led her to her most dramatic claims about racism's legacy of broad spiritual damage. She also read broadly in African American authors ("130 in all," she claimed) including the literature and sociology of W. E. B. DuBois, E. Franklin Frazier's *The Negro Family in the United States*, and Horace Mann Bond's *Negro Education in Alabama*. She praised the work of white writers, such as John Dollard's *Caste and Class in a Southern Town* and Howard Odum's *Southern Regions of the United States*, but was often skeptical of white accounts of the Civil War, which she felt only addressed the "better" white people. "What Negro," she wrote, "can ever forget that one decade of this era of good feeling which produces [historian Paul Buck's] lyricism also produced 1,035 lynchings of black men?" (qtd. in Loveland 1986, 27).

Her own writing was remarkably prolific. In 1943, as her magazine writing was peaking but before her first book was published, she was honored by the Schomburg Collection of the New York Public Library as one of six whites, along with Franz Boaz and Wendell Wilkie, on its Honor Roll of Race Relations; the Schomburg cited Smith for maintaining her liberalism in a land where it took courage to be a liberal. In addition to *Strange Fruit* and *Killers of the Dream*, the primary texts to be examined here, she published the novel *One Hour* (1959) and several books of nonfiction: *The Journey* (1954); *Now Is the Time* (1955); and *Our Faces, Our Words* (1964). Like Ralph Ellison, she also lost a massive body of writing to the 1944 fire: three manuscripts, including novels about China *(And the Water Flows On)*

---

said that although he had long opposed segregation, he was disturbed at the violence that had recently accompanied forced integration. He would, he wrote, "go on the record as opposing the forces outside the South which would use legal or police compulsion to eradicate that evil' overnight." Although *Life* did not accept Smith's reply to that letter, she did have a piece accepted at *Time* arguing with a speech by the editor of the Louisville *Courier-Journal* that equated the NAACP with segregationist U.S. Senator James Eastland, calling them both "radical."

and the South *(Tom Harris and Family);* a novella *(Every Branch in Me);* some thirteen thousand letters; sketches for future books; and all her notes from a recent six-month trip to India.

The magazine she edited with her lover Paula Snelling, known at its founding in 1936 as *Pseudopodia* and later as the *North Georgia Review* and finally as *South Today,* was brazen in its antisegregationist rhetoric; W. E. B. DuBois called the magazine "stunning and courageous" (qtd. in Sosna 1977, 182). J. Waties Waring, the South Carolina federal judge who had ruled against his state's effort to maintain the white primary, referred to Smith's denunciations of racism as among the most penetrating analyses of the South he had ever read. "If people of this country and of the world can only see and understand the disease which has long lingered under a scab of romance wrapped in the Confederate flag," he wrote, "they can and will find a way to restore to health our poor pitiful people whom you and I love and weep for" (qtd. in Sosna 1977, 193). Smith's editorial voice represented the magazine's high-water mark; in it, she developed both her literary ear and her sharp political voice. Much of her vitriol she reserved for matters of race; her commentary so infuriated her detractors that she began receiving threats not only from local and state bureaucrats, who threatened to prevent her from mailing her magazine, but from the Ku Klux Klan.

Her journalism, if rough-edged, was nonetheless powerful; her magazines were considered among the most important liberal vehicles of the decade. As an early and ardent supporter of the 1954 Supreme Court decision, a member of the board of the Congress of Racial Equality, and an admirer and associate of Martin Luther King Jr.,[6] Smith was "a standing rebuke to more timid Southern liberals and moderates. In refusing to become influential in conventional ways, she acquired a moral authority that far outweighed her institutional connections" (King 1980, 176). Her battles with Ralph McGill, the editor of the Atlanta *Constitution* and the self-styled voice of southern racial liberalism, were public and occasionally florid. Smith once wrote that

> as long as we have the sore of segregation we are going to have a foul drainage from it. If the drainage is heavy enough, repulsive enough,

---

6. King was driving her to Emory Hospital in Atlanta for a checkup when a police officer, seeing King and Smith together, pulled the car over; when King's Alabama license was found to have been expired, he was fined twenty-five dollars and given a year's probation. When he violated that probation on 25 October, 1960, he was sentenced to four months hard labor, and it took President Kennedy and Robert Kennedy to get the judge to reverse his decision.

maybe Southern liberals will finally see that there can be no health in Dixie as long as segregation is there. Maybe men like Hodding Carter, Ralph McGill, Jack Tarver, Wright Bryan will finally learn to fight the causes of our trouble and waste less time on the symptoms. (qtd. in Blackwell and Clay 1971, 78–79).

For his part, in a review of *Killers of the Dream,* McGill wrote that "Miss Smith is a prisoner in the monastery of her own mind. But rarely does she come out of its gates, and then, apparently, seeing only wicked things to send her back to her hair shirt and the pouring of ashes on her head and salt in her own psychiatric wounds" (qtd. in Loveland 1986, 104). To Richard King, McGill's rage was so acute because "hell hath no fury like a Southern moderate whose hand has been called" (1980, 104), and this Smith surely considered one of her primary functions—that of a clear-eyed, rhetorically forceful but politically marginal voice pushing the South to examine its obsession with race for what it was: dark, inextricable, spiritually damaging in the extreme.

Smith's reporting instincts, and even her language, seemed at times remarkably like those of Gunnar Myrdal, whose *American Dilemma* was published in the same year as *Strange Fruit.* In a letter she wrote to the Southern Regional Council in June 1944, later reprinted in the *New Republic,* she wrote:

> Racial segregation, political and economic isolationism cannot be considered apart from man's whole personality, his culture, his needs. Neither can man's needs be considered apart from the destroying effects of segregation. Nor can the South's major problems be solved by trying to put a loaf of bread, a book and a ballot in everyone's hand. For man is not an economic or political unit. To believe that he is, is to ignore personality and cheapen the human spirit. And by ignoring personality, we oversimplify a complex, subtle, tragically profound problem. It helps us sometimes to see this in perspective if we will look at the restricting name of segregation in terms of the needs of children.
>
> A child's personality cannot grow and mature without self-esteem, without feelings of security, without faith in the world's willingness to make room for him to live as a human being. . . . No colored child in our South is being given today what his personality needs in order to grow and mature richly and fully. No white child, under the segregation pattern, can be free of arrogance and hardness of heart, and blindness to human need—and hence no white child can grow freely and creatively

under the crippling frame of segregation. . . . We simply cannot turn away and refuse to look at what segregation is doing to the personality of every child, every grown up, white and colored, in the South today. Segregation is spiritual lynching. The lynched and the lynchers are our own people, our own selves. (Gladney 1993, 86–7)

Within this passage are all of the elements of Smith's literary work: the link between racial segregation and psychological splitting; the idea of the fragility—indeed, the illusoriness—of racial identity; and the wake of broad spiritual damage left by racist ideologues. What I want to focus on here is the notion of Smith as a writer fully engaged with what we now consider to be postmodern sensibilities; she uses notions of race to metaphorize precisely that psychological split, that fragmentation, that continues to be of such central concern to postmodern thought. In the 1961 foreword to *Killers of the Dream,* the word *segregation* stands in for all that is fractured in Smith's cultural moment.

Segregation . . . a word full of meaning for every person on earth. A word that is both symbol and symptom of our modern, fragmented world. We, the earth people, have shattered our dreams, yes; we have shattered our own lives, too, and our world. Our big problem is not civil rights nor even a free Africa—urgent as these are—but how to make into a related whole the split pieces of the human experience, how to bridge mythic and rational mind, how to connect our childhood with the present and the past with the future, how to relate the differing realities of science and religion and politics and art to each other and to ourselves. Man is a broken creature, yes; it is his nature as a human being to be so; but it is also his nature to create relationships that can span the brokenness. This is his first responsibility; when he fails, he is inevitably destroyed. (*KD,* 21)[7]

In this passage Smith is fully engaged with notions that are now considered staples of postmodern racial thought and associated with theorists

7. The ways cultural discourse damages both sides of the racial divide is also evocative of Faulkner's *Intruders in the Dust:* "All he requires is that they act like niggers. Which is exactly what Lucas is doing: blew his top and murdered a white man—which Mr. Lilley is probably convinced all Negroes want to do—and now the white people will take him out and burn him, all regular and in order and themselves acting exactly as he is convinced Lucas would wish him to act: like white folks; both of them observing implicitly the rules: the nigger acting like a nigger and the white folks acting like white folks and no real hard feelings on either side (since Mr. Lilley is not a Gowrie) once the fury is over; in fact Mr. Lilley would probably be one of the first to contribute cash money toward Lucas' funeral and the support of his widow and children if he had them. Which proves again how no man can cause more grief than that one clinging blindly to the vices of his ancestors" (Faulkner 1948, 48–49).

such as Foucault, Lacan, Hazel Carby, and Evelyn Brooks Higginbotham: first, that stable identity, coherent subjectivity, even "race" itself are myths determined by a socially constructed will to power; and second, that constructions of "otherness"—embodiments of the subject's opposite or antithesis—are not only *not* apart from the subject but are located specifically *within* the subject, are indeed something on which the subject depends for its very existence.

If Lacan focused on the relationship between male and female, I'd like to extend his thesis to include the relationship between white and black to examine just how whiteness and blackness are constructed and to what political uses these categories are put. Lacan, according to Juliet Mitchell and Jacqueline Rose, defined the objective of psychoanalysis as the effort to break "the confusion behind this mystification . . . whose conflation he saw as the elevation of fantasy into the order of truth." Woman (or black, in our case) is constructed as an "absolute category" that serves to guarantee the unified identity of the man (or white).

> What the man relates to is this object and the "whole of his realization in the sexual relation comes down to fantasy." As the place onto which lack is projected, and through which it is simultaneously disavowed, woman is a "symptom" for the man. Defined as such, reduced to being nothing other than this fantasmatic place, the woman does not exist . . . her absence or inaccessibility stands in for male lack just as he sees her denigration as the precondition for man's belief in his own soul. ("For the soul to come into being, she, the woman, is differentiated from it . . . called a woman and defamed.") In relation to the man, woman comes to stand for both difference and loss: "On the one hand, the woman becomes, or is produced, precisely as what he is not, that is, sexual difference, and on the other, as what he has to renounce, that is, *jouissance*." (1982, 47–48)

Whites define themselves not by what they are but by what they are *not*—that is, black; black is thus construed both as a "lack," an inadequacy, "what (white) is not," and a "loss," something that is at once loathed and yearned for, reviled and mourned. Black, then, is ultimately nothing more than a "fantasmatic place" onto which whites can build entire architectures of racial and political discourse. Lacan, Jacqueline Rose has written, defined the objective of psychoanalysis as the effort to break "the confusion behind this mystification . . . whose conflation he saw as the elevation of fantasy into the order of truth" (Mitchell and Rose 1982, 50). This, it seems to me, is Smith's objective as well. She aimed to cut away the cultural logic that hierarchized men and women and whites and blacks, to pressure notions of racial authority, to see how the discourse of racism damaged both races by binding them together in destructive rhetorical manacles. The breakdown of the confusion behind racial mystification was Smith's political and literary objective. She wrote *Strange Fruit,* she said, "because I had to find out what life in a segregated culture had done to me, one person; I had to put down on paper these experiences so that I could see their meaning for me. I was in dialogue with myself as I wrote, as well as with my hometown and my childhood and history and vertical exploration. It has to true itself with facts but also with feelings and symbols, and memories that are never quite facts but sometimes closer to the "truth" than is any fact" (*KD,* 13).

Strange Fruit, then, was for Smith a chance to weave together the fissures in her own psychology with the cultural scars that were the twin legacies of her experience of race in the South; for her, the personal and the political were always linked, always cross-pollinating. The novel revolves around a love affair between Tracy Deen, the white son of a prominent southern family, and Nonnie Anderson, a black college graduate returned home to the town of Maxwell, Georgia. Their romance is tormented by social restrictions on racial mixing; Tracy, in a flurry of self-destructiveness, converts to Southern Baptism, beats up Nonnie, and agrees to marry the white daughter of another well-to-do local family. Soon afterward, Tracy is found dead, setting the town aflame with rumors about the identity of his murderer. His killer, it turns out, is Nonnie's brother Ed, but it is Henry McIntosh, Tracy's black companion since birth, who finds himself in the wrong place at the wrong time and is blamed.

As the novel develops, word of the murder begins to spread through the switchboard of Miss Sadie, the town's operator, through whom all local gossip travels first.

> Miss Sadie looked out of the west window across the ballground to the swamp. Black clouds had massed up over the tree line, throwing deep shadows over the town, and by some trickery of the hidden sun clumps of palmettos stood out in startling greenness. The light, dark as the afternoon was, was so intense that she could see moss hanging from the cypress back of the Negro Lodge, something she couldn't remember being able to see before. A low roll of thunder came from the northwest. (*SF,* 276)

The colorization of the storm imagery is plain: the clouds massing menacingly over the tree line are black; they throw deep shadows over the town. To Miss Sadie, to white Maxwell, the death of a white son at the hands of what they assume to have been a black man is apocalypse foretold; it is the manifestation of their worst mythical fears, blackness spreading over their town like a biblical plague. The dark shadow Miss Sadie fears is the same one Thomas Dixon fears; the low roll of thunder that follows it is Faulknerian doom, evidence of a culture in danger, in the throes of collapse. This is Smith playing on the fears she sees manifest in her fellow whites; it raises the same polarity that Ralph Ellison acknowledges as the mythical discourse of identity. Ellison, in *Shadow and Act,* writes:

> Being "highly pigmented," as the sociologists say, it was our Negro "misfortune" to be caught up associatively in the negative side of this basic dualism of the white folk mind, and to be shackled to almost everything it would repress from conscience to consciousness. The physical hardships and indignities of slavery were benign compared with this continuing debasement of our image. Because these things are bound up with their notion of chaos, it is almost impossible for many whites to consider questions of sex, women, economic opportunity, the national identity, historic change, social justice—even the "criminality" implicit in the broadening of freedom itself—without summoning malignant images of black men into consciousness. (1964, 63)

In Ellison's essay, blackness, to whites, signifies "chaos," a malignancy; in Smith's passage, black storm clouds signify an occlusion of lightness, a haunting, an overpowering. Black is other, dangerous, perilous. Interesting also in the *Strange Fruit* passage above is the juxtaposition of the words *light* and *dark:* "The light, dark as the afternoon was, was so intense that she could see moss hanging from the cypress back of the Negro Lodge, something she couldn't remember being able to see before." Light is not separate or set off from dark, or defined by dark; it *is* dark. Indeed, the "dark light" is so intense that Miss Sadie is "able to see things she has never seen before." Darkness is not other, it is inherent in the light; otherness is tied up inextricably with subjectivity, blackness with whiteness. One does not exist without the other.

The third color in the above passage—the "startling greenness"—is equally interesting, particularly as it stands against light and black. Several chapters after this moment we find the word *green* again as Sam Perry, a black friend of the innocent Henry McIntosh, in the law office of Tom Harris, tries to convince Harris that Henry will be lynched unless he comes to his aid. As Sam presses his case, Harris repeatedly tries to convince him that Henry is safe, hidden in the one place a mob would never think to look—in the county jail. Sam will have none of it:

> "Mr. Harris," Sam's voice was quiet, "first time in my life I interrupted a white man. I've lost control—yes. Got to say it. All my life I've bowed and scraped, for the sake of the others beneath me, I thought, who needed help. I'd do it the white way, I'd say. It's worth licking a few hands for, I'd say—God!" he breathed, "God." You could hardly hear him now. He looked across the room as if he had stopped, had long ago forgot to go on.
>
> "It's more than starving . . . low wages . . ." the voice picked up words again, "more than Jim Crow—it's you white men . . . sucked as dry as your land . . . taking our women . . .yes, taking them as . . . manure, that's all they are to you . . . dung . . . to make something grow green in your life. That's all they mean to you. . . . My sister . . ." voice like wind beating palmetto ". . . my own mother . . . that's all . . .the woman I love . . . white man took her . . . used her . . . threw her aside like . . . something filthy and stinking . . . Why can't you leave them alone? God Jesus, why does the Negro have to bear this!" His voice grew suddenly quiet. "I know I can't drag God in. What would a decent God have to do with a thing like—"
>
> Tom Harris stood, struck the table hard with his hand, "Hush, you fool! You black damned son of a—" stopped as if a hand had caught his arm . . . Began again, "You've forgot, Sam," he said slowly, "there're things no nigger on earth can say to a white man!" (*SF,* 341)

This play on the word *dung* works well and is, for my argument, perfectly Lacanian. Blackness is troped as both excrement and vital to growth, both poison and nutrient, both buried to be hidden and buried to fertilize. Here, too, whiteness is troped as cotton, a particularly destructive plant sucking nutrients from and destroying the land—the black earth—upon which it feeds. Toni Morrison has written in *playing in the dark* that metaphors of blackness are frequently required to carry the weight of doubleness, and her argument fits nicely with the passage from Smith's novel:

> If we follow through on the self-reflexive nature of these encounters with Africanism, it falls clear: images of blackness can be evil *and* protective, rebellious *and* forgiving, fearful *and* desirable,—all of the self-contradictory features of the self. Whiteness, alone, is mute, meaningless, unfathomable, pointless, frozen, veiled, curtained, dreaded, senseless, implacable. Or so our writers seem to say. (1990, 59)

Morrison's comment, mirroring the thoughts of Lacan and Rose, makes clear the double-edged blade that cuts both races to the quick: not only do metaphors of virility and desire and danger demonize blacks, the other, they eviscerate the souls of whites, who are ironically denied access to the very life forces they have demonized blacks for embodying. For Smith, this system of inquiry found effective enunciation throughout her work, but it is to one particular field of vision, her treatment of women and children, that I will now turn. Her writing brims with descriptions of children who are spiritually damaged before they can even define what race is and with white women who have become utterly detached from their own physical and spiritual presences. They float through her work like disembodied ghosts, pale, shriveled, human voids. The southern offer of a detached, ambient, pervasive "glory" in exchange for sexual and spiritual neglect, it becomes clear, Smith saw as a direct outgrowth of race. Just as embodiment and specifically sexuality become troped as black, estrangement and repression are inevitably written as white.

In *Killers of the Dream,* the chapter "Three Ghost Stories" plunges into one of the South's most enduring racial and sexual images: that of a white slave master raping a black slave. Perhaps taking a cue from Faulkner's magnificent engagement with this subject in *Absalom, Absalom!* Smith writes of the debilitating consequences of such an encounter for all relationships involved—male/female as well as white/black. The first "ghost" that emerges from this bleak alliance is the ghost of miscegenation itself, with all it implies about "broken taboos and guilt too terrible to say aloud"; white women have become so "pure," so desexed, that white men turn to black women for sexual release. White women become disembodied and physically neglected, black women become troped as erotic and dangerous, and both are degraded. The second ghost represents the South's "rejected children," born of a white father and a black mother and rejected by both. Children are living testament of both the broken link between white man and white woman and of the exploitative alliance between white man and black woman. The third ghost is the relationship between white children and their black nurses, a bond that not only exploits the black woman but supplants the white mother/white child connection, damaging all three members of *that* triangle. White mothers are removed from the mothering process and are thus alienated further from their own bodies and their own families; white children are raised by black women, with whom they form a deeper bond than that with their own mothers, but at some point are told that, by dint of race, these same women—and their black children—are not worthy of respect or love.

In each of these connections, Smith writes, women and children, white and black, suffer immeasurable and unknowable spiritual damage, and it is this damage that drives much of her work. In *Strange Fruit*, Smith describes Tracy's mental image of his white fiancee Dottie Pusey,[8] as she undresses; although Tracy has had a long and rich sexual relationship with his black girlfriend Nonnie, he "had never seen Dottie undress and had no desire to" (42).

> Now the light was off. Dottie was saying her prayers. In a moment she would lie in her bed, cool, clean, composed, all of her life completely contained in the rigid little box which shut the right way to do things away from the wrong. Dottie praying. . . . What would she pray about? Sins? Tracy liked the thought of Dottie sinning. He laughed, lit his cigarette again, enjoyed smoking it. What would Dottie's sins be? In a life so neat, so orderly, like a folded handkerchief carried around all day and never crumpled—where would there be room for a life-sized sin? (*SF,* 42–43).

Dottie is the embodiment of what Hazel Carby has called the "cult of true womanhood"; she is serene, fragile, pious, utterly desexualized. More than that, however, her containment "in a rigid little box" gets to the spiritual wounds inflicted on white women directly because of their disembodiment. Tracy bitterly envisions Dottie (and his mother, who sleeps in her daughter's bed to escape her husband Tut's "masculinity" [67]) as "white goddesses, pure as snow—dole out a little of their body to you—just a little—see—it's poison—you can't take but a few drops—don't be too greedy—do as I tell you—do as I tell you now—be a good boy—do as I tell you—just a little now—Tracy!—That's not nice—that's not nice—" (*SF,* 195). Dottie and Tracy's mother are "pure" and cold as snow, goddesses untainted by physical presence or sexual appetite. Sex is "poison" among white women; a few drops are all one is allowed. The image of a "few drops" also carries with it a faint echo of the fear of miscegenation; a "few drops of ink" was all that was required to contaminate a "pure" glass of water. Sex is troped as black, alluring, deadly.

8. The name *Pusey* conjures up a vulgarity first used in 1875–80, according to the OED.

Catherine Clinton has written that the discursive vines constricting white women find their roots far back in the antebellum South. "Men were virtually obsessed with female innocence," she writes.

> The notion of white women as virginal precipitated a whole series of associations: delicate as lilies, spotless as doves, polished as alabaster, fragile as porcelain—but above all, pure as the driven snow (with its inherent connotation of coldness). Without the oppression of all women, the planter class could not be assured of absolute authority. In a biracial slave society where "racial purity" was a defining characteristic of the master class, total control of the reproductive females was of paramount concern to elite males. Patriarchy was the bedrock upon which the slave society was founded, and slavery exaggerated the pattern of subjugation that patriarchy had established.(1982, 6, 88)

Smith's own awareness of the intricacies of sexual discourse are always tied inextricably to her awareness of racial discourse. Her chapter entitled "The Women" in *Killers of the Dream* is superb in its clear-eyed look at the rending done to black and white women at the hands of an unyielding structure of white male domination. She quotes at length "one of Mississippi's politicians," whose language, in 1948, is emblematically steeped in racial and sexual mythology:

> "Now what of the ladies? When God made the Southern woman he summoned His angel messengers and he commanded them to go through all the star-strewn vicissitudes of space and gather all there was of beauty, of brightness and sweetness, of enchantment and glamor, and when they returned and laid the golden harvest at His feet he began in their wondering presence the work of fashioning the Southern girl. He wrought with the golden gleam of the stars, with the changing colors of the rainbow's hues and the pallid silver of the moon. He wrought with the crimson that swooned in the rose's ruby heart, and the snow that gleams on the lily's petal; then, glancing down deep into His own bosom, he took of the love that gleamed there like pearls beneath the sun-kissed waves of a summer sea, and thrilling this love into the form He had fashioned, all heaven veiled its face, for lo, He had wrought the Southern girl." (*KD*, 170)[9]

9. Clinton reminds us that this cult of fragile womanhood dates back to the earliest years of the plantation culture. She quotes from an 1817 letter from C. A. Hull to his niece Sarah Thomas as she prepares to leave home to begin a teaching job: "I view you on the pinnacle of an awful precipice. . . . Peculiarly delicate is the crisis, and one false step forever blasts the fame of a female. . . . Malevolence is so predominantly in the human heart, that in all, it displays the devouring jaws of a mighty Maelstrom ready on every touch to destroy the vessel that per chance may be cast into the whirlpool" (Clinton 1982, 110).

Fragility and purity, however, imply more than just innocence; like all metaphors, they are as rich for what they reject as for what they enhance. Here, images of "pallid silver" and lily petals imply not only sensitivity and grace but a disengagement from manual labor and sexual appetite. These images were, in turn, distorted, caricatured, and draped over bodies discursively unable to shed them: black women. Carby writes that this image of "true womanhood" effectively defined the parameters by which white women measured themselves against the prevailing cultural ideal. The degree to which white women tailored their dress and behavior to this model, the farther they distanced themselves from the physical labor and overt sexuality of their black female opposites, the closer they fit the ideal (1987, 23).

Whereas fragility was valorized as the ideal state of white womanhood, heavy labor, requiring other physical attributes, was associated only with poor whites and blacks. "Strength and the ability to bear fatigue, argued to be so distasteful a presence in white woman, were positive features to be emphasized in the promotion and selling of a black female field hand at a slave auction," Carby writes. "It is worth considering that a delicate constitution was an indicator of class as well as racial position; woman as ornament was a social sign of achieved wealth, while physical strength was necessary for the survival of women in the cotton fields, in the factories, or on the frontier" (1987, 25).

Smith examines at length this connection between delicacy, physical alienation, and sexlessness in *Killers of the Dream.* "The majority of southern women convinced themselves that God had ordained that they be deprived of pleasure and meekly stuffed their hollowness with piety, trying to believe the tightness they felt was hunger satisfied," she wrote.

> Culturally stunted by a region that still pays nice rewards to simple-mindedness in females, they listened to the round words of men's tributes to Sacred Womanhood and believed, thinking no doubt that if they were not sacred then what under God's heaven *was* the matter with them! Once hoisted up by the old colonel's oratory, they stayed on lonely pedestals and rigidly played "statue" while their men went about more important affairs elsewhere. (141)

More important affairs, of course, frequently meant visits to Colored Town to find the sexual fulfillment they had successfully shut off from their white women. Late in *Strange Fruit,* when Tracy visits Preacher Dunwoodie to ask about joining the church, he hears a fevered speech about the temptations of black flesh. Throughout her work, Smith saved her most viscous attacks for her assessment of religious rhetoric, and nowhere in *Strange Fruit* is it as florid as in the following passage. The conversation takes place both in Tracy's car and, later, after they unconsciously wind through country roads, under the same oak tree where Tracy and Nonnie first made love.

> "Now there's another sin. Lot of men, when they're young, sneak off into Colored Town. Let their passions run clean away with them. Get to lusting—burning up! And they get to thinking . . . they'd rather have that kind of thing than marriage. A lot rather! Scared of white girls. Scared nice white girls can't satisfy them. And they're right! Of course no decent fine white woman can satisfy you when you let your mind out like you let out a team of wild mules racing straight to . . ."
>
> Preacher Dunwoodie's voice had risen shrilly. Suddenly he stopped, Spoke more quietly. "Well, that's youth," he said and wiped his face with his big handkerchief. "This world's full of young folks wanting—strange things. That's youth and the devil," he added softly, "and sooner or later you have to face it. Funny thing," he said, "once you make up your mind to leave colored women alone and stick to your own kind, you soon get weaned." He laughed shortly. "You don't think you can. But you do. I know . . ." he sighed. "As for the colored women, they manage all right. Always have, haven't they! Most of them sooner or later get a man their color, maybe marry him. Live a fairly decent, respectable life—that is, if a nigger woman can live a decent respectable life." Voice suddenly bitter.
>
> Someone's been talking to him. He's too smooth—knows too much.
>
> "You see, Deen, you have to keep pushing them back across the nigger line. Keep pushing! That's right. Kind of like it is with a dog. You have a dog, seems right human. More sense than most men. And you a lot rather be around that dog than anybody you ever knew. But he's still a dog. You don't forget that." (*SF,* 87–88)

Here, then, is Smith conflating the three steps of "sin and segregation," one of her favorite themes. Preacher Dunwoodie, no stranger to lust or to interracial longing, wipes his face and at once mocks white female sexuality and equates black female sexuality with "strange things," "the devil," and "a dog." He at once acknowledges that white men can and must be "weaned" from black women, suggesting not only sexual desire but their reliance on black mothering, and raises himself to a pitch of overtly racist language beyond any yet encountered in the novel. He moves quickly from a discussion of black enticement to a diatribe about divinely ordained white supremacy, a move Smith recognized as all too common among southern white men. Yet his descriptions of this supremacy are labored; the reliance on a trio of adjectives to say that no "decent fine white woman" could satisfy adolescent passions seems to reveal a mind trying to convince itself more than his youthful audience. Here again is the myth of the cult of white womanhood revealed; white women are so beyond sexuality that they "scare" men. Black bodies come to stand in for this lack of sexuality and become troped, logically enough, as insatiable.

"Overt sexuality," Carby writes, "emerged in images of the black woman, where 'charm' revealed its relation to the dark forces of evil and magic. The effect of black female sexuality on the white male was represented in an entirely different form from that of the figurative power of white female sexuality."

> Confronted by the black woman, the white man behaved in a manner that was considered to be entirely untempered by any virtuous qualities; the white male, in fact, was represented as being merely prey to the rampant sexuality of his female slaves. A basic assumption of the principles underlying the cult of true womanhood was the necessity for the white female to "civilize" the baser instincts of man. But in the face of what was constructed as overt sexuality of the black female, excluded as she was from the parameters of virtuous possibilities, these baser male instincts were entirely uncontrolled. Thus, the white slave master was not regarded as being responsible for his actions toward his black female slaves. On the contrary, it was the female slave who was held responsible for being a potential, and direct, threat to the conjugal sanctity of the white mistress. (1987, 27)

One outgrowth of the cult of true womanhood, then, was a longstanding and largely overlooked tradition of white men finding their sexual outlet through the bodies of black women. It is Smith's descriptions of black women's bodies—far more erotically engaged than her depiction of white women—that reveal her awareness of these racial and sexual legacies. At one point in *Strange Fruit,* Ed encounters a group of young black girls, including one "like a jack-rabbit, a little somebody in a bright pink waist and black skirt" who "collided with him, stopped with a stumble of high-heel pumps and a twist of her torso." The girl is described as having "a perfect face the color of pine cone laughing into his. He saw a full mouth, slender neck, tipped-up breasts. He saw big laughing eyes that

looked as if they would grow solemn any minute, under a hat with three
red roses flopping on it, perched on the side of her head." Ed laughs "as
she switched her little tail in answer and ran toward the titillated cluster of
girls. Nice little rumps, hard from chopping cotton, light, bouncy, India
rubber" (12). Earlier,

> white boys whistled softly when [Nonnie] walked down the street, and
> said low words and rubbed the back of their hands across their mouths,
> for Nonnie Anderson was something to look at twice, with her soft black
> hair blowing off her face, and black eyes set in a face that God knows by
> right should have belonged to a white girl. And old Cap'n Rushton, sitting
> out in front of Brown's Hardware Store as he liked to do when in from the
> turpentine farm, would rub his thick red hand over his chin slowly as he
> watched her wheel drooling, lop-headed Boysie Brown in to see his papa.
> (*SF,* 2)

The overtly erotic language in this passage, combined with the plain
white gaze at a black body, set it off in stiff irony not only to the way white
women are described but in relation to the manner in which the novel later turns: white men, having forsaken their soulless white wives, are free to
leer at black women, but black men are forbidden from so much as speaking to white women. Here, a white man rubs his "thick red hand over his
chin" as a black woman walks by; the notion that Nonnie's sexuality "by
right should have belonged to a white girl" reveals Smith's conception that
"sexing" blackness does a double disservice: attributing eroticism to blackness not only objectifies blackness, but inherently desexualizes whiteness.
Not only does it imply that white girls do not have Nonnie's sexuality, it
implies that Nonnie must have *stolen* their sexuality. Indeed, by virtue of
the town's sexualized discourse, she has. Nonnie carries the weight not
only of white male sexual fantasy but of white female sexual repression;
she is lusted after by white men and hated by white women, who are in
turn rejected by their white boyfriends and husbands. "By the historical
'accident' of slavery, our slave holding puritan ancestors were juxtaposed
to a dark people, natural, vigorous, unashamed, full of laughter and song
and dance, who, without awareness that sex is 'sin,' had reached genital
maturity," Smith writes in *Killers.* "From all that we know of them they
seemed to have had, even as some have now, a marvelous love of life and
play, a physical grace and rhythm and a psychosexual vigor that must
have made the white race by contrast seem washed out and drained of

much of what is good and life-giving. It was natural that the white man was drawn to them. Laughter, song, rhythm, spontaneity were like a campfire in a dark, tangled forest full of sins and boredom and fears" (*KD,* 117).

Black women were not, to Smith, merely sexual vehicles caught between the sexual lust of white men and the sexual repression of white women, and it is to another "ghost," that of black women responsible for raising white children, that I now turn. Early on in *Strange Fruit,* Tracy Deen comes upon a photograph of the black nursemaid (and mother of his playmate Henry) who raised him. Wistfully, he remembers:

> her faint clean body smell like a pile of fresh-ironed sheets and he remembered her rich sweet smell on Sundays, when dressed in black silk she left the yard to go to church-meeting. He remembered her deep full breasts. There had been a time when her lap was wide enough for him and her Henry both to crawl up in. She'd sit there, knees spread wide, jogging them from side to side, singing vague sounds, breaking off, taking up after a little where she had left off, sometimes reaching for a corner of her big white petticoat to wipe one nose and the other. Knees jogging slowly, easing them back and forth, cradling them from time and its bitterness, glazing eyes with peace. Tune moving on, on, on, and body moving with it, and all the world no wider, no deeper, than the space her knees enclosed—no wider than, and no colder than the heat from her breasts.
>
> There had been a time when he was sick and no food would stay in his stomach, and Mamie had fixed little odd things, and sometimes had chewed them for him and slipped them into his mouth and he had felt better. He remembered his mother used to say after that, "The child won't eat for anybody but Mamie," or when he was hurt, "Nobody can quiet him but Mamie." (*SF,* 107)

Tracy received the mothering, the protection, the nurturing from Mamie that he never received from his own mother; Mamie is highly feminized in this portrait, compared to Smith's depiction of Mrs. Deen as a cold, neurotic, pious woman, incapable of comforting her own child. The image of a black woman chewing and regurgitating food for a white child is a powerful one; her very insides are issued up for the growth of the child. Later, when Tracy has decided to marry the frigid Dorothy, he listens to her describing the way they'll "make the old farm over" with a loveseat by the fireplace and a "beautiful old mahogany card table." Tracy's mind drifts from this scene directly to a memory of the old piano in the parlor where he used to go and hide and lay his head on the keys, until Mamie would "find you and hold you against her, saying half words through her crooked teeth—Old Mamie—you hadn't seen her in years—you must have been a funny little fool—a crazy kid" (*SF,* 185). Tracy escapes his dread of marriage to Dorothy, as he escaped his memories of an alienated mother, by imagining his youthful moments of warmth and nurturance at the hands of a black woman.

The image of white children looking to black nannies for the rare chance to become connected to physicality, sensuousness, and joy is frequently joined in Smith's writing by the image of children, white and black, playing, questioning, and suffering together. Critics and biographers alike have tied Smith's writing to her long tenure as owner of a girl's camp in north Georgia. Some of her most vivid writing, both in *Strange Fruit* and *Killers of the Dream,* relies on images of children, often conflated with memories of her own youth. If segregation represented for Smith a bifurcation of the adult personality, then the teaching or masking or explaining away of segregation began this splitting at a very early age. "Neither the Negro nor sex was often discussed at length in our home," she wrote in *Killers of the Dream.*

> We were given no formal instruction in these difficult matters but we learned our lessons well. We learned the intricate system of taboos, of renunciations and compensations, of manners, voice modulations, words, feelings, along with our prayers, our toilet habits, and our games. I do not remember how or when, but by the time I had learned that God is love, that Jesus is His Son and came to give us more abundant life, that all men are brothers with a common Father, I also knew that I was better than a Negro, that all black folks have their place and must be kept in it, that sex has its place and must be kept in it, that a terrifying disaster would befall the South if ever I treated a Negro as my social equal and as terrifying a disaster would befall my family if ever I were to have a baby out of marriage. (27–28)

Smith structures two chapters in *Killers of the Dream* around an allegorical conversation between herself and an inquisitive child asking about race. The child's wide-eyed fears and innocent questions have a visceral dimension that is reminiscent of Richard Wright's early memories in *Black Boy;* in both cases, the racial curiosities of young children are met with severe beatings at the hands of adults who have no sensible answers. "Even its children knew that the South was in trouble," she wrote. "No one had to tell them; no words said aloud. To them, it was a vague thing weaving in and out of their play, like a ghost haunting an old graveyard or whispers after the household sleeps—fleeting mystery, vague menace to which each responded in his own way."

> Some learned to screen out all except the soft and the soothing; others denied even as they saw plainly, and heard. But all knew that under quiet words and warmth and laughter, under slow ease and tender concern about small matters, there was a heavy burden on all of us and as heavy a refusal to confess it. The children knew this "trouble" was bigger than they, bigger than their family, bigger than their church, so big that people turned away from its size. They had seen it flash out and shatter a town's peace, and felt it tear up all they believed in. They had measured its giant strength and felt weak when they remembered. This haunted childhood belongs to every southerner of my age. We ran away from it but we came back like a hurt animal to its wound, or a murderer to the scene of his sin. The human heart dares not stay away too long from that which hurt it most. (*KD*, 25–26)

Here again is segregation standing in for a profound emptiness in white culture; its malevolence is haunting not only for the way it deprives a child or a community but for the violence that erupts at the slightest attempt to question it. The unspoken, the unspeakable, issue of race quickly overpowers anyone who attempts to break the silence or tries to break free of rhetorical bonds.[10] Early on in *Strange Fruit*, Tracy flashes back to a childhood moment when he and his black playmate Henry are playing on a sidewalk as a white girl rolls by on her bicycle. Rather than move out of the way, Henry tells the girl to "Move yourself." The two collide; she scratches her leg on a pedal, and Henry and Tracy collapse in laughter. A strange, violent sequence follows.

Mamie, Henry's mother and Tracy's nanny, sees the accident from her stoop, "takes Henry by the shirt, bent him over her knee and whipped him so hard that Tracy burst into sobs and covered his eyes from the sight though he could not make himself leave the sound of it." Importantly, it is not Henry who bursts into tears, but Tracy; here, as elsewhere, Smith uses the physical whipping of a black boy to express the psychological damage done to a white boy. If Henry is left only with a sore backside, his unjust whipping stands as a moment of horrific education in racial mores for Tra-

---

10. In this passage, too, Wright floats in the background like a brooding ghost; the repetition of the word *bigger* here conjures up the aura of Bigger Thomas, the main character of Wright's novel *Native Son*, published in 1940, a work that shocked white audiences in its unprecedented expression of black violence and rage.

cy; Henry's physical body is used as a vehicle to express the damage done to Tracy's spirit. But Smith does not end here; in the scene, the violence continues. When Tracy tries to speak to Mamie after the whipping, she bellows "Go! Go to your *own folks!*" Tracy runs home to his mother and sister, placidly reading a book together, and proceeds to push his sister to the ground, "expecting his mother to follow and whip him, whip him as hard as Mamie had whipped Henry. But she did not come." Tracy mistakes the reason for Henry's whipping to have been merely adolescent insolence; his awareness of the racial underpinnings come later that same evening, after he hears Mamie's husband Ten return home and violently reprimand her for whipping his son. "You goin to keep your hands offn him! You hear? You tetch him again count of white folks an I'll beat you till yo can't get offn da floor." Ten then grabs a blue-and-white glass vase that was "Mamie's one fine house ornament and hurled it to the floor, smashing it into a hundred fragments." Listening to the fight, Tracy and Henry crash into racial awareness.

> "It means I'm white," Tracy whispered, "and you're black," eyes never leaving the shed where the two stood talking, deep shadows against the lamplighted cabin. "It means," he went on and felt a new swelling pride rising in him, "I'm always right, I reckon."
>
> "How come?" Henry asked dully.
> "Cause I'm white—you heard Mamie!"
> "Do skin make the diffunce?"
> "Reckon so," Tracy said, losing his confidence a little, "yep, reckon it do."
> Black boy and white boy stood there in the darkness, watching the grown folks' trouble, and slowly Henry turned and went to the cabin, and slowly Tracy went to the big yellow house. (*SF,* 109–144)

The image of two childhood friends, one white, one black, drifting into segregated neighborhoods after watching their parents explode in the violent fallout of a harmless prank is signature Lillian Smith. White and black are distinct traits only because of their powerful capacity to alienate, to tear apart, to split; individual spirits as well as families and communities are always vulnerable to the corrosive power of race. No one escapes the damage done.

Cheese

A Conversation Between Timothy McVeigh,
Terri Nichols, the militia

Ted Wilson

black as my heart
the night grows whiter
blessed with sunny stars
born out of wedlock
if that matters
no negroes born here

ever ree buddy nose dat
aint no negrahs born here
dey just appear
raised by satan or is it
lucy fer dat be de name
on ahl deys bath certif itkats
dat be de only blessing dey gits

glory be   prays gud
glowry bee hosanna in de highest
den we saw the c...suckas balls off to see
de wizard...de wonderful
we-zard of ozzie and harriet
dat's how my boy jake were born
he be my 2nd   had-dent been dat hard
since ah made dat cullid gull go down
on me en ma-daddys barn
not even ma honeymoon were it dat hard

hell mary lee jane say if dat what killin'
one a dem aliens do den get and find 'em
at least once a week
if not ever ree utter nite
specially under de swollen
sunny sky   you know de darkest ones
with the big yeller star

her legs uzzed jism as she spoke
ran all over de floor made colored images
all over de tile   caint get away from dem
no matter what
blood on de moon   gim me a spoon
no way jo'say de moon is made of green cheese
may i have a slice please   bloods i say
on de moon   outta place never in deir
space and dey want eaqualitee
no way jo'say

no colored gov'nor in dish 'ere state
a cullid precedent   not in this millenium
i don't care how dey rap bodies   not in
my house let 'em do it at de darky town
strutter's ball   let 'em ball each utter
dey's such good at-leates   let 'em ball
each utter not my mutter
did i say mut-ter i mean utther mother i
mean my brutter's mutter   mutter's bruther
i-i-i hell you know not in dis house
i'll burn this mutter down furst

rainbows appear   is it a colition or
colation   koolaid please to cool who out
what is dis bloody mess
why all this bloody redness   dis is
moonin' time

say what
mars is red with bluish figures
gimme some cheese please
no not blue cheese   american or swiss
with a little golden moustard   don't be
coy   give it to de boy   i don't try nuttin
furst til you quench my thurst
god dammit no i don't wont no rade wine
white wine and yella cheese   now be a
mellow   fellow please
touch my soul wit ah bucket of gold
no no no my name is not judas no no no no
i'm not a priest   just de po-leece   i said
a bucket ah gold for my very soul   not ah
bag   i not play tag
judas was dat way   sweet goy but dat was
a few my lend nee ah ago
why is all dis gold red   am i dead
blood you say   pinch me   am i real
harder   make me squeal like de pig i am
what's de big deal

now   may i have anutter piece ah cheese
please   wit my negrah

Blindsided

a zuihitsu

Kimiko Hahn

They were always looking for some reason to kill us.

My heart beats in my throat in vicarious terror. Have I ever felt such an extreme emotion?

The women's psychosomatic blindness could be something I identify with. Not that I willfully do not see, but attempt to control the immediate.

The house was warm and quiet. I needed my mother's permission. I was standing right beside her and she couldn't hear me."Are you listening?" I asked repeatedly.

The incidence of women turning what I will call mad in Asian American writings is very high: John Okada's *No-No Boy*, Milton Murayama's *All I Asking for Is My Body*, Maxine Hong Kingston's *Woman Warrior*, Hisaye Yamamoto's *17 Syllables*, Bharati Mukherjee's *Wife*, Wendy Law Yone's *The Coffin Tree*.

Regardless of point of origin, date of arrival, age, etc. Not everyone is first generation. There is also Fae Ng's *Bone*, the sister's suicide driving the narrative.

They were always looking for some reason to kill us.

My village had become a prison farm.

Italicized quotations are from "They Cried Until They Could Not See," by Patrick Cooke, *New York Times*, 23 June 1991.

Of 170,000 Cambodian refugees living in the United States, half reside in Los Angeles. Local ophthalmologists noticed a high incidence of vision problems among those women who arrived in the 1980s fleeing Pol Pot's Khmer Rouge. Approximately 150 have lost all or most of their sight though there is nothing physically wrong with their eyes.

The Khmer Rouge took Chhean Im's brother and sister away. They killed her father and another brother *before her eyes.*

During the day they would take people into a big meeting hall and beat them and beat them and we all sat in a circle and were made to watch.

I am surprised they speak to an interviewer. Or perhaps a relative told their story to the doctor who told the interviewer.

From his name I assume the writer is a white male though he could be black or adopted or mixed. Like Winifred Eaton.

There is nothing wrong with their eyes. I am amazed the body can do this.

There was a draft. There was a draft from the crack in the window. I could see the curtain moving.

When the Vietnamese Army tried to liberate her village, the Khmer Rouge began massacring everybody in sight.

Perhaps there were men who lost their vision but it is unlikely any will ever be found since eighty percent of those killed were male.

The images consume me like a flame. My skin feels scorched, prickly, raw and nauseous.

For the next two years the Khmer Rouge direct Lor Poy to dig children's graves.

On learning of my work he tells me when nuns interviewed Koreans in Hiroshima after the bomb, the survivors *drew a blank.* When inadvertently questioned in Japanese, one began to wail and recall the horrors. Others could also recall it in Japanese, but not in their *mother tongue.*

The house was warm and too quiet. I couldn't avoid her any longer or wait for a better moment.

I was standing right beside her and she couldn't hear me. "Are you listening?" I asked repeatedly.

The body protects the spirit just as the spirit protects the body.

I was standing right beside him and he couldn't hear me. "Are you listening?" I asked repeatedly.

In prison camp the Khmer Rouge gave the family so little food her husband and daughter starved.

She watched her child starve. Watched her neighbor get clubbed to death. Watched another disappear.

how the mind acts to what the body perceives

"Dissociation," a state of altered consciousness. If I am on a freeway daydreaming and drive past the exit . . . If I . . .

The structure of "17 Syllables" reverses a chronological structure so we enter in the middle of the present, in the middle of an argument so to speak. We do not discover the truth of the mother's past, of her first marriage until the last two pages where we find the mother, "damaged goods" as they used to say, was married below her class in order to give her a future.

In 1919, Freud called this [physical] sacrifice "conversion disorder."

the student typed "sacriface"

What was reality for these women—how did the images affect their travel from country to country—

What of Thai children—male and female—daily prostituted, vagina and anus torn, bloody, swollen, feverish, bruised, lacerated with disease—who blame themselves for being sold? What of the men who permit themselves to wound these brown children?

Are the children's faces still lustrous as my daughters'? Will they be allowed, even by themselves, to be human? We read about them as though this only happens to Thai children or only in Thailand.

conversion disorder

Are you listening?

To see socialism in its dialectical facets, to understand the extreme disfiguration by the Khmer Rouge who used anticolonialism as a subjective means to assert an order that destroys more than builds, to see the Vietnamese as a different force, I must also explore my attraction to the concept of a planned economy.

vision and revision

disassociation

To view phenomena in more than polarities: blind but not blind.

The metaphor is not blindness. Not vision. Not hysteria. Then what? He knew a woman who brought a psychosomatic pregnancy to term. She gave birth. Then what? Psychosomatic nursing? Infanticide?

to term

The child prostitutes, rescued by a group of nuns, were telling their life stories for the first time. Mary, although sold by parents, felt she and the other children must have been bad. It is not only in Thailand.

The virgins were naturally the most expensive. Their price diminished quickly. Considered less prone to AIDS by johns, in fact their young bodies tear easily; the wounds, an open invitation to disease.

dis/ease, dis/favor, dis/member, dis/possess, dis/rupt

Rape boys and girls. Sodomize neighbors. Club them. Skin them.

A vivisection of a text. A body of work.

I don't want to see this.

I don't want to see this.

I won't see it.

I do not see it.

I do not see.

The prisoners had nothing to eat except snakes, rats, worms, and the dead.

Close your eyes—*dream.*

At first a number of social workers thought the women were attempting to con the state for public assistance. But they behaved as the blind really do, relying on sound, air movement, a sense of *what a room is like.*

symptomatic

Ophthalmologists say their machines register sight, measure brainwave activity picked up through sensors attached to the patient's head.

One of the Angka lifted an infant by the head and beat him to death against a tamarind tree.

Four of the Angka picked up [a man who had perhaps stolen a bit of rice, picked him up] by the arms and legs and threw him alive on to a big fire. After that [lesson] we all went back to work.

the need to engage with a text so personally the text becomes one's own, becomes part of one's own experience, one's own vision in fact *hysterical blindness*

My heart beats in my throat as if attempting speech.

In "17 Syllables" the three visit a family whose mother has gone mad. Of course the protagonist's father in a jealous rage takes away his wife's only pleasure, writing haiku. Apart from revealing her own history to her daughter she is completely isolated. She can speak but she will not speak.

In "The Legend of Miss Sasagawara," the woman rarely speaks to the others interned. When she finally speaks she is seen as "normal." Later in life, after the war, she is finally hospitalized and writes a long poem that refers to an authority figure who betrayed her with, ironically, his moral preoccupations. Her father, the Buddhist reverend?

I was standing right beside her and she couldn't hear me. "Are you listening?" I asked repeatedly.

In one instance the terror brought on a person's immigration. In another, in glowing expectation, the immigrant arrives but experiences various forms of abuse from inside and outside the home. The mother's sister in *The Woman Warrior* immigrates to become reunited with her husband; on finding he has begun a new family she slowly goes crazy, which includes paranoia—hearing people who are coming to get her.

Garbage ghost, mailman ghost, . . . as if turning the real less real? More, rendering them differently real; then marginalizing the inhabitants for a more central existence?

It was too warm inside and too cold outside.

When sight is cut off, how do their other senses remember?

Do the women remember more with their visual exile? as if replaying a film in a darkened theater? or do they not see *any thing?*

If a person cannot see, what do they see? Is there an awareness of black? of gray?

When I shut my eyes I am exiled into my memories and imagination. I can only leave by admitting sight.

"See? See what I mean?"

The narrator read a poem written by Miss Sasagawara in the story's conclusion. We hear the poem is tantalizingly obscure, that the man's devotion to Buddha eclipses all human relations. In her version—

version, vision—

"Are you, are you—"

When the interview is complete she turns toward the draft whistling in beneath the door.

Time, Jazz, and the Racial Subject

Lawson Inada's Jazz Poetics

Juliana Chang

> *. . . there are no calendars, no clocks.*
> *Pres holds time in his heart.*
> —*Lawson Inada, "Lester Young"*

It is no accident that the epigraph's evocation of antimetronomic time is from a poem written for Lester Young, the jazz musician popularly called "Pres," for "president." Lawson Inada's recognition of the cultural authority of the African American jazz musician participates in an African American cultural practice of counterlegitimation, a practice that implicitly critiques and refuses the authority of dominant institutions and knowledges.[1] In this figure of antimetronomic time embodied by the African American jazz musician as alternative national figurehead, Inada proposes an alternative to the dominant temporality of the U.S. nation-state. Ralph Ellison elucidates the temporality of racial difference, using invisibility as a figure for the nonrecognition of the racially subordinated subject by dominant culture: "Invisibility . . . gives one a slightly different sense of time, you're never quite on the beat. Sometimes you're ahead and sometimes behind. Instead of the swift and imperceptible flowing of time, you are aware of its nodes, those points where time stands still or from which it leaps ahead. And you slip into the breaks and look around" (1972, 8). This disjunctive racial temporality is enacted in the jazz poetics of Lawson Inada's *Legends from Camp* (1992), a volume of poetry that inscribes Japanese

I would like to thank Christopher P. Wilson, Peter X. Feng, Nicole Hickman, Jerry Miller, and Celine Parreñas for comments on earlier drafts of this essay.

1. More recent practices of naming alternative national figureheads in African American music include James Brown's "Funky President," Parliament's "Chocolate City," and Sean "Puffy" Combs's reference to singer Faith Evans as "First Lady."

American racial subject formation in the trauma of wartime internment.[2] As Cathy Caruth points out, trauma is that which one experiences both prematurely and belatedly: it occurs before we are prepared, and because shock prevents us from experiencing it at the moment of its occurrence, we can only experience it later through its recurrence. Inada's use of a jazz poetics—and of its relation to trauma, racial subject formation, and time— raises the question of what it means for an Asian American poetics to be mediated through an African American musical form.

For both historical and aesthetic reasons, Lawson Inada is a significant figure in Asian American poetry and literature. He was one of the coeditors of the landmark anthology *Aiiieeeee! An Anthology of Asian-American Writers,* first published in 1975, and has participated in efforts to recover writing by earlier Japanese American authors such as Toshio Mori and John Okada. His collection *Before the War: Poems As They Happened* was published in 1971 as one of the first Asian American single-author volumes of poetry from a major publishing house. Although jazz and blues rhythms and aesthetics have been used by a number of Asian American poets, Inada's poetry stands out in its consistency and depth of engagement with jazz. *Before the War* begins with a whimsical portrait of a Japanese American figure playing "air bass"; includes tributes to jazz musicians and singers such as Charlie Parker, Lester Young, and Billie Holiday; and ends with poems written for Miles Davis and Charles Mingus. Riffing on the term *bluesman,* Inada calls himself a "campsman," suggesting that his blues derive from Japanese American internment. He describes his project as "blowing shakuhachi versaphone" (Feinstein and Komunyakaa 1991, 261) and cites jazz as the strongest influence on his writing.

What is the attraction of jazz to a Japanese American poet addressing the history of wartime internment? Jazz is itself rooted in histories of racial trauma, and its rhythms and aesthetics of repetition, improvisation, and syncopation present for the Japanese American subject a way of reliving

2. In the current discursive context of Asian American studies, *Japanese American* is considered a category of ethnicity, whereas a pan-ethnic *Asian American* identity is considered to belong to the category of race. However, for the purposes of this essay, I find terms such as *race* and *racial formation* useful even though I discuss a specifically Japanese American history. The circulation of critical theories of racial formation has resulted in a general acknowledgment of the social constructedness of race, while ethnicity is less commonly thought of in terms of power, state apparatuses, ideology, etc. I consider the ideology that legitimated Japanese American internment—the Asian as ontologically alien to the United States—to be a racial ideology.

and transforming the pain and trauma of displacement. Focusing here on Inada's more recent *Legends from Camp*, I propose that Inada's jazz poetics work to redress the pain of racial trauma by enacting an alternative to the dominant time of the nation. Inada's poetics of repetition and improvisation enable restagings and reworkings of a troubled past, and his poetics of syncopation enact the rhythm and status of the racially marginalized subject as outside of standard national historic time. Inada's poems are sites where we can "slip into the breaks" of dominant U.S. historical time "and look around." Ralph Ellison's figure of visuality refers not only to the dominant nonrecognition of the racial other ("invisibility"), but also the particular perspective and knowledge of the racially marginalized subject, who can see from those points at which time stops or from which it leaps ahead. Jazz legitimates alternative knowledges through syncopation, a practice that allows for and makes pleasurable the peculiar perspective of the subject who is exiled from standard national time. Inada's poetics of performance is based on this experience of exile from standard time: performance is a mode that arises out of and responds to contingency.

Legends from Camp is composed of five sections, which Inada likens to musical movements, entitled "Camp," "Fresno," "Jazz," "Oregon," and "Performance." The title poem, "Legends from Camp," a kind of epic poem consisting of twenty-five parts, makes up the bulk of the first section. The term *legends* signals Inada's project of myth making, taking us into a mythological time that is different from historical time. The first, second, and fourth sections map particular spaces, communities, and histories. Fresno, California, is the town in which Inada grew up, and a number of the poems in the section "Fresno" are told from a child's point of view. After attending the University of Iowa, he settled in Oregon and has taught at Southern Oregon State College since 1966. Although the section "Camp" also maps a particular time and space, it does not evoke the sense of belonging, grounding, and home that "Fresno" and "Oregon" do. "Camp" does not even begin with a poem; that is, we are not immediately grounded in the words of the poet. It begins with a reproduction of the poster that ordered the relocation and internment of Japanese Americans during World War II. We begin the book in medias res, immediately and suddenly plunged into disruption and loss, without even knowing what has been lost. (Below, I provide a reading of the first poem "Instructions to All Persons" as a response to this document.) We may also more generally consider the last four sections of the book to be a response to the trauma of the first section. "Fresno" and "Oregon," as mappings of place, enable us to get our bearings again. "Jazz" and "Performance," as terms that highlight contingency, however, unsettle our sense of time and place as fixed and settled. "Jazz" consists mainly of poems named after particular musicians: "Louis Armstrong," "Lester Young," "Billie Holiday," and so on. The poems in the final section, "Performance," were written to be performed in specific contexts. Inada's poetics of performance posits his art not as an object that transcends time, but as a process that shapes time. Calling live performance his favorite form of "publishing" (*LC,* 148), Inada appropriates the value ascribed to a finalized, written text for a mode that is oral and more contingent. In *Blues People,* Leroi Jones's comment about the suppression of certain African/American cultural forms and the survival of others suggests the importance of contingency and improvisation in African American culture: "Music, dance, religion do not have *artifacts* as their end products, so they were saved" (1963, 16). Jones argues that cultural forms that are more performative, that are adaptable to unpredictably changing contexts, had more of a chance of survival than those that relied on objects that could be confiscated or destroyed. The trauma of Japanese American internment included dislocation from home, dispossession of personal property, and forced relocation to a radically different environment. We can see that improvisation and performance are valued in Inada's poetics not only as survival tactics, but also as practices that reshape time and thus, as in Ellison's formulation of nonstandard time, legitimate subordinated knowledge and enable rearticulations of subjectivity and power.

If we consider the arrangement of Inada's book to be based on a jazz aesthetic, the poems within each section comprise variations on the theme named in the section title. The poems in "Jazz," for example, are mostly tributes to individual jazz musicians, whereas the poems in the section "Oregon" present particular Oregonian landscapes. Within particular poems, Inada's characteristic phrasing is to create a musical rhythm with similar-sounding, repeated, or polysyllabically rhymed words; examples include the phrases "cornerstone course and chorus" ("Louis Armstrong"); "the scripture of the structure" ("John Coltrane"); and the following lines from "Blue Monk":

> as a result of recognition,
> as a consequence of confirmation,
> as an accomplishment of affirmation—
> (*LC,* 64)

in which repetition and rhyme occur both between lines and within lines: the anaphoric "as a[n]," the similar-sounding final words of each line, the repetition of "re," "con," "a" within each line. These poetic forms correspond to the emphasis on percussion, repetition, and chordal structure, rather than (primarily) on melody, in jazz. A melody typically develops in a more linear fashion, but the musical structure of variations on a theme evokes a more layered sense of time, in which a particular moment (a particular musical phrase) may be experienced or recalled differently from different points in time and from different subject positions. Inada's use of this structure indicates that there is more than one way to tell a story, that there are many stories embedded within a given story or within what we know as history. This layered and contingent sense of time implicitly critiques the notion of a standard time that is equivalent for all subjects. Two of Inada's poems in particular shape time as contingent, variable, and layered: part II of Inada's poem "Two Variations on a Theme by Thelonious Monk as Inspired by Mal Waldron" and the last poem of the book, "Red Earth, Blue Sky, Petrified."

"Two Variations" is a piece responding to Thelonious Monk's piece "Blue Monk," divided into an introduction and two parts: "I. 'Blue Monk' (linear)" and "II. 'Blue Monk' (percussive)." Part II consists primarily of words whose prefix *re-* denotes repetition and whose suffix *-ing* denotes process; repetition and process are also enacted by the very form of the poem. Beginning and ending with centered lines consisting of single words followed by colons, while the middle section groups together several lines consisting of several words, the poem is shaped like a drum.

Ricochet:

Radius:

Radiating:

Reciting:Realizing:Referring:Recapturing:Repercussion
Revolving:Reflecting:Returning:Reconstituting:Republic
Reshaping:Restructuring:Reversing:Reclaiming:Religion
Respecting:Removing:Reforming:Receiving:Reality:
Refining:Reducing:Refreshing:Regenerating:Resource:
Regarding:Relating:Relaxing:Revering:Remembering:
Renewing:Revising:Repairing:Replacing:Residing:
Reviewing:Respecting:Resolving:Reviving:Responsible:
Retaining:Resuming:Revealing:Rehearsing:Resulting:

Restoring:Retrieving:Regaining:Recovering:Relying:
Redeeming:Replying:Reminding:Rewarding:Resounding:

Reverberating:

Remarkably:

Releasing:

Remaining:

Repeating:
(*LC,* 68)

When I saw Inada perform the piece, he inserted the beginning word *ricochet* at various points and at various intervals throughout the reading of the poem, so that the text functions as a musical score that may be used as a departure point for improvisation. As James Snead notes, "Without an organizing principle of repetition, true improvisation would be impossible, since an improviser relies upon the ongoing recurrence of the beat" (1984, 68). We might think of the performative in Judith Butler's theory of subject formation (1994) as analogous to the improvisatory. The performative and improvisatory are often thought of as acts of pure agency and freedom, but are in fact enabled by the constraining framework of repetition. The temporality of repetition, the interval that is opened up by the act of repetition, provides an opportunity for the rearticulation of what is "given." Inada's poetics of repetition operate against closure: the final word of the poem, "Repeating," and its punctuation mark of the colon with its similarity to the musical coda signifier of repetition indicate the end as a return to the beginning.

James Snead describes the "cut" in African American music as a return to the beginning, a figure of repetition. The last poem in the book, "Red Earth, Blue Sky, Petrified" (1984, 67–69), performs such a cut, a response to the text that returns to and repeats the text. As in the poem "Instructions to All Persons," this poem consists of words and phrases excerpted from another text and reconfigured. Here the original (or referenced)[3] text is the very book *Legends from Camp*. Inada describes the poem as a Navajo-inspired "weaving," in which fragments of the book are woven together, us-

3. Tricia Rose notes that African American and Caribbean musical practices such as sampling and "versioning," in which old and new pieces are mixed into "narrative reformulations," redefine traditional notions of authorship and originality. The appropriations and transformations performed in jazz music and Inada's poetry raise similar questions. I borrow Rose's substitution of "referenced" for "original" (1994, 90).

ing a syntax of juxtapositioning. Placing words and phrases next to each other without the conventional connectives of prepositions and conjunctions opens up the possibilities of relations between these words.

> Securely. Plainly. Numbered. Accordance.
> Kind. Personal. Substantial. Accepted.
> Given. Let us bring. Let us have.
> Friends, neighbors, colleagues, partners.
>
> Spirits. Land. Dreams. Visions.
> Sand. Creek. Moon. Black. Red.
> Denver. Sacramento. Hiroshima.
> Battle. Creek. America. Planets.
> Marysville, Placerville, Watsonville.
> The blue tricycle left in the weeds.
>
> Buddha. Buddhas. Down the rows, rows, rows.
> Calligraphy of echoes. At Amache Gate.
> Sit. Listen. Love. Sing. Concentrate.
> (*LC*, 176)

The short phrases present flashes of images, suggesting a nonlinear, non-continuous sense of time. Short, discrete phrasing results in an increase of stressed syllables, creating a rhythm of strong percussive beats. Reading this poem after reading the book as a whole brings back memories of one's previous reading: one experiences time as layered and sedimented, rather than as consisting of separate, discrete moments. This palimpsestic text highlights the spectral nature of language, reminding us that every use of a word recalls prior moments. What Inada's poems stage is this very recall, the return to prior moments in order to rework these moments.

Inada's poem "Rayford's Song" (*LC*, 43–45) presents the problem of how our use of language is subject to other histories and other forces. As the poem begins, "Rayford's song was Rayford's song, / but it was not his alone, to own." The scene of the poem is the classroom as a site of subjugating racial knowledge. Rayford is a black third-grade student who takes the initiative in the music classroom and sings a song that is not on the agenda of the music teacher. Inada describes Rayford's rendition of "Swing Low, Sweet Chariot" as lumiscent and awe inspiring, but the teacher, Miss Gordon, responds only with a stern "correcting" of Rayford's pronunciation into standard English. She asks if anyone else would like to sing "a song of their own," but this apparent act of solicitation conceals the power she has already exercised to silence the students. "Our songs, our songs, were there— / on tips of tongues, but stuck/in throats . . . / songs / of other lands, in other languages, / but they just wouldn't come out. / Where did our voices go?" In response to this subjugation of knowledge, Inada and his classmates construct their own codes of literacy, knowledge, and community that are alternative to those legitimated by the educational system.

The introduction to the section "Jazz" describes the social and cultural marginalization of West Fresno's colored youth, whom Inada refers to as the "ABCs of life—Asians, Blacks, Chicanos," a formulation that proposes a racialized mode of literacy. Inada recalls, "The music we most loved and played and used was Negro music. It was something we could share in common, like a 'lingua franca' in our 'colored' community. And in our distorted reality of aliens and alienation, it even felt like *citizenship*" (*LC*, 57). The phrase "aliens and alienation" is an example of Inada's musical structure of chords and repetition, in which the sound and meaning of the two words counterpoint and illuminate each other. The repetition of the sound *alien* calls attention to the second half of the latter word, in which *nation* is a suffix denoting the process of being alienated, in contrast to the inherent nature implied by the noun *alien*. *Nation* is also the term signifying the entity that produces this alienation.

Inada observes that he and his classmates feel little connection to the sanctioned and legitimated discourses of their civics class—that, for them, the announcement of Charlie Parker's death is by far the most relevant civics lesson. This redefinition of *civics* highlights how this youth subculture creates alternative networks of cultural literacy and cultural belonging in response to their exclusion from official discourses of national citizenship.

> Ah, to be so "culturally deprived"! The poor West Side—we had no library, no galleries, no museums, no civic orchestra, no ballet company! . . . being an illiterate lot, we squandered our money on entertainment, on music, mostly. . . . We were quaint, ignorant, primitive, and deprived. . . . It was our community's fault. It was the fault of the jukeboxes, which were our libraries, it was the fault of the Chinese-owned record stores; it was the fault of all those touring minstrel "revues" that kept us where we were—incorrigible, unimproved.
>
> We didn't know anything. And all we knew—in detention, on suspension, in special education, on probation—were obscure irrelevancies, certain "tunes" by a Big Joe Turner, by a T-Bone Walker, by a Sister Rosetta

> Tharpe, by a Hamp, by a Bullmoose, a Cleanhead, a Bird, a Dizzy, a Pres.
> (*LC*, 57–8)

This collective self-characterization as "illiterate" and "ignorant" is of course tongue-in-cheek, as is the pinpointing of popular music as the cause of such youthful incorrigibility. The patronizing characterization of these youth as "culturally deprived" from a dominant standpoint, mimicked and apparently internalized by the speaker, is undercut by the knowledgeable listing of musicians whom the speaker invests with cultural authority. His use of their nicknames indicates his own authoritative status as cultural insider, so that lack is now positioned on the side of the outsider who is ignorant of *his* (the speaker's) culture. The musicality, sound, and rhythm of Inada's poems present knowledges alternative to those sanctioned by dominant narratives of nation, time, and history.

The layered meanings suggested by the words in part I of Inada's poem "Looking Back at Camp" demand that we approach the temporality of reading not as linear, but as repetitive: to understand this short and deceptively simple poem fully, we must return to it after a first reading and reread.

> I. The Fresno Assemly Center [*sic*]
>
> To get into the fair,
> You have to pay admission.
>
> We got in for free
> To the Fresno Family Prison. (*LC*, 29)

The initial, literal reading of the poem that Inada intends is the message that the speaker got a bargain: his family, unlike the universal "you," did not have to pay admission to the fair. The irony of this apparent privilege becomes evident in the final three words: the fairgrounds, a public space of family and community recreation, have been transformed into a space of imprisonment for specific racial families.

The rhythm of the poem points to the racial collective that is set apart and produced by this act of imprisonment. The rhythm of the first lines of each couplet and of the second lines of each couplet are roughly similar to each other; the major difference is the noticeable beginning of the second couplet with a stressed syllable: "*We* got in for free." The stress on the "we" stands in contrast to the unstressed "you" of the normative general public in the line "You have to pay admission," a difference that parallels the marked character of those racialized as "colored" and the unmarked, transparent, universalized character of whiteness. The parallel structures of the first lines and the second lines, of each of the two couplets, as well as the off rhyme and near rhyme of the ending words of these lines suggest that we consider the relation between the pair "fair" and "free" and the pair "admission" and "prison." "Admission" to the fair connotes a compliance with one's desire to enter—that is, it implies a voluntariness; "prison" makes explicit the coerciveness, the involuntariness, of this space of racial confinement.

The Japanese American family getting in for "free" makes reference to the ideological construction of racial immigrants entering the United States and using without deserving its national resources, as well as to racial others in general "getting over" on these national resources. However, interiority in this poem is not a privileged space of inclusion and admission to membership in a community or nation, but a space of imprisonment and exclusion. The poem reverses the dominant ideological positioning of interior and exterior space in terms of value as marked by degrees of freedom and privilege. Other inversions of value and meaning in the poem include the act of getting in for "free" as resulting in the absence of freedom, while the word *fair* highlights this act as the opposite of ethical fairness. If the initial, literal reading of the poem iterates dominant ideological constructions of a racial economics, in which the racial other apparently enjoys an undeserved privilege at the expense of the normative white subject, the act of rereading performs a reiteration by revealing what this surface meaning/ideology conceals: racist practices paid for by the freedom of the racial other.

Like the reinterpretation of prior musical texts in jazz, Inada's poems engage and transform dominant discursive meanings through a practice of citation and reiteration. "Instructions to All Persons" is a poem that recalls in order to reconfigure prior discursive moments. The section "Camp" opens with a reproduction of the poster in which the state orders the evacuation and relocation of Japanese Americans in Los Angeles. What legitimates this mass incarceration is a specific kind of racial criminalization: the assumption of racial treachery. The Japanese American subject, projected as alien, is positioned as a threat to national security, a threat that demands containment. Inada's poem "Instructions to All Persons" faces this document. The opening poem of the book, it is an explicit response to this prior text, Executive Order 9066. Inada's juxtapositioning of these two texts may be read as a representation of the dialectic of Japanese American subjectivity: racial formation by the state, and a response to such racial formation.

The form that this response takes is that of repetition, a citation that is a reinterpretation and reterritorialization. Repetition, to paraphrase Saidiya V. Hartman, returns us to the breach that engenders the racialized Japanese American subject (Hartman 1997, 75). Not a simple acquiescence to or refusal of the demands of the state, this form of response interrogates such demands by acts of apparent mimicry and internalization that are not, however, acts of identification. The poem consists of words and phrases excerpted from the poster, uprooted from their original context and reconfigured from instructional sentences into a call-and-response structure. The linear is transformed into the percussive, and a unidirectional imperative becomes dialogic in form. Framing these citations is a liturgical voice that calls into being a congregational collective and provides a tone of ritual, a repeated enactment of what has come before. The poem appropriates the language of state force, contesting dominant meanings and transforming this text of punitive racialization into an occasion for racial community building.

> Instructions to All Persons
>
> Let us take
> what we can
> for the occasion:
>
> > Ancestry. *(Ancestry.)*
> > All of that portion. *(Portion.)*
> > Within the boundary. *(Boundary.)*
> > Beginning. *(Beginning.)*
> > At the point. *(Point.)*
>
> . . .
>
> Let us bring
> what we need
> for the meeting:
>
> > Provisions. *(Provisions.)*
> > Permission. *(Permission.)*
> > Commanding. *(Commanding.)*
> > Uniting. *(Uniting.)*
> > Family. *(Family.)*

Presidio of San Francisco, California
May 3, 1942

INSTRUCTIONS
TO ALL PERSONS OF
JAPANESE
ANCESTRY
Living in the Following Area:

All of that portion of the City of Los Angeles, State of California, within that boundary beginning at the point at which North Figueroa Street meets a line following the middle of the Los Angeles River; thence southerly and following the said line to East First Street; thence westerly on East First Street to Alameda Street; thence southerly on Alameda Street to East Third Street; thence northwesterly on East Third Street to Main Street; thence northerly on Main Street to First Street; thence northwesterly on First Street to Figueroa Street; thence northeasterly on Figueroa Street to the point of beginning.

Pursuant to the provisions of Civilian Exclusion Order No. 33, this Headquarters, dated May 3, 1942, all persons of Japanese ancestry, both alien and non-alien, will be evacuated from the above area by 12 o'clock noon, P. W. T., Saturday, May 9, 1942.

No Japanese person living in the above area will be permitted to change residence after 12 o'clock noon, P. W. T., Sunday, May 3, 1942, without obtaining special permission from the representative of the Commanding General, Southern California Sector, at the Civil Control Station located at:

Japanese Union Church,
120 North San Pedro Street,
Los Angeles, California.

Such permits will only be granted for the purpose of uniting members of a family, or in cases of grave emergency.

The Civil Control Station is equipped to assist the Japanese population affected by this evacuation in the following ways:

1. Give advice and instructions on the evacuation.
2. Provide services with respect to the management, leasing, sale, storage or other disposition of most kinds of property, such as real estate, business and professional equipment, household goods, boats, automobiles and livestock.
3. Provide temporary residence elsewhere for all Japanese in family groups.
4. Transport persons and a limited amount of clothing and equipment to their new residence.

The Following Instructions Must Be Observed:

1. A responsible member of each family, preferably the head of the family, or the person in whose name most of the property is held, and each individual living alone, will report to the Civil Control Station to receive further instructions. This must be done between 8:00 A. M. and 5:00 P. M. on Monday, May 4, 1942, or between 8:00 A. M. and 5:00 P. M. on Tuesday, May 5, 1942.
2. Evacuees must carry with them on departure for the Assembly Center, the following property:
 (a) Bedding and linens (no mattress) for each member of the family;
 (b) Toilet articles for each member of the family;
 (c) Extra clothing for each member of the family;
 (d) Sufficient knives, forks, spoons, plates, bowls and cups for each member of the family;
 (e) Essential personal effects for each member of the family.
All items carried will be securely packaged, tied and plainly marked with the name of the owner and numbered in accordance with instructions obtained at the Civil Control Station. The size and number of packages is limited to that which can be carried by the individual or family group.
3. No pets of any kind will be permitted.
4. No personal items and no household goods will be shipped to the Assembly Center.
5. The United States Government through its agencies will provide for the storage, at the sole risk of the owner, of the more substantial household items, such as iceboxes, washing machines, pianos and other heavy furniture. Cooking utensils and other small items will be accepted for storage if crated, packed and plainly marked with the name and address of the owner. Only one name and address will be used by a given family.
6. Each family, and individual living alone, will be furnished transportation to the Assembly Center or will be authorized to travel by private automobile in a supervised group. All instructions pertaining to the movement will be obtained at the Civil Control Station.

Go to the Civil Control Station between the hours of 8:00 A.M. and 500 P.M., Monday, May 4, 1942, or between the hours of 8:00 A.M. and 5:00 P.M., Tuesday, May 5, 1942, to receive further instructions.

J. L. DeWITT
Lieutenant General, U. S. Army
Commanding

SEE CIVILIAN EXCLUSION ORDER NO. 33.

U.S. Government poster during World War II about Japanese ancestry. In Lawson Inada's *Legends from Camp* (1971, 4), facing the poem "Instructions to All Persons." Courtesy of the United States Government.

Let us have
what we have
for the gathering:

> Civil. *(Civil.)*
> Ways. *(Ways.)*
> Services. *(Services.)*
> Respect. *(Respect.)*
> Management. *(Management.)*
> Kinds. *(Kinds.)*
> Goods. *(Goods.)*
> For all. *(For all.)*

Let us take
what we can
for the occasion:

> Responsible.

Individual.

Sufficient.

Personal.

Securely.

Civil.

Substantial.

Accepted.

Given.

Authorized.

Let there be
Order.

> Let us be
> Wise. *(LC, 5–6)*

The occasion—meeting, gathering—is this poem, a text that conjures historical subjects, a site where readers are called on to participate in a collective ritual of memory.

The recontextualization of words by this poetic act of appropriation highlights the repressive use of language in the original, historical document. "Uniting," for example, evokes the name of the nation that in fact separates out and punishes racial others from the national "family." The notion of private property is parodied in the phrase "Goods. / For all." Japanese Americans were dispossessed of their property, save for what they could carry. Remaining property was distributed among others ("for all"),[4] in some cases "given" away under duress. The phrase "Let us take / what we can" may be read literally, for they could in fact take *only* what they were physically able to carry with them to the camps. The term *ancestry,* used in the original text in a biologistic fashion, is reclaimed as imagined kinship, temporally vertical community. The term *order,* which recalls the command of Executive Order 9066 and how it reinforced the ordering of a racial hierarchy, becomes in this poem part of a spoken rite of spiritual clarity and meaning: "Let there be / Order. / / Let us be / Wise."

Repetition occurs not only between the poster and the poem, but within the poem itself, in which the parenthetical, italicized repetitions provide the effect of an echoed response. This repetition is a rearticulation that indicates a refusal to simply accept the racialized dicourse of the state. Improvisation, that quintessential jazz practice, produces the difference that arises from this practice of repetition. In Michael Jarrett's phrasing, jazz "starts with what is given and spins off new melodies, rhythms, and harmonies" (1999, 3). With his jazz poetics of repetition and improvisation, Inada takes what is "given" (*LC,* 6) in this dominant discourse and transforms it. This practice of citation and reiteration, of repetition with a difference, acknowledges that power is constitutive of the subject, rather than external to it, but also that power is not deterministic, for the subject may also rearticulate power and potentially turn it against itself (Butler 1997, 1–30).

Inada's poetics of repetition also conveys how internment is not confined to a discrete moment in the past, but is a trauma that returns to haunt the present and future, a haunting that he describes in Part III of "Looking Back at Camp":

> III. Amache Camp
>
> I work on campus.
> I try to concentrate.
>
> Still, things sneak
> up to remind me:
>
> "This is *not* Amache!" (*LC,* 30)

The contradictory double entendre of *concentrate* is precisely an example of such haunting: the history of the word ("concentration camp") is the con-

---

4. I thank Jean Wu for this reading.

dition of its own impossibility of enactment (concentration as focusing on something else). Inada's reference to his work as a poet as the imperative to "concentrate," recalling Gwendolyn Brooks's formulation of poetry as "life distilled," posits his writing as inextricably linked to his racial history. The effects of internment continue to be powerfully felt, even, perhaps especially, in its very absence. Its return in ghostly form is experienced as involuntary, a kind of possession of the subject by an other.

Part XXI of "Legends from Camp," "The Legend of Block 6G Obake," describes this kind of haunting as unspeakable:

> I still don't mention his name in public.
> . . .
> . . . all he did was go around our block
> banging a stick on a garbage can lid
> and chanting, droning, *"Block 6G Obake."*
>
> He did that every evening, when the ghost
> to him appeared—his personal ghost,
> or whatever it was that haunted the camp.
>
> He was punctual, persistent, specific.
> And then I guess he either moved or died.
> Whatever it was, we never spoke of him.
>
> Because the thing is, he was right.
> Amache really was haunted. As it still is.
> Amache was, is, are: Nightly, on television
> (*LC*, 22–23).

The television screen, with its racialized images, becomes an everyday (or, rather, every night) screen for involuntary flashes of the viewer's memory. The act of looking at this screen of cultural images provokes the "looking back" that Inada refers to in the title "Looking Back at Camp." And the phrase "looking back" recalls Ellison's proposed act of inserting oneself into a node or break in time and "looking around." Looking is here a figure for confrontation with particular moments in time. The haunting of the subject by memories of Amache Camp forces such a confrontation with and return to prior moments. This return then forces another question: If Amache is what haunts the subject, *what is it that haunts Amache?* I approach an answer to this by considering how the racial trauma of internment disrupts but also exposes the logic and the time of everyday racialization.

When Asian Americans are framed as analogous to European immigrants to the United States, they are placed within the temporality of Americanization, which posits immigrant populations as subjects to be transformed through and by time from alien to American, not only politically but culturally. What the act of internment highlights, however, is how racial difference is expelled from and remaindered by this teleology. The historical time of settlement or citizenship becomes nullified by racial difference. In this act of spatial displacement, Japanese Americans are also temporally displaced, exiled from the historical time of the nation. The title of Inada's first book, *Before the War,* indicates wartime internment as the node or break in time that Ellison refers to: life is divided for the Japanese American subject into prewar and postwar. The shock of uprooting, displacement, and incarceration is experienced as an absolute break in linear, everyday, continuous time. The rhythms of daily life—the everyday, historical sense of "homogeneous, empty time"—are interrupted and suddenly wrenched into the disorienting time-space of a bewildering confinement, an uprooting of the subject and the disappearance of the familiar. One's sense of temporal continuity is dependent on the stability of space, specifically a space of home that one returns to on an everyday basis. In the poem "Legends from Camp," Inada repeatedly refers to the space "out there," a space where home has now become unattainably located. Incarcerated by the state, surrounded by barbed wire, and surveyed by armed soldiers, the internees experience not only a radical discontinuity between inside and outside, but space being turned inside out, so that home is incomprehensibly exterior, and interior space is permeated by the constant threat of state violence.

If we think analogously of turning a body inside out, it becomes clear that this kind of spatial reconfiguration is experienced as grotesque and shocking. To turn something inside out is to expose what should remain hidden, in this case the explicitness of racialized state violence. The shock produced by this exposure is felt as a break in a comprehensible narrative of experience. It is this disturbing visuality, the revealing of the underside of the everyday, that produces trauma. Although the internment is experienced as a disruption of the everyday, what is traumatic is in fact the realization that the internment is also *a continuation of the everyday.* Recall that in the passage from the introduction to "Jazz," racial discipline and punishment structure the rhythm of daily life for colored youth in West Fresno: "in detention, on suspension, in special education, on probation" (*LC*, 57). Inada's evocation of this racialized, punitive, everyday rhythm enables us to comprehend the wartime incarceration of Japanese Americans as a more dramatic continuation of everyday racialization, rather than as an aberration, an exception to the everyday.

Drawing from Slavoj Žižek's observation that at certain moments "social reality becomes nothing more than a fragile symbolic tissue which can be torn . . . by the intrusion of the real" (1997, 21), I would posit Japanese American internment as an eruption of the real of U.S. nationalist desire and fantasy. The real here signifies that traumatic kernel of the subject that cannot be incorporated into or accounted for by the symbolic. Underneath the "simpl[e]" everyday Japanese American experience of "living in America 'among others'" ("Legends," *LC*, 8) are the racial fantasies, desires, and anxieties that project Asians as aliens threatening the U.S. nation-state. Asian racial difference is here that traumatic kernel for the nation-as-subject. This is what the old man of "Block 6G Obake" both recites and embodies: the Japanese American subject as site and symptom of national trauma. His everyday practice of rhythm and percussion, chanting and repeating "Block 6G Obake," evokes the uncanny for the inhabitants of camp. "Block 6G" uses the parlance of camp to refer to a space that is home, yet not home. *Obake,* the Japanese word for ghost, is familiar to them linguistically, yet also strange and dreaded, for Japaneseness is what implicates them as threatening to the U.S. nation-state and therefore to be punished. Not only in its repetition, but also in its linguistic content, the old man's chanting evokes a temporality of haunting. Japanese-ness belongs to the past, referring to a time before the brutal and coercive Americanization of the camps. What is Japanese must be disappeared, yet it returns in ghostly form, and the site through which it reappears is the site of its violent banishment: the home/not-home of the internment camp.

The old man may have been haunted, but he also haunts; in speaking the unspeakable, he himself becomes unspeakable. It is common for Japanese Americans whose parents were interned to say that their parents did not speak of this experience. Countering conventional constructions of this silence as "cultural," I read this silence as referencing the unspeakable at the intersection of the political and the psychic. I return here to the question of how jazz allows for a speaking that cannot otherwise be spoken. Inada's emphasis on performance indicates the importance of the artist's direct interaction with an audience. His poems often utilize jazz musical structures that explicitly assume intersubjective relations, such as the dialogic form of call and response. His awareness of audience and his engagement in poetic conversation with jazz mentors indicate his sense of poetry as dialogic and public, rather than lyrical and private. Countering the conventional separation of the aesthetic from the social, critic Ingrid Monson reminds us that jazz is a mode of social action that musicians selectively employ in their process of communication (1994, 285). James Snead also describes the beat in African/American music as "social" (1984, 68). Dialogism in jazz can take place within a particular piece, as when members of an ensemble anticipate or respond to each other's music, or, more diachronically, as when an artist interprets and revises a piece another artist previously performed. This dialogic time allows for and enables response.

Inada begins the introduction to the section "Camp" with an imagined telephone call: "Hello, Lawson? This is President Roosevelt speaking. Now, as you may know, son, we're at war with Japan, so I'm going to have to put you and your family in camp" (*LC*, 3). The telephone call as trope for Executive Order 9066 dramatizes the effect of the government order as interpellation by the state "hailing" and calling into being the racial subject. The paternalistic use of the term "son" demands obedience on the part of the infantilized racial subject, an apparent invocation of a protective and benevolent kinship that conceals the nonrecognition and violation of the subject's status as citizen, as well as the subject's expulsion from membership in the national family. The only response expected is acquiescence, for the racial subject cannot speak from the position of the adult citizen-subject.

In counterpoint to this U.S. nationalist claim of kinship that expels him from the status of speaking subject, Inada describes in "Jazz" an alternative kinship that recognizes and enables him to rearticulate his subject position. He describes his youthful encounter with Billie Holiday, who responds to his quietly reverent request for an autograph. "Her face lights up as she smiles: 'Why certainly, son! What's your name?' He tells her, and she pronounces it, somewhat 'sings' it, as she writes in the book. . . . And before he knew it, he was writing poetry" (*LC*, 58–9). In contrast to the obedient silence that the presidential use of "son" demands, the singer's recognition of him as a part of a jazz community—her musical pronunciation of his name rearticulating his subject position from that named by President Roosevelt—facilitates his entrance into a jazz-influenced poetry.

The poems named after and written for Louis Armstrong, John Coltrane, Bud Powell, Thelonious Monk, Charlie Parker, and Billie Holiday in "Jazz" illustrate Inada's practice of what Ralph Ellison refers to as the artist's prerogative of choosing his ancestors (1964, 140).

Inada describes the call and response of African American cultural tradition as that which not only includes but stimulates participation of the one(s) addressed: "It *called* me, *called* me by my name: 'Laaawwwson! Laaawwwson!' . . . the music spoke to us and we spoke back—laughing and carrying on among ourselves in a quaint code of 'jive' and 'hepcat' talk about 'boogie' and 'bebop' and being 'cool.' Mexicans, Negroes, Orientals—talking that talk!" (*LC,* 57). Inada's inversion here of the ordering in his previous phrase "Asians, Blacks, Chicanos" is in tandem with its transformation from properly legitimate into more improper and vernacular form, signaling a mode of speaking from within a group, an insider's knowledge of how to "talk that talk." The cultural authority that the racial subject acquires from these counterlegitimated knowledges enables him to return to the breach that engenders him, to respond to the presidential "call." In part I of the poem "Two Variations on a Theme by Thelonious Monk as Inspired by Mal Waldron," the subject is inspired by Monk's song "Blue Monk" to

> . . . stick it in the phone,
> sending it out via satellite:
>
>> *"Hello, Mom? Dig this song!"*
>> *"Hello, is this the White House?*
>> *Listen, I've got a solid*
>> *new anthem for the shaky republic!"* (*LC,* 66)

His employment of advanced technology for the return of the presidential phone call signifies on the role of electronic technology (phonographs and radio) in the circulation of jazz. Benedict Anderson describes the singing of national anthems as an experience of "unisonance" (1991, 145). Inada's proposal of a jazz piece as national anthem is his alternative to such national unisonance. Rather than the temporality of equivalence in simultaneity that unisonance demands, the dialogism, syncopation, and polyrhythms of jazz enact a temporality that recognizes and allows for the articulation and rearticulation of racially subordinated and marginalized subject positions.

I would like to end by turning to the questions raised by framing Inada's poetics as cross-racial practice. How do we think through Asian American subject formation as mediated through African American culture in this text? What are the implications of the Asian American subject's being enabled by an African American cultural form to redress racial trauma and rearticulate power? What are the ethics and economics of this cross-racial practice? Inada's jazz poetics is a site of cross-racial identification that enables us to think beyond the centering of whiteness that the binary of "colored versus white" produces. In its engagement with a predominantly African American music, his writing provides an alternative to thinking of the *American* in *Asian American* as white American culture. However, I am not proposing Inada's poetics as a model of cross-racial cultural hybridity that conflates and flattens out the differences between two very distinctive modes of racialization. Cross-racial cultural identification in Inada's writing is not simply assumed because of one's analogous status as a racially subordinated subject, but rather is earned through practice as the labor of learning how to read and produce codes of alternative knowledges.

Given the history of the commodification and consumption of African American culture, and the ascription of a symbolic value to African American culture that does not translate into political power, a non-African American writer's use of African American cultural practices provokes an interrogation of the economics of cross-racial cultural appropriation. In their more pernicious forms, culturally appropriative acts use the culture of a subordinated group to compensate for some perceived lack in one's own subject position and culture, while disavowing and reproducing the power inequalities that constitute such "cultural differences." Inada's jazz writings acknowledge the centrality of African American culture to the formation of U.S. national subjects that are not necessarily African American. However, Inada is very explicit about the specific racial history that has engendered the Japanese American subject. He does not disavow or abdicate his own subject position. His identification with African American culture is not so much compensatory or substitutive as it is affiliative. For the subject of *Legends*, jazz provides a sense of belonging that other forms of U.S. culture or politics do not provide. The introduction to the section "Jazz" describes the institutional forces and material contexts that produce and are experienced by racially subordinated young people. Although they are excluded in racially specific and distinctive ways from dominant U.S. culture and politics, they respond to this disenfranchisement by building alternative codes of legitimation, codes that they use to signal networks of affiliation with each other. Cross-racial identification is not a given, but is articulated through practices of knowledge formation and code reading. The introduction to "Two Variations on a Theme by Thelonious Monk" begins with a quote—"I can't do that right. I have to practice that"—which Inada ascribes to "Thelonious Monk, composer, to his pianist (himself)." The introduction then takes us through three decades of Inada studying the prosody of Thelonious Monk and ends with the poet saying, "Prosody—yeah. I have to practice that" (*LC,* 62). The reference to Monk's pianist as "himself" links cultural production and cultural practice, and practice is figured in this poem as labor that is repeated over time. Cultural authority is not simply invested in a subject because of his ontological status as "colored," but is earned through the commitment of practice, which is also a commitment of one's time.

Describing the inscription of his name by Billie Holiday as the moment that inaugurates his poetic practice is Inada's figure for jazz as that which has enabled him to speak what would otherwise remain unspoken and unspeakable. His poems respond to this act of naming with similar acts of naming and rearticulation, bringing the signature style of various African American musicians into poetic language. Jazz practices such as repetition, improvisation, and syncopation allow for this kind of metaresponse—that is, responses to the art form itself. If jazz enables the Japanese American subject to return to the site of racial trauma, if jazz is what the subject "can take" for this occasion (*LC,* 5), Inada's poetry also returns to jazz this very articulation of a Japanese American culture and poetics. When Inada begins the introduction to "Jazz" by saying "The music speaks for itself," he implies that his writing does not speak *about* or *for* the music, but *to* the music. Speaking for or about is an act that dichotomizes and hierarchizes a relationship between subject and object of knowledge. Inada's subject is positioned not as an analyst of or expert on jazz, but as a respondent who is an inseparable part of the music. His dialogic response enacts what Paul Gilroy calls "an ethics of antiphony" (1992, 315), in which his writing gives back by participating in the building of the culture that has given him an enabling practice. Inada's jazz poetics of citation and reiteration, dialogism and syncopation produce moments of cross-racial affiliation that provide alternatives to dominant formations of race, knowledge, and time.

Friendly Town, being #10

Safiya Henderson-Holmes

maria goes to town
with almost mom.

maria's face doesn't turn
many heads in woolworths'

or a&p. maria can stand
near cookies and cakes

and only be accused of hunger,
not stealing.

my absence protects maria.
it is the power of my darkness.

maria will bring me dulce.
i watch the station wagon

take them away. the car rattles
and limps. I wonder about the death

of this car. how its passing may bury
almost mom on the farm. her bingo turkeys

won by free women. almost dad's
slinging cow shit. the sons are at boys

club. pig and i snort and stand.
what else is piglike about me?

i dig a hole in the dirt, spit,
think of hunting barbra again.

it's been four days since the last
failed search. not a scent of glover's mane,

not one pink sponge curler,
or one hotcomb in grass anywhere.

but we hadn't been to the river,
and the river's where any self-respecting

colored would surely be.
it's part of every escape, every prayer.

barbra must be at the river.
i wave to pig and run,

pass barn and piles of cow shit,
pass oak, maple, sumac, mushrooms,

mud. the river: dulce con dulce.
over a small hill of pine needles,

cones, loose earth, i slide
onto shoulder of river.

the river's head on my knees.
i wait and wish.

air undresses everything:
naked and shameless.

baptized in the name of
a salamander's swiftness.

barbra? no barbra.
my hands cradle rocks.

i don't ask them to hide me.
i wait and wish until sun and river speak.

they say barbara's been
and gone.

barbra's been washed
clean and gone.

sun embraces river.
river sucks sun

purple.

Negotiating the Differences

Anna Deavere Smith and Liberation Theater

Kimberly Rae Connor

> *"People are people through other people."*
> *—Xhosa proverb*

On the same day in September 1993 that Yasser Arafat and Yitzhak Rabin shook hands on the White House lawn, members of a Palestinian and an Israeli theater group also shook hands in an agreement to stage an unprecedented collaborative production of Shakespeare's *Romeo and Juliet*. They chose the story of the doomed lovers because, as Israeli director Eran Baniel explained, the play sends a critical message: "There is only one alternative to peace—death" (qtd. in Blumenfeld 1994, C1). As the group worked to achieve its goal, ironies deep inside Shakespeare's text took on their own dramatic life and small symbols became potent reminders of the perils inherent in collaboration. Conflicts over the appropriate site to stage the production led to an unsatisfactory compromise to hold the play in an old warehouse in Jewish West Jerusalem. When the company first moved in, the building was inhabited by doves. Unable to trap or scare away the noisy and messy birds, they finally called in an exterminator. When the actors arrived the next morning for their peace project, they found the doves, wings twitching, dying on the stage.

Cultural differences necessitated that every aspect of the production be discussed and negotiated. They decided the Montague and the Capulet families would be represented by Arabs and Jews, respectively, and each family would speak in their native tongue among each other, but when speaking outside the family all would speak Hebrew, the language of the occupation. Weapons used during the Intifada would be used during fight scenes. For the ending, they decided that in lieu of the reconciliation scene between the families, the cast would gather and repeat the compelling words of the prologue. This change suggested a recognition on the part of the actors that although their gesture in mounting the play was significant, there are no simple solutions to the problems that have for so long divided these people, for unlike the "two households, both alike in dignity" who from their children's death learned to "bury their . . . strife," the actors knew from experience that the tragedy of Romeo and Juliet was bound to be repeated as it had been for many years.

Despite financial problems and opposition from both Israelis and Palestinians—including death threats issued from both sides—the group continued and eventually mounted a production in the summer of 1994. Although we may never know what effect this production had on the people for whom it was performed—indeed, even members of the cast claimed to still be unable to set aside preexisting hostilities and prejudices—the show went on, and a message was sent. Critics were, for the most part, unimpressed with the aesthetic merits of the production. But the cast clung to their belief that their efforts were successful if only in bringing together the actors. Those involved in the production held on to the hope that they might have had a personal effect on those who viewed the production—by bringing people out together and by causing them to think about what their toil strived to mend, what our impatient ears tend to miss.

Sending such a message is also the motive behind the theatrical work of the African American playwright and performer Anna Deavere Smith. Smith is also a student of Shakespeare who in interviews repeatedly draws attention to the fact that "if it hadn't been for Shakespeare, I wouldn't be where I am because it was my Shakespeare teacher who got to me" (Martin 1993, 55). Through her study of Shakespeare, Smith became fascinated with how the spoken word works in relationship to a person's psychology. "It's the *manipulation* of the words that creates the character [Connor's emphasis], not just the words, not just the emotions. . . . In Shakespeare, the words held not just the psyche of the person but also the psyche of the time" (qtd. in Lahr 1993, 90). Her encounter with Shakespeare she also describes in religious terms as a kind of epiphany or "transcendental experience" (Martin 1993, 56) that combined both terror and mystery. A search to re-create this experience of *mysterium tremendum* led her continually to explore language and its effects, with Barbara Lewis observing that "Talk, the word, is central to Smith's theater" (1993, 55).

159

Although Smith admits that she never duplicated her epiphenominal experience in actual ways, she describes how she came to make connections between language and the desire to explain her feelings. For example, while reciting dialogue of the nurse in *Romeo and Juliet*—a character who "goes all around the block to say a simple thing" (qtd. in Lewis 1993, 59)—what struck her was how the nurse remembers Juliet's age by remembering the expression on Juliet's face when she no longer desired to breastfeed. Act 1, scene 3: "And she was weaned (I never shall forget it), / Of all the days of the year, upon that day; / For I had then laid wormwood to my dug, / Sitting in the sun under the dovehouse wall. / My lord and you were then at Mantua. / Nay, I do bear a brain. But, as I said, / When it did taste the wormwood on the nipple / Of my dug and felt it bitter, pretty fool, / To see it tetchy and fall out with the dug!" Reciting the lines impressed on Smith the recognition that "the process of being in the world is a process of learning the world as a place full of attractive and unattractive and warm and frightful things. The power of life is that we're always in that friction. It's never heaven. If there's a heaven, it's never pure bliss" (Lewis 1993, 59).

Smith's attempts to explore the relationship between words and human psychology are best represented in the series of theater or performance pieces she has written, produced, and performed all across America for more than a decade entitled "On the Road: A Search for American Character." Smith creates the pieces by interviewing people in select locales and later performs them using their own words. As she describes it, her goal "has been to find American character in the ways that people speak" (*FM*, xxiii). She believes that if she can find a way to "inhabit the words of those around me," then she can "learn about the spirit, the imagination, and the challenges of my own time, firsthand" (*FM*, xxv). Her desire is to hold a mirror up to diverse groups to expose the motives and meanings behind their association and in the process to generate for the public at large what Gayle Wald calls "theatrical compassion" (1994, 8).

Smith describes her work as not just theater, but also "community work . . . low anthropology, low journalism; it's a bit documentary" (Lewis 1993, 56). Accordingly she has been characterized as a performance artist, a cultural anthropologist, a documentarian, and a biographer. The director at the Mark Taper auditorium even calls her "the closest thing to a professional athlete I know. There's a willingness to go out into the field of play and just do it" (qtd. in Lahr 1993, 92). Her choice of "On the Road" as the title for her enterprise elaborates and extends two familiar endeavors associated with the same title—the novel by Jack Kerouac and the television program created by Charles Kerault. Her work has also been compared to the documentary writings of Studs Terkel. But she goes beyond the exploratory hedonism of Kerouac, the nostalgia of Kerault, and the reportage of Terkel to explore in her "theater of testimony" not just issues of ethnicity and American character, but fundamental issues of identity that underlie all these investigations. "Theater of testimony" is how playwright Emily Mann characterizes her own documentary dramas, which are similar in form and function to the work of Anna Deavere Smith. Although Mann (who directed the world premier of *Twilight* at the Mark Taper Forum) does not play all the roles herself, like Smith she conducts interviews and uses the actual conversation of involved people to consider issues such as the Vietnam War, the murder of gay activist Harvey Milk, the Holocaust, and most recently her celebrated adaptation of the reminiscences of Sadie and Bessie Delaney, all of which she hopes have something to contribute to healing and reconciliation in America (*Washington Post* 1995).

An associate professor of drama at Stanford, Anna Deavere Smith has a background that is conventional in most respects. She was born in Baltimore, Maryland, the eldest of five children, and her family was solidly middle class. Smith claims that although she was a mimic as a child, she never wished to grow up to be a movie star. Rather, she pursued acting because she was "interested in social change" and unwittingly ended up in acting class, where she was "stunned at how the process of acting was about transformation." Part of her exploratory personality she attributes to growing up amid the "experiment" of integration (Lewis 1993, 62). Being a product of this experiment, she learned that the world can be an indifferent place and that even in the communities of the academy and the theater where she is most at home, "the dominant culture decides when we will be hidden and when we will be seen" (Lewis 1993, 62). After college, she made her way to New York. It was there, while supporting herself with sporadic appearances on soap operas, that Smith began conducting acting workshops, developing her method and discovering her mission.

While conducting these workshops around the theme of language and character, she began developing the method that would lead to "On the Road" as exercises to teach students to experience language more fully. Smith began approaching people she encountered who resembled participants in her workshop, hoping they would agree to be interviewed so their words could be used or spoken by her students. In exchange, the interviewees were invited to see themselves performed. In her first such experiment, there were twenty people on stage and twenty people in the audience. Smith persisted in employing the interviewing technique, but rather than asking a troupe of players or students to create each character, she began to assemble one-woman shows in which she would play all the parts herself. Despite her singular presence, Smith maintained a sense of inclusion by using the pronouns *us* and *we* in relation to everybody. Her reasons were two-fold: so she wouldn't appear confrontational and so that she could force the audience to "feel that it's you and me. My experience of the interviews I included was that there was an 'us' before I left." From these simple exercises her ambition has evolved into an enterprise wherein she seeks to "capture the personality of a place by attempting to embody its varied population and varied points of view in one person—myself" (Martin 1993, 48).

The goal of "On the Road" Smith describes as creating a kind of theater "that would have a different relationship to the community than most of the theater I was seeing. It would be a kind of theater that could be current . . . capture a moment and as quickly as possible give that moment back to the people" (qtd. in Kaufman 1993, G11). In developing pieces for "On the Road," she observed how "inhibitions affect our ability to empathize" and traced this inhibition to the lack of vision engendered by racism and prejudice (*FM,* xxvii). She is blunt in her refusal to allow any standard of privilege—be it race, class, or gender—to relieve people of the responsibility to see clearly, but she believes that the theater, despite its sometimes exclusionary practices, is an ideal place to confront these issues. By opening up the world of the theater to new voices and visions, Smith makes a larger statement about the quality of democracy in America. As she writes, "If only a man can speak for a man, a woman for a woman, a black person for all black people, then we, once again, inhibit the spirit of the theater, which lives in the bridge that makes unlikely aspects seem connected. The bridge doesn't make them the same, it merely displays how two unlikely aspects are related. These relationships of the unlikely, these connections of things that don't fit together are crucial to American theater and culture if theater and culture plan to help us assemble our obvious differences" (*FM,* xxix).

One especially useful way to appreciate Smith's enterprise is offered by Victor Turner's concept of "social dramas." In his anthropological study of symbolic human action in society, Turner probes the ways in which social actions of various kinds acquire form through "the metaphors and paradigms in their actors' heads (put there by explicit teaching and implicit generalization from social experience)," which in certain intensive or conflict-ridden circumstances generate new forms and metaphors to reflect social concerns (1974, 13). These intensive periods arise when society is "betwixt and between" agreed upon systems of order or in a state Turner defines as "liminality." In a liminal state, one can stand outside personal and social positions to formulate alternative social arrangements and encourage others to assent to innovation. Furthermore, although these times invite innovation, they also become occasions to reaffirm "root paradigms" of culture—ideals such as liberty, justice, and equality—and to reinvest them with new meaning.

The social dramas that emerge in liminal times do so from abstract cultural domains or "fields" where paradigms are formulated, established, and come into conflict, but it is in specific "arenas" or concrete settings that abstract paradigms are transformed into symbolic metaphors by the actions of "lead actors" in these social dramas. The wished for result of such actions is the generation of a new feeling of commitment, where the persistence of cherished values is recognized as "a striking aspect of change" (Turner 1974, 32). The liminality of episodes of conflict, therefore, is a "sacred" time in Turner's formulation because it provides the opportunity for self-conscious reexpression of theological and philosophical values—root paradigms—that people lose sight of when society is stable and complacent. "Communitas or social antistructure" is the creative alternative to structure, and it is generated by conflict, which is the other side of cohesion. "Structure is all that holds people apart, defines their differences, and constrains their actions" whereas *communitas* is "often a sacred condition or can become one" (Turner 1974, 47). The coherence of a completed social drama is a function of *communitas* and that is what Anna Deavere Smith provides in the domain of theater.

The episode of conflict that erupted in Crown Heights made this location an appropriate "arena" to go to in search of American character, and out of this incident Smith created the *communitas* of *Fires in the Mirror*. The play concerns the racial strife that erupted in the Brooklyn neighborhood of Crown Heights in August 1991. Smith interviewed six hundred people in just eight days—two months after the riots abated—and from the gathered recollections she crafted her performance. Blacks and Jews had clashed following a car accident in which a Jewish van driver, steering one of the cars in a procession carrying the Lubavitcher Hasidic rebbe believed by his followers to be the Messiah, ran a red light, hit another car, and swerved onto the sidewalk. The car struck and killed a young black child, Gavin Cato, and seriously injured his cousin. Further aggravating the situation in the minds of the black residents were rumors that the children had been left lying on the sidewalk while a private Jewish ambulance helped the driver and his passengers. That evening, a group of young black men fatally stabbed Yankel Rosenbaum, a twenty-nine year-old Hasidic scholar from Australia. The three-day riots that followed were a culmination of years of resentment between the Orthodox Jewish sect and the Crown Heights black majority. Blacks cited white racism as playing a critical role in the conflict. Many believed that the Lubavitchers had received preferential treatment in the community from police and other city agencies, and they reported that some Lubavitchers threatened and harassed them. According to Jews, black anti-Semitism also played a role, as they cited reports that they were frequent victims of black street crime and verbal abuse such as "Heil Hitler" or "Kill the Jews."

The conflict, therefore, represented more that what actually transpired during the specific event. It also reflected the pain, oppression, and discrimination these groups have historically experienced outside their own communities. Many in the Crown Heights black community were Caribbean immigrants who faced discrimination because of their color and their national origin. Their identity, therefore, could not be conventionally affirmed as African American in the local sense only, but in the more complicated diaspora sense where old and new worlds were more readily in tension. And the Lubavitchers—members of a 250-year-old messianic Hasidic sect that fled the Nazi genocide in Europe—were particularly vulnerable to anti-Jewish stereotyping because of their religious style of dress and insular community. The resulting trials—in which no one directly involved was convicted of a crime—and the media coverage that polarized the people involved made it difficult, as Anna Deavere Smith writes, "for people to develop an understanding of the Crown Heights situation that acknowledges the experiences of all people involved" (*FM*, xiv).

The tension between these two groups Smith identifies as inevitable in America because it is "the tension of identity in motion, the tension of identity which is in contest with an old idea, but a resonant idea of America" (*FM*, xxxiv). Yet this characteristic tension was not a tension that was moving identity forward in a collective way. As Smith explains, the prevailing idea of American character may have been developed initially by white men, but it has constantly been adapted by marginal populations. The tension that results when different notions of American character come into conflict presents an opportunity she describes in the following metaphor of motion that recalls at once the historical success of the Underground Railroad and the present failure of the Crown Heights episode: "like a train [it] can pick up passengers and take them to their destination . . . or be derailed onto a sidewalk where some innocents are waiting to get struck down" (*FM*, xxxiv).

Returning to Turner's terminology, one can see how the play's exploration of ethnic relations reveals our "root metaphors" and demonstrates how in America "identity is always being negotiated" (*FM*, xxxiii). In Crown Heights, Smith saw two clearly different groups of people who were "defining in every breath they took the melting pot idea of American character" (qtd. in Kaufman 1993, G11). Yet in an interview with Carol Martin, Smith also observes that in Crown Heights "everyone wears their beliefs on their bodies—their costumes. You can't pass," and she comes to the seemingly paradoxical conclusion that "Crown Heights is not a melting pot and I really respect that" (1993, 46). Taken together, these remarks underscore the basic tension between individuals and their communities that her dramas explore in contemporary settings but that emerge from historical conditions and eternal human conflicts.

The incident in Crown Heights was, therefore, essentially a social drama, a narrative that revealed "more known traditions that we can draw from—for example, the language of African Americans that draws up images of slavery and the language of the Lubavitcher that draws up images of the Holocaust. And the whole nation understood those images" (qtd. in Kaufman 1993, G11). So in the play Smith tried to display authentically the apparent ethnicity of people as a way to underscore the basic humanity of people in all their difference. By showing how issues of race and difference figure in the character equation of creating identity, Smith demonstrates that she understands the condition author Thomas Keneally described when he observed that in the natural and necessary process of self-definition, we tend to locate ourselves as members of a particular "tribe" with its own mores and, furthermore, find ourselves "tempted to believe in the inferiority of the culture and mores of other groups." Keneally thus concludes that "prejudice is the hairy backside of what we all need: a sense of identity" (1994, A7).

Smith's effort in creating *Fires in the Mirror* is directed not just at observation but at solution. Her notion of giving back to the community is the way she suggests what Charlayne Hunter-Gault calls "a creative approach to issues we're all struggling to handle" (qtd. in Kaufman 1993, G11). But Smith is careful not to set herself up as one with the answers. Her interest lies in revealing "the complexity of the issue, not trying to solve it" (Kaufman 1993, G11). Her goal is to get people where she finds herself: engaged—paying attention to each other and, if possible, talking and becoming able to reconsider attitudes. "What I want to do is to invite people to listen differently. I want to have people in the same room who normally would not spend five minutes with each other. It's important that people come together to do this thing called theater" (qtd. in Kaufman 1993, G11). Smith is trying to present a standard of "truth" that is not actual in a metaphysical sense, but representational in a contextual sense. By drawing our attention to different perspectives on truth she also shows us what is possible in terms of social justice and action. The critic John Lahr asserts that "in this heroic undertaking, she is conducting one of the most sophisticated dialogues about race in contemporary America" (1993, 90).

Smith believes that "the process of creating literature is natural. It isn't dependent on a pen and paper. It's a person using their voice and the making of words to come to the consciousness of what they know" (qtd. in Lahr 1993, 90). Convinced that everyone has a poem in them, she interviews subjects for as long as it takes for them to "come into character . . . to discover their own personal literature"(qtd. in Kaufman 1993, G11). She views her method as a collaboration, actually writing a poem with her characters; hence, that is how she sets down dialogue for publication, falling unpunctuated down the page. All the people she depicts are actual people who played some role in the social dramas she explores and whose words she has collected in interviews she speaks verbatim. Although she is dependent on "the kindness of strangers" to offer up their stories willingly, Smith nonetheless found that everyone she interviewed wanted to talk:

"Everybody felt there was something unsaid" (qtd. in Kaufman 1993, G11), indicating their need to express their feelings and also testifying to Smith's interviewing skill, which "like the Billie Holiday song . . . asks heartache to come in and sit down" (Lahr 1993, 90).

When Smith conducts interviews, her interest lies not so much in *what* is said as *how* it comes out. She rehearses with earphones on and plays back unedited talk and speaks the words until images and gestures emerge from rhythms. Smith's performances are meticulous as she assumes not just the actual speech of her characters but also their speech patterns and mannerisms, believing that "speech is a physical act" and that "the body has a memory just as the mind does" (*FM,* xxv). Smith's investigation into how different characters embody or inhabit language differently creates a style of performance Carol Martin calls "hypernaturalistic mimesis—in which [Smith] replicates not only the words of different individuals but their bodily style as well" (1993, 45). Yet she does not consider herself an impersonator or impressionist. "The big difference," Smith explains, "is that when you impersonate someone . . . you give an intelligence to what may seem to be random gestures, and once you point out to the audience that the person does this or that, an impersonator is going to be tempted to exaggerate. . . . I don't do that. What I try to do is create a kind of document of what the person said, and the physical part follows" (qtd. in Kaufman 1993, G11). Just as she "wears" characters' words and mannerisms, so too in her productions does she rely on scant props and minimal clothing changes to convey symbolically something about the characters she represents. A change in headgear may be all it takes to transform her from a Lubavitch rebbe to a rapper.

Fires in the Mirror: Crown Heights, Brooklyn, and Other Identities was scheduled to open in New York on April 29, 1992, the same day of the uprising in Los Angeles that followed the announcement of the verdict in the trial of police officers charged with beating Rodney King. The opening was canceled, and Anna Deavere Smith herself joined demonstrators in Times Square to protest the verdict. While Los Angeles burned, the images of fire and light that surround the text of *Fires in the Mirror* took on a wider scope of meaning. The musings of A. M. Bernstein—an MIT physicist whom Smith interviewed and portrays in the play—became especially pertinent. Imagining the idea of a mirror large enough to accurately reflect the true nature of the universe, he describes how if you want to focus on the stars without getting caught in a circle of confusion, you need a telescope big enough to gather in a lot of light. Gathering light enough to see through a dark scene becomes the metaphor for Smith's enterprise in this piece.

Mirrors are a recurrent image in the play, but as the author points out, "there isn't just one mirror." She goes on to explain that "we don't stand on a surface like a chorus line, all going across with the same legs. We've got different lengths and many different mirrors. The reason I use the image of the mirror is that we think of the stage as the mirror of society, the thing that shows us back what we are, that shows us our identity, and right now fire is in the mirror. There are plural fires, not just one fire; fires are in the mirror" (Lewis 1993, 57). Thus, another metaphor Smith adopts is the image of a fire truck answering distress calls and making many stops but never quite attending all the needs. "They're just putting out the little fires" (Lewis 1993, 57). Fire is light, power, warmth, and, like a mirror, a reflective agency. Smith sees "the fires of social unrest that we've had as evidence of power secreting, power insisting, power igniting, power that has been dormant coming up and surfacing. Whether it's bad power or good power, or disruptive or not, it's power. It's voice. It's also danger, because it's the result of friction" (Lewis 1993, 57). To underscore the relevance of these metaphors of reflection, fire, and light, the set for *Fires* was highlighted with mirror fragments in which the audience was reflected. Large screens were also used to project the characters' names, and halfway through the piece a montage of photographs taken during the riots was shown. These technical adaptations are part of Smith's entire theatrical enterprise, which is aimed at shedding as much light as possible while also recognizing the virtue of putting out the little fires.

In accordance with her notion of adapting concepts of American character, Smith structures her text in such a way that issues related to character and identity formation are investigated in a circular fashion, from the general to the particular. The first two sections, "Identity" and "Mirrors," offer broad and speculative reflections on not just identity but how one sees or discerns the reality in which identities are constructed. From there, Smith locates specific issues higlighted by the section titles "Hair," "Race," "Rhythm," and "Seven Verses" (a biblical allusion) to structure the dialogue pertaining to how the African Americans and Jews of the community come to describe and define themselves and each other. The drama concludes with the unambiguous "Crown Heights, Brooklyn, August

1991" section, which offers different perspectives on the actual events and their meanings.

Smith performs in simple garb that is accentuated for each character by some distinctive addition—a yarmulke, a Kente cloth cap, a glittery sweater, a wig—that marks her transition from character to character. Because each character is based on an actual person who speaks his or her own lines, "there were unresolvable contradictions in the multiple versions of truth," but this "did not diminish the conviction of each character that what they said was true" (Martin 1993, 45). Each character gives voice to a multitude of feelings seldom expressed at all and if so, rarely in the same space. But as the drama moves from general reflection to the specific issues that led to the incident documented, the audience confronts more difficult discussions of specific racist attitudes and the "reification of those ideas" (Laris 1993, 119). It is only the continuity of Smith's presence that undercuts the authority of one group over another or of one individual over another. With Smith functioning like a diviner through whom many voices travel, all the characters speak together while their presence and words, as Carol Martin observes, "mark the absence and silence of the two people around whom the drama revolves, Gavin Cato and Yankel Rosenbaum" (1993, 46).

Smith begins the play with Ntozake Shange because she recognizes that although the play is about race and difference, it is also about identity. Shange's definition of identity—knowing who and what you are regardless of where you are—Smith finds especially relevant. As she explains, "who owns what of what culture and how that becomes part of another culture is in many ways at the bottom line of how we negotiate who and where we are" (Lewis 1993, 55). Smith's use of Shange is also a way for her to tap symbolically into all Shange represents in terms of the theater, the way she declared her own identity and made a place for herself in American theater with her ground-breaking portrayal of black women in *For Colored Girls*. Still, Smith is careful to distinguish herself from any specific tradition, identifying herself as one who has "always been on the outside . . . an observer who steps in and then steps back out" (Lewis 1993, 56).

Following Shange, Smith steps into two characters who discuss their own painful struggles with the social conventions that would define their identity. An anonymous Lubervitcher woman relates how an orthodox injunction prohibiting her from turning off the radio on the Sabbath affects her young black neighbor's view of her. Although usually articulate, the accomplished director George C. Wolfe is portrayed stumbling his way through a recollection of how when he was a child, segregation prevented him from seeing a Disney movie. From this early recognition of how race circumscribed his identity, he reflects on how his blackness affects others' perception of him, ranging from the "insignificant" to the "extraordinary." His own "confused, complex, demonic, ridiculous" perception of himself is revealed in his stuttering speech as he tries to articulate that his blackness "does not exist in relationship to your whiteness" (*FM*, 10).

Smith moves to portray characters whose sense of identity is clearly articulated and expressed by their external characteristics—in particular by their relationship to their own hair. Their attitudes about hair reveal human commonalties in small details of personal style. Basic concerns of appearance and identity are vital to a thirteen-year-old black girl gazing at herself in a mirror. She is utterly satisfied with her blackness and her appearance, and chastises others—black, Puerto Rican, and white girls—who don't seem to be able to develop their own style but "bite off" (*FM*, 17) or appropriate the style of others. Al Sharpton describes somewhat defensively his allegiance to James Brown, whom he honors by adopting the same hair style. Noting that the once fashionable look is now associated largely with him and Brown, Sharpton claims it as a badge of honor, a "personal thing between me and James Brown" (*FM*, 21) and a way for him to pay tribute to the man who played a significant paternal role in Sharpton's life. Finally, Rivkah Siegal confesses her discomfort with the artificiality inherent in her religion's mandate for wigs. She claims wearing them is "fake . . . not me" (*FM*, 25) and yet she continues to do so—to displace her own individual sense of self in honor of a larger communal identity, despite her apparent discomfort.

In a section titled "Race," Smith steps back from the particular and portrays Angela Davis articulating her own evolving attitude about the idea of racial communities. Davis observes that once race and community were synonymous, but she now sees that race is an obsolete way of constructing communities. Race, she believes, emerged from racism, so she uses the term "in quotes." Recalling divisions in the black community, she asserts that she is looking for new ways "of coming together in a different way." To explain her vision she selects the metaphor of a rope that is attached to an anchor of community but cautions that the rope "should be long enough to allow us to move into other communities to understand and to learn" (*FM* 32). The section "Rhythm" follows and introduces a young rap, artist who offers another strategy for survival than the one set forth by Davis. Big Mo is unsparing in her criticism not just of racism, but of the sexism that permeates the black community and that also plays a role in the declining African American sense of community Davis observed. Big Mo articulates her response in her chosen art form—rap—which "breaks down" rhythm and poetry in order to create a particular kind of expression that creates conditions wherein self-esteem is bolstered in one's attempts to become "def," a slang expression for "the epitome of the experience . . . and you have to be def by your very presence" (*FM,* 38–39).

Following these examples of contemporary responses to the systemic problems of racism, in "Seven Verses" Smith includes the reflections of leading African American and Jewish cultural critics, who provide an important historical context for what transpired in Crown Heights. She begins by portraying the controversial university professor Leonard Jefferies, whose promotion of an Afrocentric perspective on history has been challenged for being anti-Semetic. Jefferies is firm and unapologetic in claiming his position, willing to take on not just whites and Jews but other African Americans as well. Reflecting on his role as an advisor to the television production of Alex Haley's *Roots,* Jefferies cites it as yet another example of Jewish media control over the representation of black history. The anti-Semitism and the images of slavery recalled by Jefferies are picked up in Smith's portrayal of Minister Conrad, a Muslim who graphically describes the Middle Passage and the historical suffering of blacks, which he contrasts with the Holocaust, claiming that it in "no way compares with the slavery of our people" (*FM,* 54). Conrad cites as the most egregious crime against black people the way slavery robbed people of their identity by cutting them off from knowledge and their past to the point that only indigenous blacks have a "contextual understanding of what identity is" (*FM,* 55). He concludes with the statement that the Muslim claim to be the chosen people of God is more valid than that of the Jews, who base their claim on only "seven verses" in the Bible.

What the convenant between God and humanity offers in actual terms, how choseness is expressed in history, is complicated by the facts of slavery and the Holocaust. This is where the feminist writer Letty Cottin Pogrebin steps in, citing the role Jews have played in black liberation movements, yet also how Jews have constantly been picked as scapegoats. In a moving recollection of her cousin Isaac's Holocaust experience and resulting death, Pogrebin offers his experience as a metaphor for how we fail in advancing liberation. After physically surviving the Holocust, Isaac died once he had "spoken the unspeakable" to all who would listen to his story. In this instance, Pogrebin calls into question not just what "survival" means, but also the effectiveness of testimony, of storytelling as a strategy for not just survival, but creative endurance. Her worry is summed up in the comment that "we're trotting out our Holocaust stories too regularly . . . we're going to inure each other to the truth of them" (*FM,* 59). The role language plays in both advancing and obstructing conflict resolution is also articulated by Robert Sherman, a city bureaucrat who was not at all surprised by the episode in Crown Heights. His observations of the community reveal not a simple cultural conflict or black/Jewish dichotomy, but what he calls a "soup of bias—prejudice, racism, and discrimination" (*FM,* 64). This murky soup is the result, he claims, of "lousy language" that does not clearly identify the complexity of the social problems American society faces.

It is this "lousy language" that Smith attempts to rehabilitate while also not denying its presence and effect. The constituent ingredients that make up the soup of bias are revealed in the final section, which explores from a variety of perspectives actual reflections on the specific incident itself. From theorizing and reflecting on the systemic conditions that generate the ingredients for a soup of bias, Smith's portrayals of different individuals involved demonstrates how these ingredients were blended in Crown Heights. Among those chosen to speak are several clerics of different faiths, social workers and community organizers, and anonymous residents who observed the conflict at various stages of its development, from the incident itself to the resulting riots, rallies, and funerals. Each character's recollection is informed by some past experience or opinion, emphasizing that the conflict was not just a spontaneous outburst but the result of perceived and ongoing oppression of one group or another. Tribal loyalties come to the fore in allusions to prior episodes of justice denied or favors proffered to one group or another. The distances between people that at first seemed academic and diffuse become actual and precise, and seldom is a note of ambiguity interjected in the comments of any of the characters.

What also becomes apparent is that those who become the spokespersons for one position or another are conferred this privilege by their ability to manipulate language to create the specific effect of uniting people in a particular formulation of their identity. Sharpton's defiant challenge on behalf of the black community that "If you piss in my face I'm gonna call it piss, I'm not gonna call it rain" (*FM*, 116) and the assertion by Norman Rosenbaum (the Jewish victim's brother) that "I'm here, I'm not going home, until there is justice" (*FM*, 96), drown out the calmer observations of Rabbi Hecht that "we're all children of God" (*FM*, 111) or Richard Green's pledge to "pray on both sides of the fence" (*FM*, 118). What all the characters share, however, is a recognition of difference and an unwillingness to give up different aspects and expressions of identity that define who they are. This attitude is best expressed in the Jews' continuous historical references to images of the Holocaust—pogroms and ovens—and blacks' repeated references to slavery—its origin and its ongoing effects—that are not even fully understood by those who possess the greatest rage.

It is Carmel Cato, the father of the child who was killed and the final character Smith portrays, who most overwhelms one with his ability to use language as a way to focus in on the locus of identity. Smith remarks that precisely because he "crossed so many worlds" (Lewis 1993, 64), he is able to make a "journey in language across so many realms of experience" (Martin 1993, 52), an accomplishment the others don't seem to be able to achieve. As Smith remembers her interview with Cato, he began giving facts but soon moved into his own belief system, drawing on his own sensitivity and spiritual power to discuss his premonition that his son's death "was upon us" (Lewis 1993, 64). Unable to eat or function normally, Mr. Cato felt "something is wrong somewhere but I didn't want to see, I didn't want to accept. . . . I could feel it, but I didn't want to see" (*FM*, 137–38). Smith observes that here Cato is speaking not just about his own personal tragedy and loss but also about the denial that pervades society. In this regard, he is seeing for all of us. By ending his comments with a description of the circumstances of his birth—being born feet first, which he believes makes him a "special person" who cannot be overpowered—Cato's speech is structured "in the way classical drama is structured. It crosses different worlds, different feelings, and articulates his view of his existence in a really short span of time" (Lewis 1993, 64). There is also an African element to this structure that, by ending with reflections on birth, affirms the myth of eternal return where the cycle of life renews itself, suggesting that even out of the ashes of Crown Heights a new mode of existence could rise. That a new existence might rise is alluded to by Sonny Carson, who recognizes "tonight by nighttime it could all change for me. So I'm always aware of that, and that's what keeps me going today and each day" (*FM,* 105).

What keeps Anna Deavere Smith going is her belief in what theater can accomplish by way of human liberation. In apparent contrast to what goes on "outside" the theater, Smith creates a sacred space for equal representation, wherein not only issues of identity are broken down, but also customary distinctions between high and low art are deconstructed. In the liminal space of the theater, she is able to explore the more subtle contradictions in speech that customary public arenas won't allow. She replaces the stylized language of the theater with the no less stylized language of everyday speech. In so doing, she uses the theater as an objective space to explore the complications that emerge when people, in the midst of conflict, are unable to hear any voice but their own.

Although Smith might be perceived as employing a technique that involves theft—the appropriation of others' voices—she can also be perceived as practicing the art of giving—a mode of re-presenting or returning others' voices to them. The words she amplifies are precisely those that are lost in journalistic accounts and indeed those that describe events that result precisely when words themselves do not suffice. In the process of eliciting everyone's personal literature, Smith is also making a larger statement about the condition of those traditionally seen as oppressed. Oftentimes we deny that those who are oppressed have the need to seek opportunities for imaginative expression, assuming that mere survival constitutes the whole focus of their lives. By revealing the hidden poetry that emerges out of the most conflict-ridden situations, Smith shows us that this assumption is just another way to objectify the oppressed and deny them full humanity.

To appreciate fully what Anna Deavere Smith contributes to our cultural dialogue, we must view her mission and method as inextricably bound. Her missionary zeal is rooted in a complex and thoughtful appreciation of aesthetic theory and dramatic performance techniques. She describes her fascination with and repeated references to the relationship between language and character as just like a photographer who wants to capture a character in physical image; she wants "to capture character linguistically, to capture what the spoken word has to offer us about character" (qtd. in Kaufman 1993, G11). The basis for her notion of theater is rooted in speech-act theory and her own Africanized or spiritualized version of method acting.

In developing her philosophy of theater, Smith encountered Stanislavsky and applied some of his theories of method acting; for example, she describes her goal as an interviewer as persisting until a psychological through-line is reflected in language. But she also resists what she sees as the limitations of this approach. "The through-line always made me feel bad in teaching, reading, and trying to write plays" (qtd. in Martin 1993, 50). She objected in particular to aspects of Stanislavsky's technique in which objectives—little and super—are graphed with straight lines and arrows. Her reasons for discomfort became apparent to her when she began reading a book about African philosophical systems "and saw a picture of a wheel that had all these little spikes with arrows pointing towards the center. I knew then that I wanted to try to find a way of thinking or a structure that was more like that" (Martin 1993, 51).

Smith goes on to connect this circular structure with the black church in America, which she sees as "not only about speaking to one God. The whole thing is supposed to be an occasion to evoke a spirit" (Martin 1993, 51). In resisting the linear through-line, she refined her method and began to see her thought processes as more organic and circular. Remembering her grandfather's words, "that if you say a word often enough it becomes you" (Martin 1993, 51), Smith believes her power as an artist comes from not just *what* people tell her but *how* they tell her something that makes a whole-soul impression on her psyche, an experience she describes as becoming "possessed, so to speak, of the person" (qtd. in Martin 1993, 51). Acting "is becoming the other" and using the other rather than the self as a frame of reference. Smith's technique, which strives to begin with the other and come to self, empowers the other in contrast to method acting techniques that "come to a spiritual halt" precisely because they are so self-oriented and see self "as the ultimate home of the character. To me, the search for character is constantly in motion. It is a quest that moves back and forth between the self and the other" (*FM,* xxvi–xxvii).

Thus, what Smith is after is "not psychological realism. I don't want to own the character and endow the character with my own experience. It's the opposite of that. What has to exist in order to try to allow the other to

be is separation between the actor's self and the other" (Martin 1993, 52).
This kind of enterprise involves struggle, Smith reminds us,

> as well it should—the struggle that the speaker has when he or she speaks
> to me, the struggle that he or she has to shift through language to come
> through. . . . Psychological technique is built on metaphors for a reason. I
> believe it's quite organic. You listen to some of the characters and you be-
> gin to identify with them. Because I'm saying the stuff over and over again
> every night, part of me is becoming them through repetition—by doing
> their performance of themselves that they do. I become the "them" that
> they present to the world. For all of us, the performance of ourselves has
> very much to do with the self of ourselves. That's what we're articulating
> in language and in flesh—something we feel inside as we develop an iden-
> tity. (Martin 1993, 57)

Her final goal is that somehow the transference she experiences as a performer will be passed on to the audience.

How this transference might be accomplished Smith explains by
speech-act theory:

> Theater is action, but in the beginning was the word. And the word was
> all. And speech is action. Theater is action. . . . The way action happens in
> the theater is through the propulsion of words. The text is spoken to push
> action forward. . . . And on a less obvious level, on a less literal level,
> there's a visceral action that's going on so that the words you hear in the
> theater don't just go to your head, but they go into your whole system,
> and if there's a catharsis it's because the words get into you. (Lewis 1993,
> 58)

Smith appreciates a concept central to speech-act theory—that words do
things and actions say things. Words, for example, are "expressions whose
function is not to inform or describe but to carry out a 'performance,' to
accomplish an act" (Felman 1993, 12). Furthermore, Smith observes that
the power of the speech of people backed up by crowds can frighten people, as they did in Crown Heights. People with the power of the word
know that their words cause action, and so theater is speech as action, but
in a context where individuals have agreed to participate in the language
of the other and to work toward adopting a communal language.

Still, Smith believes "that at the same time we speak communally, we
also speak specifically," and that the specificity of individual voices must
not be lost or appropriated. As she explains, "part of the glory of humanity

is the potential for understanding the specific and coming together around it. If we kept our ears clean, we could speak more in the specific and wouldn't have to think that the only way to speak is in this communal way" (Lewis 1993, 58). What Smith tries to offer everyone is a way to "read" the "texts" that are implicated in ways of seeing, believing, and feeling. Events such as the one that occurred in Crown Heights require an interpretative framework that allows for both individual expression and communal understanding. As Smith says, she is "trying to find the tools for thinking about difference as a very active negotiation rather than an image of all of us holding hands" (Martin 1993, 53).

It is only by understanding how text "travels"—how it remains contextual and nonneutral, as Edward Said asserts—that any theory or method can be applied to the most volatile struggles for cultural hegemony. Smith shares with Said a profound recognition of how identities that emerge out of specific contexts travel by way of text. Said observed in *The World, the Text, and the Critic* that "texts have ways of existing that even in the most rarefied form are always enmeshed in circumstance, time, place, and society—in short, they are in the world, hence worldly" (1983, 35). His concept of borrowed or "traveling theory," therefore, is an acknowledgment that ideas can and do move from place to place and across boundaries of time; but it also describes what happens when the formulations of an activist witness and participant in a particular historical event pass into the realm of pure academic discourse. These formulations run the risk of being watered down or entirely disconnected from the human life that created them.

Because Said identifies himself as an "exile," one who is not "at home" in his own culture of origin or in his present location, he believes his view engenders a complex mode of identity that can tolerate the polyphony of many voices playing off against each other without the need to reconcile them. Accordingly, Smith strives to close the historical and actual gaps between people without destroying the differences between each moment and between individuals. Like Said, Smith employs images of motion as she attempts to discern who can move in space, how people "pass" between borders of identity, at one point even recalling the liberating image of the underground railroad (Martin 1993, 54). Smith's performative mimicry is designed to show us how to pass in by diminishing the critical detachment that prevents one from seeking direct engagement with others. In the process she indicts those who do not recognize that in James Snead's words, "the dominant 'I' needs the coded 'other' to function" (1994, 4).

By facilitating a radical empathy, Smith enables the viewer a transformative slippage across socially produced identities of race, nation, gender, and class. Or as she expresses her intent in the introduction to *Fires in the Mirror*, "The spirit of acting is the travel from self to the other" (xxxvi). Travel from self to the other requires that all voices be heard, but few hear any but their own voice or the voices of their chosen representatives. Still, the very boundaries that divide people also provide them safe support and valuable constructs of identity, so taking them down is not always easy or even desired. Like Said, Smith suggests we select a mode of being that develops "multifaceted identites" and a more "complex language," because her liberation theater has convinced her that "identity is in some ways a process towards character. It is not character itself" (*TL*, xxv).

Said's call for a fluid identity that can tolerate and initiate change while also being bound to time and circumstance is embodied in Anna Deavere Smith's theater. Although her notion of identity is performative and shifting, constructed in and by "identifications" and articulated in narrative as a kind of affiliation or re-presentation of that which we encounter, her singular presence serves as a metaphor for how such diversity can also be grounded and unified, so that what we encounter can be incorporated into the self. By activating her imagination, she identifies with others in such a way that she can reproduce the historical specificity of the feelings she engages without descending into distant discourse. Furthermore, the challenge of representing identity as fluid or as character in process, she claims as a spiritual commitment by using language characteristic of an African American theological aesthetic: call and response. She sees her work as "a call to the community," whereby she could be part of the examination of their problems by demonstrating the need for eclectic groups of people actively to "break the silence" about race and participate in dialogue (*TL*, xxiv).

To achieve this aim, Smith drew on her experiences "as a girl in the Black church . . . not just talking back to the preacher, but talking to God" (qtd. in Cain 1992, 66). By utilizing a call and response method, she hopes to "provoke a lot of other people to create theater that inspires the audience to participate. And I hope my work will also inspire people who don't come to the theater to come to the theater" (qtd. in Cain 1992, 66). By ritualizing empathy, Smith urges all who view her dramas to see self as other, but also to change the way they see self, too. And if those who enjoy entitlements are willing to pay the "price of the ticket," they can, through the magic of the theater, participate in the same experience. Her reliance on the movement of spirit, her belief in the transformative power of language and the healing aspects of performative experience lead critics and scholars to describe her work in religious terms.

Carol Martin describes Smith's performative language as "conjuring" (1993, 46) and her method as that of a "spirit doctor" who "brings ancestors or other spirits in contact with the living—in the presence of the community of the audience" (45). Richard Schechner writes of how Smith's way of working is less like that of a "conventional, European-American actor," but more like an African, Native American, or Asian "ritualist" or "shaman." Schechner goes on to explain that he observes Smith working "by means of a deep mimesis, a process opposite to that of 'pretend.' To incorporate means to be possessed by, to open oneself up thoroughly and deeply to another being" (1993, 63). In a memo Smith wrote to one of the dramaturges of *Twilight* (a production similar in form and intent to *Fires in the Mirror,*) she explains she was seeking to create for her audience

> points of empathy *with themselves.* . . . To create a situation where they merely empathize with those less fortunate than themselves is another kind of theater. . . . My political problem is this: Privilege is often masked, hidden, guarded. This guarded, fortressed privilege is exactly what has led us to the catastrophe of non-dialogue in which we find ourselves. I'm not talking about economic privilege. I'm talking about the basic privilege of white skin which is the foundation of our rare vocabulary. (qtd. in Lahr 1993, 90)

To accomplish her goal, therefore, she brings "unoffical" language into public debate by way of an aesthetic mode. Katie Laris describes her method in the following way:

> In a provocative and involving displacement, the audience assumed the part of Anna Deavere Smith as she in turn took on the role of the interviewee. Placed in this position, we are asked to read the text of the situation as closely as she has, to see what is really there, not what we have imagined or what has been fed to us by the media. Her success in creating a dialogue between different races, though contained within herself, offers a

blueprint for racial harmony, an invitation to, as she has said, "negotiate the differences." (Laris 1993, 119)

That Smith not only engenders this response but generates and embodies it herself is what makes her work unique. Because she and the people she portrays all remain visible, individuality is asserted while at the same time difference is called into question. In the process, she forces us to reconsider what constitutes not just theater, but also literature and text itself. For her, texts to be studied are not preexisting literature but other human beings. By finding the poetry in people's everyday speech she redirects our studied theater gaze back out to the streets from which it emerged. As Schechner describes her method, Smith composes her performances much as a ritual shaman might investigate and heal a diseased patient. By closely consulting with the "patients"—opening to their intimacy and listening to and looking closely at those whom she interviews—Smith goes beyond the process of interviewing to create a more spiritual encounter. She shows respect and looks and listens with empathy, a sensibility Schechner describes as "going beyond sympathy . . . the ability to allow the other in, to feel what the other is feeling" (1993, 64).

Smith demonstrates this empathy not just in her investigative techniques, but in her performance—the way she absorbs the gestures, the tone of voice, the look, and all the details of the personalities of those she interviews. Accomplishing this effect without parody or insult is not easy, but that Smith does so is evidence not only of her fine technique but her genuine commitment. As Schechner concludes in his review of *Fires in the Mirror:* "Smith's shamanic invocation is her ability to bring into existence the wondrous 'doubling' that marks great performances. This doubling is the simultaneous presence of performer and performed. Because of this doubling Smith's audiences—consciously perhaps, unconsciously certainly—learn to 'let the other in,' to accomplish in their own way what Smith so masterfully achieves" (1993, 64). Double consciousness, of course, is not a new concept when applied to African Americans. But Smith's theater reveals a new aspect or way to interpret the crisis DuBois identified—to negotiate the difference and use the tension for creative result rather than paralysis—and in the process she teaches us something new about ourselves.

Still, the final line of "Anonymous Young Man #2—Bad Boy" in *Fires in the Mirror* serves as caveat for Smith and her entire enterprise. When Bad

Boy tries to explain to Smith "how it is" he says: "That's between me and my creator." As Smith observes in this statement, Bad Boy is asserting his dignity. "He doesn't appropriate his own culture" (Martin 1993, 59). Smith's appreciation of Bad Boy's caveat reveals how her theatrical enterprise is full of personal risk. As she candidly admits, she cannot afford to have an opinion and must strive to show all sides while favoring none. To have an opinion would diminish, perhaps even silence the very voices she is trying to amplify. But by not taking an opinion, Smith risks that her "willingness to walk in other communities will reflect badly on me in my own community" (qtd. in Kaufmann 1993, G11). How Smith negotiates this risk is by honoring her community, aligning herself with several African American aesthetic traditions.

Like a folk artist, she creates out of what is available, using "found objects" such as dialogue culled from interviews or basic elements of wardrobe. She animates the subjects that are too often perceived as objects and reveals the spirits within. She takes the lives that society would throw away or ignore and invests them with value. Like a quilt maker, she creates a verbal patchwork of pieces that she sews together with her own constant bodily presence. But despite the temptation to surrender their everyday use to be museum pieces, her "quilts" retain their intended function, becoming a cover that envelopes in intimate conversation characters and audience members who most likely would never share the same room together. As one critic explains, "In making the audience hear the characters, Smith is also showing it how to listen to the strangers in its midst. She creates a climate of intimacy by acknowledging the equality of the other" (Lahr 1993, 93). Finally, like a jazz musician, Smith adopts an improvisational style as each performance of "On the Road" and each subject matter she tackles "comps on the head" or improvises on the theme of identity and difference. She adds or subtracts characters to suit the needs of particular audiences or her own evolving ideas so that each performance is unique and cannot be fully duplicated. Like a jazz composition, her performances are, by definition, always works in progress.

Thus, all the while Smith proudly claims an African American identity and demonstrates and celebrates in her work a profound knowledge of African American and African cultural traditions, she is sensitive to not only her own temptation to appropriate aspects of this culture but how she may lead others to do the same. It is only through her uncanny ability to make connections with other cultural and ethnic influences, to allow anything that comes into her orbit to enrich and deepen her perception of the human condition, that she both honors and challenges the people she strives to represent. As Cornel West describes her efforts in his introduction to *Fires*, Smith demonstrates how art can constitute an empowering public space because she functions as a *citizen* who knows that we cannot address problems of ethnic strife "without a vital public sphere and that there can be no vital public sphere without genuine bonds of trust"; and she functions as an *artist* who knows that "public performance has a unique capacity to bring us together—to take us out of our tribal mentalities—for self-critical examination and artistic pleasure" (*FM*, xxii).

By her ability both to "race" and "erase" language, Smith shows us how we can move beyond exclusive forms of identification. In the process, she reaffirms that creation in the midst of endurance is what constitutes genuine survival, transforming both victim and oppressor into characters entitled to the fullest measure of humanity. When those on the margins dance to the center and those at the center relinquish their space, the result can be community rather than chaos because "American character lives not in one place or the other, but in the gaps between the places, and in our struggle to be together in our differences" (Smith qtd. in *FM*, xli).

A Letter to My Soul

For Lex

Kathy Engel

I won't leave you standing
in the rain
like that.

You gave me
your raincoat
I wore it like a sister
wrapped around me.
Proud
I announced
its origin.

That's the way we wear
each other
right?
Loose or tight
we never let go.

You gave me a bureau
big and dark
full of drawers
for your goddaughter

it's yours baby
you said

and we filled it with dreams
and wished it into life

a bureau with wings.

You gave me a ring
is it okay
you asked
purple for love
silver for courage
how'd you know I wanted a ring

you laughed
from Buffalo
on a bus
that musical lilt of a laugh

tiny ankles
encircled by shells
never giving way

You walked
through penned out volumes
calligraphic histories
bloodscript.

You gave me a glimpse
into your soul
I safekeep it
look into it
for vision
hold it for comfort
touch it for strength.

You gave me
faith in myself
how'd you do that
when I should've had it anyway?

We give each other
salt
blood
love

two rivers
out of two sea- mouths
foreigners
from the same ancient mama sea.

Rivers run tough
some days
crash around rocks

then give themselves over
leeched dry as scale
the wetness soaked thirsty
into another life.

Rain can talk mean.
Even the ground seems scared.

Some days rivers just cry.

We traveled to the war
together
came home warriors.

We traveled to peace
together
came home singing.

Looked up and found
too many soldiers dead
too many sisters gone.

What you gave me
is safe
a promise.

I talk to your grandmother
sometimes, say her name
like a stream in the mountain

Ruby Hill, I say,
we never spoke,
but I buried you too.

We're related,
remember?

This is a letter to my soul:
standing there
shaking

I'm putting your goddaughter to bed
we cross fingers
build a new world.

As a child Dad's Mom saved pennies
for a piano lesson
on the Lower East Side.
Mom's mom wore silk.

Ruby Hill, you told me,
was a schoolteacher down South.
Jobless in New York
she washed a white woman's sheets.

Could've been my grandma's
could've been . . .

The sheets on our beds
sting

Africa to Palestine
Harlem to Tribeca
Buffalo to Bridgehampton.

We keep washing them
and laying down in hope.
These nights you wake in fright.

I'm singing your goddaughter to sleep
off-key
determined to keep dreaming.
She asks about waterbeds, Buffalo, your house.

I show her a photo.
We bought our homes the same week in May.
Ashamed of my comfort,
you urged me on.

You, poet, sweep all fifteen rooms
of your Buffalo dream house
methodically.

Whoever might clean for pay
could be someone's grandma.

I can't sew
like my mother
but thumb over thumb
we stake out
a new stitch.

I'm reading your goddaughter to sleep
in her new house
she tells me
your poem "Race& Class& Da Canine Xperience"
laughing about the dog and the shit!

That old stick
of fire
still pokes around sparks,

are we crazy, outdated
to think of a life where poems
do feed

birds, at least,
cure disease, maybe?

I'm kissing your goddaughter goodnight
and tell her a story
about women,
about making something together,
believing together,
a story of friendship.

This is what lasts
I tell her.
Ideals we work for.
Love makes it real.

We are married
my husband tells a friend
about you and us.
That's how we know each other
in this dark corridor.

This is a letter to my soul:

You gave away your raincoat
you gave away your bureau
you moved away from home
you kept your faith
you followed your path
you broke the rules
you sweated

you shine like the Egyptian sun
offering gifts of light
gift after gift

you buried too many

you didn't tuck yourself in
sing yourself a lullaby
you opened your soul

and saw too much.

What you gave me
is safe:
Here, hold on.

Now

For Safiya

Kathy Engel

1.

> *you sift*
> *the blue*
> *for the agate*

a line you dreamed
I wrote

each word
clay between us

in the conscious light of day
things are meant to make sense

we trade metaphor
no flash, no map

a flag of colors and language
startling the sky we draw with a pencil

an intractable
desire

for a truth
we wrap ourselves around

2.

just as serious
the quest for beauty:

privet in musky bloom—your favorite
a perfect line,

historical,
sensuous

adornment . . .
suede pants

sliding down our thighs
almost cashmere sweater

*"rooted
in culture"*

with that permission
we culture deeper

lay away
our deepest fears

for a moment or two:
what we leave won't show

*we sift the blue
for the agate*

3.

when your grandson
holds your face to his

sucks you into his one year marvel
you sift the blue for the agate

those years you healed with your hands
the branches of your fingers

diligent
each stroke a villanelle

when you poet
long limbed, sinuous

open eyed
exquisite in what you know

the blue for the agate
sifts through

the work doesn't change
it moves

the sifting is how we travel
alone, together

alone again

the agate
is what you see

the blue
is your truth

your triumph.

Part Three. Contesting Identities

A Legacy of Healing

Words, African Americans, and Power

Keith Gilyard

To claim that "words will never hurt me" is the all-time number one act of denial. Only a person profoundly hurt by words would attempt this psychological maneuver. I have, in fact, been rather adept at the sticks and stones competition, but have been nicked quite a bit, along with others of my ethnic group, by the master narrative in which inferiority is ascribed to those of darker hues. I plead no special case here. African Americans aren't the only ones who don't fare well in the American script of exploitation—just a prominent example. My aim, therefore, is not merely to highlight the victimization of African Americans but to explore adaptive responses to that victimization along the axis of language. In other words, I am considering the healing qualities contained in the counterstory about language that has been central to the African American intellectual and expressive traditions. I don't argue that language alone oppresses or that a magic combination of syllables could alone secure full empowerment. I simply choose to pay particular attention to the Word, even as I acknowledge that Word and Deed inevitably interact to shape destiny.

Imagine the first African slaves ever captured by Europeans. As soon as they were called *totally out they names,* they had to know they were up against a different game. They weren't losers in a mundane intracontinental conflict; they were to be subjected to the largest program of dehumanization ever seen in the Western Hemisphere, complete with tales and labels, sanctioned by respected intellects, that rationalized enslavement. *Nigger,* because of the variety of powerful reactions it can spur and because of the particular history and present it inscribes, remains to this day the most potent word in the American vocabulary.

Although captured Africans were suffering huge losses in the skirmish about self-definition (we did call ourselves Negroes well into the twentieth century), they managed some impressive gains along other verbal fronts. Patricia Turner points out in *I Heard It Through the Grapevine,* her fascinating study of rumor in African American culture, that the 1839 mutiny aboard the *Amistad* probably began because Cinque and other Africans believed the rumor that they were about to be literally eaten by their captors. That slavers were cannibals, in more than the obvious metaphoric sense, was an idea widely held by Africans. When Cinque and company made their move, therefore, they were propelled toward their eventual freedom by a specific linguistic form. So, although rumor generally connotes negativity, it has functioned systematically in the African American community, as Turner carefully and brilliantly documents, as a method of protection and resistance. Recent and popular rumors suggesting that there is an ingredient in certain fast food chicken to sterilize black males, or alleging Ku Klux Klan ownership of clothing companies such as Troop, or asserting that Reebok sneakers were manufactured and/or distributed in South Africa circulate as sites of teaching and survival.

The Reebok rumor even convinced supposed empiricists like my wife and me. The Boston-based manufacturer was, in fact, the first major U.S. shoe company to pull its products *out* of South Africa. But when some folks told us about the South Africa angle, and when we pondered how South African the word *Reebok* sounded, we soon vowed never to buy a pair of Reebok sneakers as long as South African apartheid existed. This really bothered our children. It was:

"Mommy, Daddy, but the sneakers is phat!"
"Yeah, but you not gittin em."

Through dialogue about sneakers, a very powerful channel, we taught our children much about colonialism, the Mandelas, and boycott. And to communicate this most effectively, all I had to do was not purchase a few pairs of sneakers, which cost too much anyway. In fact, when one considers that every other major sneaker company has been hit by a rumor connecting it to the predemocracy South African government or the Ku Klux Klan, one understands that some folk are doing fine cultural work in trying to discourage African American youth, an audience specifically targeted by these manufacturers, from so intently, and sometimes perilously, accumulating so many pieces of overpriced leather and rubber. Health is one of the issues here, and not all the rhetoric can be pretty. As Turner concludes, "like a scab that forms over a sore, the rumors are an unattractive but vital mechanism by which the cultural body attempts to protect itself from subsequent infection" (1993, 220).

I'm not trying to start any trouble, but Crooked I, a company that produces malt liquor and fruit drinks, may easily be hit by a rumor. Some brother or sister may notice that the company's juices, whatever the flavor, are packaged in black cans and are available almost exclusively in the African American community. Someone else may notice that the product is produced in North Carolina and then associate it with the Ku Klux Klan. Another may discover the ultimately damning scoop, that is, if you dissect the company logo, the Crooked I, vertically, which you can do, say, by covering half of it with your finger, you will clearly see three Ks. Opinion then spreads that in KKK-owned Crooked I products there is a chemical (beyond, but clearly connected to, the alcohol in the malt liquor our youth drink too much of) designed to destroy African Americans.

The grapevine also extends to literature. In his 1967 novel, *The Man Who Cried I Am,* John A. Williams has a character discover a document describing the King Alfred Plan, a "final solution" for African Americans in case of continued racial unrest. Agencies such as the FBI, CIA, National Security Council, Department of Defense, and local police forces are to coordinate their efforts in order to neutralize black leadership and then "terminate, once and for all, the Minority threat to the whole of the American society, and, indeed, the Free World" (*MC,* 372). This conspiracy theory grabbed hold of the mass black imagination. Black folk skipped past the first twenty-seven chapters to get to this King Alfred Plan they had heard about. They didn't care anything about Harry Ames or Max Reddick or Marion Dawes. The Black Topographical Society based a three-hour political awareness session, one I sat through in the early 1970s, on a version of the proposal. Speakers would explain, for example, that super highways such as the Dan Ryan Expressway in Chicago were always routed through black ghettoes to facilitate eventual military operations against those communities. I told one of the presenters that the King Alfred Plan came out of a novel. He replied that the novel was just telling the truth. And it is certainly easy to comprehend why it could ring true for anyone who had witnessed the suspicious assassinations of Martin Luther King Jr., Malcolm X, and a long list of others, and who had seen or been a part of the post-Watts wave of inner-city uprisings.

Although it provided ample grist for the rumor mill, Williams's novel is, in addition, firmly linked to texts in the African American literary tradition. The Wright-like figure Harry Ames asserts that "I'm the way I am, the kind of writer I am, and you may be too, because I'm a black man; therefore, we're in rebellion; we've got to be. We have no other function as valid as that one" (MC, 49). The story is—as most stories in the tradition are—largely about the tension between the expression and repression of the black voice. This dynamic is manifest, for example, in the very first novel by an African American published in the United States, Harriet Wilson's *Our Nig; or, Sketches from the Life of a Free Black* (1859).

After being abandoned by her mother at the age of six, Frado begins a period of indenture in the New England home of the Bellmonts. She quickly becomes a favorite of men working around the farm, who "were always glad to hear her prattle" (*ON*, 37). However, Frado is soon silenced. When young Mary Bellmont accuses Frado of pushing her into a stream, Frado's true account of events is ignored. Mrs. Bellmont, with the aid of her daughter, beats Frado, props her mouth open with a piece of wood, and locks her in a dark room. Frado cannot even talk things over with herself as many of us are wont to do in times of extreme distress.

As Frado grows older, the Bellmont's son, James, Aunt Abby, and Mr. Bellmont himself, all try to shield her somewhat from Mrs. Bellmont's cruelty. But her mistress only becomes more selective and clandestine about the beatings, never failing to warn Frado that she wouldn't hesitate to "cut [Frado's] tongue out" if Frado exposed her (*ON*, 72), threatening to do physically to Frado what she has been accomplishing symbolically all along. Frado tells anyway as her voice, encouraged by her advocates, is gaining in strength, which prompts a desperate Mrs. Bellmont to resort to one of her favorite techniques. She forces a wooden block into Frado's mouth and whips her with a rawhide strap.

Frado is undeterred. She reads and continues to converse with those willing to entertain her. And in the novel's climactic scene, when Mrs. Bellmont raises a stick to strike Frado because she feels Frado is taking too long with her chores, Frado loudly declares that if struck, she will never work again. Mrs. Bellmont, amazed at the direct verbal challenge, declines to test Frado's resolve. Frado, her period of indenture nearing its conclusion, becomes intensely interested in a wide range of reading material and pursues literacy with vigor. She keeps a book nearby even as she toils.

Charles W. Chesnutt explores nineteenth-century expression/repression conflict against a Southern backdrop, particularly in his Uncle Julius tales. He illustrates how tightly the voices and literate behaviors of slaves were monitored by slave owners. Dave, the central character in "Dave's Neckliss," hardworking and obedient, encounters no special problem with his master until he is found reading the Bible. Dave uses his wit, however, to escape trouble. Mars Dugal, in contrast, cunningly attempts to reinforce control. As Julius narrates,

> "'Dis yer is a se'ious matter,' sezee; 'it's 'g'in de law ter l'arn niggers how ter read, er 'low 'em ter hab books. But w'at yer l'arn out'n dat Bible, Dave?'
>
> "Dave w'an't no fool, ef he wuz a nigger, en sezee: "Marster, I l'arns dat it's a sin fer ter steal, er ter lie, er fer ter want w'at doan b'long ter yer; en I l'arns fer ter love de Lawd en ter 'bey my marster.'
>
> "Mars Dugal' sorter smile' en laf' ter hisse'f, like he 'uz might'ly tickle' 'bout sump'n, en sezee: "'Doan 'pear ter me lack readin' de Bible done yer much harm, Dave. Dat's w'at I wants all my niggers fer ter know. Yer keep right on readin', en tell de yuther han's w'at yer be'n tellin' me. How would yer lack fer ter preach ter de niggers on Sunday?'" (DN, 134)

When Dave later is framed for a theft, his Bible is taken away and burned by the overseer.

African American writers have never lost sight of the language problematics posed by Wilson and Chesnutt. Toni Morrison, for one, always foregrounds, perhaps most notably in *Beloved,* the dialectic of expression/repression. Sixo, one of the Garner slaves, a bit more fiery than Dave, decides to stop speaking English because he sees no future in doing so. One can sympathize with Sixo's position after witnessing the conversation, a thoroughly postmodern one, between him and schoolteacher when Sixo is accused of stealing a pig:

> "You stole that shoat didn't you?"
> "No, sir. I didn't steal it."
> Schoolteacher smiled. "Did you kill it?"
> "Yes, sir. I killed it."
> "Did you butcher it?"
> "Yes, sir."
> "Did you cook it?"
> "Yes, sir."
> "Well, then. Did you eat it?"
> "Yes, sir. I sure did."
> "And you telling me that's not stealing?"

"No, sir. It ain't."

"What is it then?"

"Improving your property, sir."

"What?"

"Sixo plant rye to give the high piece a better chance. Sixo take and feed the soil, give you more crop. Sixo take and feed Sixo give you more work." (*B*, 190)

Schoolteacher beats Sixo anyway to show him that, as the authorial voice puts it, "definitions belonged to the definers—not the defined" (*B*, 190). Of course Sixo knows this by then, and he seeks to become a definer. So he leaves the masters their language, resorting to English again only while formulating plans to escape. His plan is defeated, but he goes to his death singing his own song, laughing, and calling out because his Thirty-Mile Woman (not her master's label) is pregnant, "Seven-O! Seven-O!" (*B*, 226).

Baby Suggs also practices self-definition. After her freedom is purchased by her son and she is escorted out of bondage by Mr. Garner, she asks why she was always referred to as Jenny. Garner informs her, naturally, that the name on her invoice is Jenny Whitlow. She bitterly rejects it. Another of the story's free elders has cast aside his given name of Joshua and renamed himself Stamp Paid because he feels he has settled any debt he might have owed in this world.

If Zora Neale Hurston and Ralph Ellison have written the most artistic "discovery of voice" books in the African American literary tradition, then *Beloved* will probably go down as the most accomplished "claim your name" book. It is *The Bluest Eye,* though, that conveys most powerfully Morrison's concern with both the debilitating and therapeutic aspects of overall language practices.

The story opens with a paragraph that could have been excerpted from a typical primer: "Here is the house. It is green and white. It has a red door. It is very pretty. Here is the family. Mother, Father, Dick, and Jane live in the green-and-white house. They are very happy" (*BE*, 7).

The major trouble with primers is that characteristically they have depicted the happy, white, suburban nuclear family, which discounts the reality of most of the nation, including, of course, African American children such as Pecola Breedlove, who wishes for, above all things, a set of blue eyes.

In the second paragraph of the novel, Morrison repeats the wording of the first, only she removes standard punctuation marks. The spaces between the lines of type are smaller. In the third paragraph, she removes the spaces between the words and even ignores conventional syllabification.

The reader soon realizes, even more so as similar phrases are repeated at the outset of later chapters, that a narrative of domination contributes directly to Pecola's plight and eventual insanity. Undeniably there are other crucial factors: neglect, abuse, incest, rape. But the fact that no voice is stronger to Pecola than the one that encourages self-loathing is an essential element. So is the fact that her father, Cholly Breedlove, who eventually passes the sickness of his life to her, hasn't grabbed hold of an enabling tale. In describing Cholly's relationship with his wife, Morrison pens a line reminiscent of the description of *Native Son*'s Bigger Thomas: "He poured out on her the sum of all his *inarticulate fury and aborted desires* (*BE*, 37, emphasis mine).

Contradistinct to the inadequate language system most available to Pecola are the rich verbal experiences shared by Claudia and Frieda MacTeer, who habitually tune in to the vibrant verbal interplay of their mother and her friends. As Claudia narrates:

> Their conversation is like a gently wicked dance: sound meets sound, curtsies, shimmies, and retires. Another sound enters but is upstaged by still another: the two circle each other and stop. Sometimes their words move in lofty spirals; other times they take strident leaps, and all of it is punctuated with warm-pulsed laughter—like the throb of a heart made of jelly. The edge, the curl, the thrust of their emotions is always clear to Frieda and me. We do not, cannot, know the meaning of all their words, for we are nine and ten years old. So we watch their faces, their hands, their feet, and listen for truth in timbre. (*BE*, 16)

With ready access to a collaborative, self-affirming language community, the MacTeer girls have a shield against the dominant narrative.

Morrison's work advances significantly the African American literary project. Although not all characters in the tradition successfully counteract repression, many do achieve autonomy, expressive and otherwise. African American literature as a whole, much like protective African American rumor mechanisms, has been a grand gesture toward healing.

Rap, at its best, is on the same mission. A blend of urgent beats and reinvigorating black orality, rap is recent testimony that the contesting black voice in every generation will somehow force itself upon a broad audience. Ready or not, brand new flava will be kicked in your ear. Referring to the "Stop the Violence Movement" and HEAL (Human Education Against Lies), and to stars such as KRS-One and Chuck D, Houston Baker argues that "these positive sites of rap are as energetically productive as those manned by our most celebrated black critics and award-winning writers" (1971, 59–60). Baker, one of those celebrated critics, sees the connection between "this DJ be Warren G" and "this PHD be Houston B." He adds that "rap is the form of audition in our present era that utterly refuses to sing anthems of, say, STATE homogeneity" (1993, 96–97).

Tricia Rose, one of the most informed people on the planet about rap, amplifies Baker's comments:

> Rap music is, in many ways, a hidden transcript. Among other things, it uses cloaked speech and disguised cultural codes to comment on and challenge aspects of current power inequalities. Not all rap transcripts directly critique all forms of domination; nonetheless, a large and significant element in rap's discursive territory is engaged in symbolic and ideological warfare with institutions and groups that symbolically, ideologically, and materially oppress African Americans. (1994, 100–101)

Obscenity trials, widespread media attention, and the multibillion dollar scramble over rap revenues indicate the power and importance of this verbal form. Also interesting is the elbowing over who gets to tell the most persuasive academic story about rap. The participation of Skip Gates in the 2 Live Crew trial is called careerism by Baker, who sees Gates as an uninformed outsider pimping the music for publicity. Baker, in turn, is criticized by Rose for marginalizing the female voice in his version of rap's origin and development. And Tricia, just beware. I don't know who is right on these questions, but it's amusing and gratifying to see rap on the agendas of professors at Harvard, Penn, and NYU.

General African American literacy initiatives have run parallel to folkloric and artistic concerns with language power. Immediately after the Civil War, black folk took the lead on the issue of literacy and schooling for the newly freed population. Black illiteracy had been state sanctioned, so it is little wonder that a widespread black literacy project was conceived primarily as a self-help endeavor. These educational pioneers understood that to be literate was to be able to construct textual knowledge for oneself. They didn't want former slaves to be tricked by the textual interpretations of others as was often the case during slavery when a literate ruling class would lie to slaves about the content of abolitionist writing. It is common nowadays to hear the slogan "knowledge is power" associated with African American educational campaigns, but Thomas Holt reveals that the phrase has been in use at least since 1865, when the South Carolina black men's convention used it in the preamble to a resolution to establish schools (1990).

Holt also demonstrates quite clearly that there has been no greater dedication to the ideal of popular education in this nation's history than that made by the African American community in the South. The secret schools that operated during slavery, the free schools that were founded shortly after the war, contributions of money that were an amazingly high percentage of contributors' incomes, abundant in-kind resources made available, even the institution of voluntary tax collection systems to support schools when federal and state monies were withheld—all constitute remarkable commitment.

The African American literacy project even survived, though barely, both the postreconstruction white backlash and the subsequent attempts of philanthropists such as Rosenwald and Rockefeller to gain control of the agenda and ensure that blacks received only the type of education that kept them "in place," so to speak, in southern society—a sort of Booker T. Washington deal. W. E. B. DuBois, as one probably would suppose, was prominent among the African American leadership who countered this idea. But, as Holt writes, opposition came also, and perhaps more importantly in terms of history, from another formidable source: "Resistance also came from students at Tuskeegee, Fisk, Howard, and Hampton who, during the 1920s, went on strike against their school administrations and in many cases succeeded in getting new leadership. In the long run, all those struggles laid the basis for the student warriors during the civil rights movement in the late 1950s and early 1960s, because, next to the church, Southern colleges were the most critical to the success of that movement" (1990, 99).

One thing that now has to happen is that we tap into the fundamental valuation of education that exists to this day in the African American community. Although African Americans have become highly skeptical about certain educational practices and remain dismayed because even institutional certification ensures equal opportunity for them only sporadically, they still view effective schooling to be a key aspect of communal healing. It still represents great possibility.

Language professionals can help to improve educational practice by bringing clarity to discussions of language-related matters. They can share state-of-the-art knowledge about language acquisition and verbal processing, and assess how instructional designs are consonant or inconsistent with this information. In addition, they can indicate some of the social variables that affect language instruction and stress—above all, the importance of honoring the language varieties that students bring to school. The teacherly impulse to eradicate specific dialects, for example, is wrong, as Peter Trudgill cogently argues, on grounds of psychology, sociology, and practicality (1974, 80–81). Such corrective attempts usually send the message that students are inherently deficient and fail to facilitate expansion of students' verbal repertoires. Students may, in turn, understanding the message clearly, make language a site of resistance and thus reject standard English so as to solidify their rebellious identities. Some think that these concerns, particularly as they relate to African American students, were laid to rest back in the 1970s. However, that is not the case.

On November 28, 1992, the *New York Times* ran a front-page story entitled "Caribbean Pupils' English Seems Barrier, Not Bridge." The article dealt with the poor performance of students from the English-speaking Caribbean, who were enrolling by the thousands in New York City public schools. To some extent, dialect was cited as the cause of failure, and I was reminded of the black English debates of previous decades (which continue today, though more quietly). Wary about the impact this article could have, I was eager to author a response and shake things up a bit.

Fortuitously, a reporter from the *Carib News* visited me to solicit my opinion. I told him that if folks are committed to discrimination, they can almost always use language as a pretext. I further asserted that the problem was one of method, not language. It has been demonstrated repeatedly, especially during the celebrated King case (or black English trial) in 1979, that inappropriate *responses* to language diversity, not language diversity per se, are a major educational problem. I definitely favored committing as much support as possible to helping the students in question; linking dialect with deficiency is what I was mainly arguing against.

I am fully aware of and do not want to minimize differences among black English and a variety of Caribbean dialects. On the other hand, I feel a diasporic view with regard to African-derived language forms yields the most compelling analysis. Only diaspora esthetics can properly explain rap, for instance, which could not have started as it did without Kool DJ Herc and other Jamaicans. And both black English and black Caribbean dialects are examples of what linguist John Holm terms *Atlantic Creoles* (1988, 1999). The *Times* article, in fact, in describing the language patterns of Caribbean students, reported that "Many forgo the past tense, drop the verb to be (he tall; she a princess) and switch subject and object pronouns (I tell she; him say). They express plurals and possessives differently (two house, or de house—dem; this is mines). Their words often carry different meanings, pronunciation varies greatly and sentence stresses fall in different places" (*New York Times* 1992, 22). Every item mentioned here, with the possible exception of "de house-dem" is familiar to anyone who knows black English.

Unfortunately, the reporter lumped my response with those of several other interviewees, not all of whom shared my views or academic background, in a piece entitled, "American English Experts Respond!" As a group, we sounded as if there were no real problem at all. I wasn't surprised, then, when "Caribbean English Specialists Respond" appeared in a subsequent issue of the paper. A Caribbean scholar took us to task for being unqualified to address the matter; for buying into West-Indians-as-cream-of-the-crop mythology; for failing to properly understand the realities of bilingualism and bidialectalism; and for ignoring the fact that the children were doing abysmally in school, scoring very low on standardized test, and sitting in special education classes in disproportionate numbers.

I responded with a letter to the editor, which was graciously printed. I emphasized again my objection to any belief that dialect differences alone can account for the rate of so-called failure in our schools. I conceded the fact of bilingualism, as there is the issue of mutual unintelligibility between English and a certain varieties of Caribbean creoles. But I warned that we must not conflate bilingualism with bidialectalism.

I remain supportive of serious attempts to enhance the academic performances of Caribbean students both in class and on standardized tests. Programs that recognize the uniqueness of the Caribbean immigrant experience and build upon strengths in that experience make sense to me. But a reassessment of standardized tests is also required, as is the deconstruction of special education. It's easy to wind up there if you're black, no matter which sounds come out of your mouth.

I don't pretend that my analysis has drastically effected change. It's merely illustrative of the insight that language professionals can offer. To fully implement correct, not simply corrective, language pedagogy, a varied action agenda is needed along with participation from many types of individuals and groups. Schools ultimately are sensitive to occurrences in the larger society. Anyone working toward positive social change is to some extent helping to strengthen language instruction.

One more flashback as we move forward. Arna Bontemps explains that during the eighteenth century, when even greater than usual pressure was being applied to repress the literacy of slaves, the beautiful, gorgeously double-voiced spirituals were born (1969). As noted earlier, the contesting black voice will find a way. Marveling at that achievement, James Weldon Johnson paid homage to those artists in "O Black and Unknown Bards," some of which goes:

> There is a wide, wide wonder in it all,
> That from degraded rest and servile toil
> The fiery spirit of the seer should call
> These simple children of the sun and soil. (1969, 123–24)

It's a beautiful poem, but it's also a script we want to flip. We want to bring all the righteousness of African American expressive and intellectual output to bear full force upon the creation of more black *known* bards whose production will be wide and wonderful as well.

"Nothing Solid"

Racial Identity and Identification in
Fifth Chinese Daughter and "Wilshire Bus"

Wendy Motooka

Recent assessments of Jade Snow Wong's *Fifth Chinese Daughter* (1950) have found the work to be, in Elaine Kim's words, "rather pathetic" (1982, 72). The editors of *Aiiieeeee!* (1974) pronounce it complicitous in the "anti-Japanese" sentiment of the war years, and therefore not really "Asian American" (Chin et al. 1983, xiv). Kim agrees, though she tempers her judgment by recognizing that Wong's choices were impeded by prejudice: "Wong's assertion of her Chinese identity was restricted to identification with whatever was acceptable about it to white society, and the Chinese identity that Wong defined involved whatever was most exotic, interesting, and non-threatening to the white society that was her reference point" (1982, 66). Shirley Lim reads Wong alongside Maxine Hong Kingston's *Woman Warrior*, at first defending Wong against the male bias of the *Aiiieeeee!* critics, but eventually abandoning her as a failed woman warrior; *Fifth Chinese Daughter*, she concludes, ultimately expresses "an earlier generation's submergent subjectivities and eventual submission to patriarchal discourse" (1992b, 264). It is thus ironic that Jade Snow Wong's autobiography has been a subject of controversy, for her critics all seem to agree that her work suffers from being too compromising.[1] Generally, they see her as someone too eager to please the white and male dominant culture, one who offers distorted or even "fake" representations of Asian American female identity, one who never fully liberated herself as a racialized and gendered subject (Chan et al. 1991, xi–xii).

Failed self-liberation and its meanings are the focus of this essay. De-

---

1. For a summary of this controversy, see Sau-ling 1992, 248–79.

spite Wong's critical reputation, she and her critics are not so different. They share important common ground in their mutual desire for individual expressive freedom, moral certainty, and self-validation against a background of externally imposed identities. True self-expression, they agree, can be attained only by resisting imposed identities: compromise equals failure. With the personal stakes so high, disputes—such as the one pitting race against gender—rage on,[2] and the Asian American critical enterprise succeeds merely in reproducing what Nancy Armstrong and Leonard Tennenhouse have called "the violence of representation," a rhetoric of uncompromising individuality that sustains itself by maintaining specious divisions between the powerful and the powerless, and by forcing this schema onto others: "We tend to think of ourselves as outside the field of power, or at least we write about 'it' as if it were 'out there,'" rather than considering 'it' as *us,* a product of our thoughts, our actions, and our expressions" (1989, 10). Such representations of powerlessness invite us to hold others responsible for social mischief and injustice, to blame someone "out there." This representational strategy, Armstrong and Tennenhouse suggest, "constitutes a form of violence in its own right in so far as it maintains a form of domination" (1989, 3)—in this instance, the ability to castigate and cast out authors whose self-representations conflict with "our" collective critical expectations. Jade Snow Wong has felt this violence; her compromises have irritated critics into casting her "out there," making her not like us, but of "an earlier generation" (Lim 1992b); not Asian American like us, but an "Americanized Asian" (Chin et al. 1983); not prepared to defy the dominant culture like us, but reluctant "to launch such an assault" (Kim 1928, 266); not like us because of her compromises, because of her failures.

The rhetoric of uncompromising individuality thus forges identity by fostering disidentification, promoting a critical methodology that sidesteps serious discussion of complicity and its meanings. Such an approach curtails inquiry into the very areas in which Asian American literature—itself a motley coalition of texts—may have particular relevance and insight. Hisaye Yamamoto's "Wilshire Bus" (1950), for example, subtly depicts "the violence of representation," the collaborations and complicities that accompany the identity politics of liberation through self-definition. Pub-

2. On the race/gender debate, see Cheung 1990; Kim 1990; Lowe 1991; and Lim 1992.

lished the same year as *Fifth Chinese Daughter,* "Wilshire Bus" has been critically ignored. Yet, placed in historical context, Yamamoto's short story speaks frankly of the shifting nature of racial and ethnic allegiances in the 1940s, illuminating the indirect means through which Wong addresses the issue. Read together, these two texts point to the difficulties and costs of equating uncompromising individuality with liberation.

Toward the end of her autobiography, Jade Snow Wong establishes her pottery business by renting a space in a small store, to which she draws curious customers via the spectacle of her throwing pots on the premises. As Wong explains in her marvelous narrative tone—so naïve that it could be satiric—"Jade Snow Wong discovered that one had only to get into a window to attract spectators" (*FCD,* 243). The source of much critical discomfort, this impulse toward display creates an "outside" and an "inside," a spectator and a spectacle, reducing Jade Snow to a mere sideshow. Looking through the window, the viewer sees "a 'special' American, one who can do more tricks, speak more languages, and serve up more exotic and appealing dishes than 'ordinary' Americans" (Kim 1982, 61) Wong's efforts to "create better understanding of the Chinese culture on the part of Americans" as the introduction to her book claims (*FCD,* vii), leave little doubt as to who her intended audience is. Having begun in college "to formulate in her mind the constructive and delightful aspects of the Chinese culture to present to non-Chinese" (*FCD,* 161), Wong establishes an opposition between China and America in order to narrate the path of her own self-liberation, a progress measured by her movement away from Chinese cultural encumbrances toward budding (white) Americanisms.

For Jade Snow Wong, the most important Americanism is individual expressive freedom—that liberation through self-definition that her recent critics so value as well. The Chineseness of her family is Wong's primary obstacle in the autobiography; in discussing the "struggle . . . between her and her family," Wong asserts that the "difficulty centered around Jade Snow's desire for recognition as an individual" (*FCD,* 90–91). Jade Snow's most pained moments come when family members dismiss her individual achievement: when her excitement about skipping two grades in school is crushed by her father's impassive response, "That is as it should be," followed shortly by her mother's concurrence (*FCD,* 19); when her joy in her brother's birth is marred by the realization that he is more important to her parents than she could ever be, because he is a boy (*FCD*, 27); when her youthful dream of becoming a dressmaker is toppled by her older brother's cruel reply, "Since you ask me, you'll never be a successful designer . . . you need imagination to design clothes; you need personality to meet people and sell to them, and the trouble with you is that you're so mousy, you lack both of these needed qualities" (*FCD*, 92). Individual recognition is rare in Chinese families, Wong intimates. "I want to be more than average," Jade Snow proclaims while pleading with her father to help her through college (*FCD*, 109). When she is unceremoniously rebuffed, her bitterness wells up: "I am a person, besides being female! Don't the Chinese admit that women also have feelings and minds?" (*FCD*, 110). As this last pronouncement makes plain, Jade Snow specifically associates her gendered oppression with her Chinese heritage. Chinese families impose unfair, unwarranted constraints on female individuality.

The Land of the Free, in contrast, imposes no unreasonable restraints. When told by her (white) American boss, "Don't you know by now that as long as you are a woman, you can't compete for an equal salary in a man's world?" Jade Snow does not protest angrily, demanding to know why her "feelings" and "mind" are not being respected. Rather, she acknowledges this piece of advice as "good" and "a practical lesson in economics" (*FCD*, 234).[3] In a similar vein, she first realizes the joy of "individual expression" in college (away from her Chinese family), where she discovers that "her grades [are] consistently higher when she [writes] about Chinatown" (*FCD*, 132). It does not occur to Jade Snow that her "individual expression" may be just as limited by her (white) American professors' expectations as by those of her Chinese American parents'. Likewise, when she sets up shop as a potter, "Caucasians came from far and near to see her work, and Jade Snow sold all the pottery she could make. . . . But the Chinese did not come to buy one piece from her" (*FCD*, 244). The cause of this racially imbalanced clientele, Wong suggests, is Chinese prejudice against women potters. "Look, here comes the mud-stirring maiden," the Chinatown shopkeepers chortle: "Sold a pot today? Ha! Ha!" (*FCD*, 244). Wong feels no need to offer an explanation as to why Caucasians *did* buy her pots.

3. Wong's insistence on identifying gendered oppression with Chineseness is rendered all the more questionable by the historical context of her autobiography. Through the 1940s, because of the Depression, the war, and reconversion, gender roles—particularly women's place as a wage earner—received much attention as a mainstream American issue (Honey 1984).

Emphasizing "Chinese" misogyny while entirely overlooking its blatant "American" counterpart—in other words, opposing American individualism to Chinese "cultural disregard for the individual" (*FCD*, vii)—Wong contrives to maintain strict divisions between her two worlds, "old and new, past and present, Orient and Occident" (*FCD*, 1). Her autobiography concludes happily when, having "found herself and struck her speed," Jade Snow can "stop searching for that niche that would be hers alone" (*FCD*, 246). Now assured of her individuality, Wong has successfully progressed from Chinese to American. Her personal liberation is simple, a linear progress between two poles that results in assimilation.

It should be clear at this point that for Wong, Chinese American identity and assimilation do not conflict. She equates the identity she "finds" with the identity that mainstream America has prepared for her, thus liberating herself to be exactly who she has been allowed to be. Despite attempts to reread *Fifth Chinese Daughter* as a more imaginative and "masterful" work,[4] Wong's self-representations do—as the *Aiiieeeee!* editors have maintained—reproduce the stereotypes and propaganda that the popular press promoted about the Chinese during the 1940s (a point I argue in greater detail below). At issue in the controversy stirred by Wong's assimilation, then, is the validity of those pan-ethnic identities known as "oriental" and "Asian American," for the assimilative success Wong celebrates in her autobiography was only possible for her as a Chinese, not for her as an Oriental. Other Orientals, such as Japanese Americans, could not at this time conflate identity and assimilation as Wong could. The identity politics of the early 1940s, which sought to distinguish between Chinese allies and Japanese enemies, promoted Chinese American assimilation while barring Japanese American assimilation. "Orientals" thus stood in an estranged relation to one another, a state of simultaneous identification and disidentification that can be seen in Wong's text. The *Aiiieeeee!* critics' reductive designation of this ambivalent identity as mere "anti-Japanese sentiment" greatly oversimplifies the identity politics of the period and the politics of representation in general by refusing to acknowledge the complexity of racism and the ambivalence of identity.

Jade Snow Wong is ambivalent. She is Chinese. She is Oriental. She is Asian American. And she appears to see little difference among these iden-

4. See, for example, Swee and Paulson 1982.

tities. As late as 1989, Wong happily recounts how her book has brought her rewards "beyond expectation": "I recall a handsome young paratrooper in full military dress who appeared at my San Francisco studio on his way to Vietnam. He came to thank me for writing the book, which he had read in a Texas military base, for he would better understand the Asians where he was going" (*FCD,* vii). Wong here invites readers to conflate Chinese with Vietnamese, oddly considering such conflation a reward. The image of the "handsome young paratrooper" becomes all the more unnerving when one realizes that his task in Vietnam was probably not to "understand" Asians. A similar moment occurs within the narrative of *Fifth Chinese Daughter,* when Jade Snow, living in the dean's house at Mills College, invites some friends up to the house for dinner. Her invitation includes "a Japanese girl from Tokyo" named Teruko: "Teruko did not hesitate. 'Could we have Chinese food? I have been so homesick for Oriental food'" (*FCD,* 158). Here, "Chinese" metamorphoses into "Oriental," and Teruko is homesick for the culinary delights of a culture foreign to her home.[5] Like the passage about the handsome young paratrooper, this passage blithely presumes Asian pan-ethnic ("Oriental") identification at a moment in history that produced vastly different experiences for different Asian groups. Wong speaks as an Asian to a paratrooper "in full military dress" bound for Vietnam and speaks as an Oriental with a Japanese girl just prior to the war against Japan. Each case offers Wong the opportunity to display her American patriotism as the United States heads into conflict with Asian peoples from whom she can distinguish herself. The rhetoric of Asian pan-ethnicity notwithstanding, there are differences. After the dinner at the dean's home, Teruko—though supposedly one of Jade Snow's best friends—disappears from the narrative, never to be heard from again (why?), whereas Jade Snow goes on to get a job working for the defense industry, a position all the more important to her because of her ambiguous status as "Oriental."

Consider how carefully Wong represents her Chinese—not Oriental—identity as she describes her efforts to secure employment after graduating from college in 1942. Jade Snow's exchange with and reaction to the college placement officer portray her full outrage at the prospect of being

5. The slippage between "Chinese" and "Oriental" is particularly noticeable in the context of cooking, for the cooking of Chinese food figures importantly in the construction of Jade Snow's identity (Cobb 1988; Sau-ling 1992).

misidentified, a sentiment she manages to convey without even naming the dreaded Oriental other.

> "Oh yes, I can give you some good advice," her interviewer retorted. "If you are smart, you will look for a job only among your Chinese firms. You cannot expect to get anywhere in American business houses. After all, I am sure you are conscious that racial prejudice on the Pacific Coast will be a great handicap to you."
>
> Stung and speechless, Jade Snow felt as if she had been struck on both cheeks. The numbness gave way to the first anger she had felt against any of the college staff. She had been told that because she was Chinese, she could not go into equal competition with Caucasians. Her knowledge that racial prejudice existed had never interfered with her personal goals. She had, on the contrary, found that being Chinese had created a great deal of favorable interest, and because of its cultural enrichment of her life she would not have traded her Chinese ancestry for any other.
>
> No, this was one piece of advice she was not going to follow, so opposed was it to her experience and belief. She was more determined to get a job with an American firm. (*FCD*, 188–89)

Though the interviewer specifically tells Jade Snow to look for jobs only "among your Chinese firms," his or her reminder to Jade Snow of the "racial prejudice on the Pacific Coast"—in the spring and summer of 1942—hints at the bias against Japanese Americans, who superseded the Chinese as the immigrant race to be despised in California and who at the time of Wong's job search had recently been interned. (Whatever happened to Teruko?) Jade Snow's "numbness" and "anger," her feeling that she had been "struck," Wong informs us, arise from her being "told that because she was Chinese, she could not go into equal competition with Caucasians." In fact, she seems to have been told no such thing. The placement officer recommends a Chinese firm because of the "racial prejudice on the Pacific Coast," probably meaning that she would be better off where coworkers would not mistake her for or associate her with the Japanese. Rather than admit this interpretation, Jade Snow scrupulously ignores the Japanese (she won't even mention them), eluding the identification earlier implicit in Teruko's homesickness for "Oriental food." Unwilling to trade "her Chinese ancestry for any other" at a time when Japanese Americans were burying, burning, and forgetting their ancestry,[6]

6. Such desire to destroy one's Japanese past finds repeated expression in autobiographical accounts of the Japanese American internment. See, for example, Sone 1979, 154–56, and Hous-

Jade Snow claims that her outrage stems from the very idea of Caucasian prejudice (which does not really exist, as she will demonstrate by getting a job with an "American firm") against the Chinese, *not* against Orientals.

Thus, Wong racially identifies herself only ambivalently, sometimes acknowledging her fellow Orientals, sometimes ignoring them entirely. In doing so, she replicates the mainstream American understanding of race and ethnicity during the early 1940s, choosing to inhabit the simplistic, stereotypical, and inconsistent roles imposed on her as a Chinese Oriental. The extent to which she wholeheartedly conforms to these stereotypes may be illustrated by the numerous points of comparison—including an ambivalence about race and identity—between her autobiography and the descriptions of the Chinese that mainstream publications such as *Life* magazine popularized.

Jade Snow Wong graduated from Mills College in 1942, a year that saw a crisis of racial and cultural identification in America. Japan had bombed Pearl Harbor, becoming the declared enemy of the United States, while China was a U.S. ally. Americans suddenly had to distinguish between the Chinese and the Japanese and (in the context of the eventual internment) between Chinese Americans and Japanese Americans.[7] Shortly after the attack on Hawaii, both *Time* and *Life* ran articles stressing the importance of making these distinctions and assisting puzzled readers in the science of racial and cultural taxonomy.[8] The *Time* version, "How to Tell Your Friends from the Japs," shows comparative pictures of young and middle-age Chinese and Japanese faces, while warning readers that "[t]here is no infallible way of telling them apart, because the same racial strains are mixed in both" (*Time* 1941, 35). Those "same racial strains," constituting the Oriental ("no . . . way of telling them apart"), complicate accurate ethnic identification. The article nonetheless goes on to mention a "few rules of thumb," which include not only physical characteristics pertaining to height, weight, build, and hairiness, but also some allegedly distinguishing

ton and Houston 1973, 5. Yamamoto briefly discusses her own family's destruction of Japanese things in Cheung 1994, 80.

7. The Chinese American experience of World War II was quite different from the Japanese American experience: "Japanese America was debased while Chinese America was promoted," Daniels has argued (1988, 187).

8. Both *Time* and *Life* were edited by Henry R. Luce, whose energetic interest and powerful influence popularized the image of an Americanized China (Jespersen 1996).

cultural features. For example: "Most Chinese avoid horn-rimmed spectacles"; "Those who know them best often rely on facial expression to tell them apart: the Chinese expression is likely to be more placid, kindly, open; the Japanese more positive, dogmatic, arrogant"; "Japanese walk stiffly erect, hard-heeled. Chinese, more relaxed, have an easy gait, sometimes shuffle" (*Time* 1941, 33). Although the mixing of racial strains might stump even "an anthropologist, with calipers and plenty of time to measure heads, noses, shoulders, hips," the cultural signs are more revealing; Chinese and Japanese may all look alike, but they do not all act alike. The aversion to horn-rimmed glasses(!), the serene and benevolent facial expression, and the subservient walk ("sometimes a shuffle") all point to the Chinese as "Your Friends" (*Time* 1941, 33). *Life*'s version of the article, published the same week, explains:

> In the first discharge of emotions touched off by the Japanese assaults on their nation, U.S. citizens have been demonstrating a distressing ignorance on the delicate question of how to tell a Chinese from a Jap. Innocent victims in cities all over the country are many of the 75,000 U.S. Chinese, whose homeland is our staunch ally. So serious were the consequences threatened, that the Chinese consulates last week prepared to tag their nationals with identification buttons. To dispel some of this confusion, LIFE here adduces a rule-of-thumb from the anthropometric conformations that distinguish friendly Chinese from enemy alien Japs. (*Life* 1941b, 81)

Perhaps Jade Snow's college placement officer had this report in mind when he counseled her to seek employment only in Chinese firms. Though the two "races" may easily be misidentified, the article makes the primary cultural differences clear: the Chinese "homeland is our staunch ally," and they are "friendly," whereas the Japanese are "enemy alien[s]." Though the *Life* essay does go on to enumerate "the special types of each national group," its attempts to do so ultimately collapse. "[A]ristocratic Japs," we eventually learn, look like northern Chinese; Chinese, when "middle-aged and fat . . . look more like Japs"; and Admiral Nomura and Emissary Kurusu of Japan, in fact, look "atypical" and "European" (*Life* 1941b, 81). Oriental identities are difficult to distinguish. The more certain way to tell, the article hints, is to have the Oriental person self-identify. Beneath the smiling photo of an Asian man wearing the badge, *"CHINESE REPORTER, NOT JAPANESE PLEASE"* is the caption: "Chinese journalist, Joe Chiang, found it necessary to advertise his nationality to gain admission to a White House press conference." Joe Chiang's self-identification was deemed sufficiently newsworthy to be mentioned in the *Time* article, too ("In Washington, last week, Correspondent Joseph Chiang made things much easier by pinning on his lapel a large badge reading 'Chinese Reporter—NOT *Japanese* — Please'" [1941, 33]), while his photo also ran that same week in *Newsweek*, above a caption reading "No Mistake, Please" (1941, 67). Acknowledging his similarity to his fellow Orientals by simultaneously insisting on his difference, Chiang strikes the same pose as Jade Snow Wong, assuming with apparent cheer the role of helpful Chinese informant.

A glance through the pages of *Life* magazine for the later weeks of 1941 and the early months of 1942 reveals a sustained effort to identify differences between Japanese and Chinese Orientals. Aside from the news articles describing Japan's military efforts in Asia and the Pacific, the magazine also ran stories emphasizing Japanese treachery and imitativeness. Though the latter characteristic—still a current stereotype—may seem a bit odd in this context, it was central to the way *Life* magazine understood and represented the unassimilable Orientals. "Today, as the whole world stands aghast at the strength and cunning of the Japanese, it is instructive to realize that all this is the end result of one of the most remarkable national efforts in the history of any nation," one article asserts, identifying imitation as the key to Japan's success: "The Japanese raised themselves from a state of feudal isolation to their present power by deliberately copying the methods and machines of the West" (*Life* 1942d, 80). Prior to this analysis, a photo essay called "Modern Industrial Japan Needs Steel, Oil and Machine Tools" had already alerted *Life* readers to Japan's technological advancement (*Life* 1941e, 36). Yet Japan's acquisitiveness is not limited to industry alone; it includes all aspects of culture. In fact, the magazine suggests, Japan has no culture of its own. An essay on jujitsu mentions that "[l]ike most Japanese culture, jujitsu was an import, having been practiced originally in China" (*Life* 1942a, 70.) An article introducing Americans to the game of Go begins, "The national game of Japan is called Go. Like many Japanese things, it was borrowed from another country, from China where it originated 4,000 years ago" (*Life* 1942e, 92). Everything Japan has it has borrowed, even its country: "The modern Jap is the descendent of Mongoloids who invaded the Japanese archipelago back in the mists of prehistory, and of the native aborigines who possessed the islands before them" (*Life* 1941b, 81). Japan's oft-mentioned imitativeness is but another way to refer to its colonial ambition; everything Japan has—culture, land, industry, and technology—is borrowed. Japan first imitated Chinese ways, then later invaded China, and now Japan has begun to copy the methods and machines of the West. The Japanese do not assimilate. They colonize.

A sinister foretaste of the Japanese invasion emerges in the *Life* pictorial report of 250 Japanese diplomats enjoying southern hospitality far from "the teeming streets of Tokyo" (1942f, 68–69). Too crowded in their own capital, the text suggests, the Japanese have sought out "the peaceful inviting scenes on these pages." True colonialists, they luxuriate in a deluxe hotel "at the expense of the U.S. Government," which foots the exorbitant bill of more than two thousand dollars per day. With the Japanese now in residence, the regular guests no longer come; the "700 waiters, maids, and bellboys, porters, chauffeurs, gardeners, chefs, butchers, bakers, laundresses, craftsmen, game wardens, masseurs and hostlers" serve only the Japanese delegates, who eat in the big dining hall, stroll "among the palms in the long lobby" from which "a big American flag" has been removed, see free movies, empty the hotel shops, swim in the hotel pool, and mostly stay indoors. Though they pay no money, these new Japanese masters have managed to supplant the regular clientele. They lounge about in luxury (not even exerting themselves to go outdoors for pleasure) and command hundreds of servants. The absent American flag gives the scene an eerie look of successful invasion. The name of the hotel? The Homestead. Perhaps most ominous, the Japanese are reproducing themselves on the Homestead: "One baby was born and christened Spring" (*Life* 1942f, 68–69). At the close of the article, the Homestead's president sends "his regular patrons . . . a hopeful message: 'By the time spring returns to our valley, all traces of alien visitation will be gone'" (69). Ending in such a manner, the article grimly hints that only the outcome of the war will determine whose vision of "spring"—Japan's or the Homestead's—will prevail.[9]

The image of the Chinese in these same pages of *Life* is altogether dif-

---

9. Henry Luce's publications had mastered the techniques of insinuation and innuendo, biasing their reporting to a degree that alarmed even some of Luce's editors. One such editor resigned in protest. Even Franklin D. Roosevelt wrote directly to Luce to complain about what the president perceived to be Luce's deceptively insinuating reporting practices (Jespersen 1996, 12–19).

ferent. China and its people, as the *Newsweek* article advises, wear a benevolent expression. "The Story of Christ in Chinese Art: Scholars at Peking Make a Christmas Portfolio for *Life*" reminds readers of the similarity between the Americans and the Chinese (1941f, 40). The paintings of Christ's life, which scholars at the now Japanese-occupied Catholic University of Peking produced, "are a touching affirmation that China, even in the midst of battle, holds to the spiritual and cultural values which America and China alike are now fighting to preserve." Greater cultural identification could be expected between the Chinese and the (white) Americans than between the Chinese and their Japanese fellow Orientals. "*Life* Goes to a Wedding in the Soong Family: The Youngest of China's Great Family Takes a Wife in a San Francisco Episcopal Cathedral" informs readers that this great family's founder was an American success story: "a foundling named Charlie Jones Soong who shipped to America on a clipper in 1879, took its captain's name. A self-made man, Methodist Charlie Jones came back to China to trade and teach Western ideas" (*Life* 1941c, 87).[10] In case Charlie Jones Soong's life story and name are not enough to convince readers of his and his family's basic American-ness, further details are provided: "The Soongs are a sternly Christian family . . . [the] wedding was a thoroughly American rite performed by an Episcopal bishop." Chinese and American cultural interests merge in the receiving line: "Bride and groom greeted guests at reception in the Fairmont Hotel. At their request, wedding-present money went to allied war chest." China and the United States were compatible in matters military as well as marital, as shown by *Life*'s cover picture of a Chinese cadet on the 4 May, 1942 issue. The accompanying article, "Chinese Pilots: At Arizona's Thunderbird Field They Are Taught Lessons of Aerial Combat," marvels at the speed with which the Chinese cadets are completing the program, but lest anyone interpret their impressive aptitude as mechanical, alienating, and foreign, the article pauses to add: "But life has not been all study for the Chinese cadets. They are as fun-loving and mischievous as any American youth" (*Life* 1942b, 59). The Chinese, even amidst their extraordinariness, are never too unlike (white) Americans. In fact, the fundamental, democratic principles of their society approximate American culture, without ever threatening to supersede it.

"A Chinese Town: Little Market Towns Make China Unconquerable"

---

10. Charlie Soong's daughter, Soong Meiling, gained the admiration of Americans as Madame Chiang Kai-shek (Jespersen 1996, 82–107).

presents the case succinctly. Focusing intently on "the little Chinese village"—exemplified by a community called Lung Chuan I—this pictorial essay conveys an image of the Chinese that directly contrasts with the image of the masterful Japanese strolling easily through the Homestead. Chinese society, at heart, is unassuming and democratic: "Their distinction is not hereditary, hence the gentry of China have no tradition of rule like that of the Japanese and British aristocrats. In bargaining for a ride on the street . . . with the ricksha boy . . . [the Elders] are on a basis of equality with the boy. Democracy in China applies to the daily small concerns of life" (*Life* 1941a, 85.) Moreover, the friendly Chinese pose no threat to America not only because their cultural values are basically the same, but also because their society is quite backward. "Fixed in [a]ncient [f]orms," the Chinese are ultimately inferior to Westerners. "In looking at Lung Chuan I, its ancient techniques and moral codes, Americans may see what it is that Lung Chuan I has lacked," the *Life* article continues: "Fundamentally, it has lacked the Western man's drive to become master of his environment. As a result it lacks machinery, scientific education, meat, good doctors, electricity (1941d, 86–87). Readers then learn that a generation gap is developing, for young Chinese "are determined to give [China] the techniques and material progress of the West and to cut it in on the continuous revolutionary process that is the genius of the West" (87). With industrialization and the drive to become masters of the environment constituting the "genius of the West," the necessary inferiority of the Orient becomes apparent: China is backward, though morally admirable, because it *does not* imitate the West well; Japan is modern, though morally degenerate, because it *does* imitate the West well. China can be praised for its quaint ways, applauded as "[u]nconquerable," and generally treated as a younger sibling, a miniature version of America, an assimilable entity. Japan, however, in borrowing so effectively from the West (and from China), seeks to out-West the West (and out-China China), to *become* the West (and to *become* China)—in short, to colonize the homestead and supplant "the spiritual and cultural values which America and China alike are now fighting to preserve."

If these examples from *Life* are indicative of a wider American pattern of racial and cultural representations in the 1940s,[11] then *Fifth Chinese*

11. The immense popularity of *Life, Time,* and the other productions of Henry Luce's media empire (Jespersen 1996, 12–13, 19–23) argues that Luce's particular vision of culture and race did indeed have broad appeal.

Daughter can be read as Jade Snow Wong's earnest effort to inhabit the re-
configuring boundaries of her Oriental identity. Because *racial* differences
between the Chinese and Japanese ultimately collapse both before "rules
of thumb" and before anthropologists "with plenty of time," *cultural* distinctions between Orientals assume greater importance, intensifying pressures on Chinese Americans to display the normative identities that these
clumsy attempts at Oriental identification require: "No Mistake, Please."
Tuned to the teachings of popular culture, *Fifth Chinese Daughter* fits in
well with the *Life* descriptions of "the Chinese": the antiquity, even backwardness, of their customs and their susceptibility to generational conflict
such as the one brewing in Lung Chuan I—Jade Snow "was trapped in a
mesh of tradition woven thousands of miles away by ancestors who had
had no knowledge that someday one generation of their progeny might be
raised in another culture" (*FCD*, 110); their fierce devotion to independence—seen both in Jade Snow and in her father, who emigrated from China because he prized individuality (*FCD*, 72, 246); their amazing yet
humane aptitude for learning—like the Chinese cadets at Thunderbird
Field, Jade Snow accelerates through her educational programs while still
being fun-loving and mischievous;[12] even their patriotic wedding fi-
nances—Jade Snow carefully notes that at her sister's wedding banquet,
the host "was making a most generous donation to the funds for China
war relief" (*FCD*, 142). If we compare *Fifth Chinese Daughter* to *Life* magazine articles on Orientals during World War II, Jade Snow Wong emerges as
typically Chinese and distinctly not Japanese.

Wong's willingness to conform to this normative Chinese identity,
now recognized as a stereotype, has brought upon her the anger, disap-
proval, and pity of her critics. Yet despite her model-minority appearance,
there is little to suggest that Wong herself felt forced into a submissive
role. Elaine Kim has argued that Wong accommodated rather than challenged mainstream "distortions about Chinese Americans" in order to be
accepted by white society and that the U.S. State Department interest in

12. Jade's skipping of two grades and her parents' casual response, "That is as it should
be," have already been discussed. Her fun-loving and mischievous side emerges most noticeably
in the chapters called "Saturday's Reward and Sunday's Holiday" (Jade Snow enjoys movies and
leisurely walks), "One Who or That Which Slips" (Jade Snow shows off her "gay new slippers"),
"Cousin Kee" (Jade Snow goes fishing), "Girl Meets Boy" (Jade Snow learns how to dance), and
"Alas, She Was Born Too Tall" (Jade Snow intentionally embarrasses her parents as they try to
arrange a marriage for her).

sponsoring Wong on a speaking tour in Asia in the early 1950s reflects the success of her subservient strategy (1982, 60–61). Wong, however, was hardly the submissive lotus blossom on that trip. The foreign service dispatches and airgrams recording her journey are filled with bureaucratic hand wringing over her uncooperative independence: she brought her husband along on the trip, whose presence made her interest in Asian pottery appear to be commercial rather than artistic in nature (NA a, c, d); she insisted on canceling many of her scheduled lectures, much to the embarrassment of the United States Information Service (in Wong's words, her original schedule was so heavy that she was "living off aspirin and brandy") (NA b, e); she refused many social invitations that the U.S. consuls thought she should have accepted (NA e); she refused to lecture in Chinese (NA e, f); she objected to the use of an interpreter because she believed her ideas to be too complicated for the interpreter to convey; she refused to lecture to children because she did not think her lectures could be adapted to that level (NA e).[13] Some readers today may find Jade Snow Wong too accommodating, but it is unlikely that the U.S. State Department in the 1950s would have agreed. Wong appears to have been a confident and assertive young woman, who was unafraid to risk the displeasure of others. Her acceptance of the normative, virtuous Chinese identity popular at the time may be owing not to any craven attempt to curry favor, but to the power of her experience and the strength of her own beliefs: she may have recognized this Chinese identity as authentically hers, not as a cultural and political choice.

Ironically, Wong's detractors insist that she did indeed have a choice by denying the validity of the choice she made. Like Wong herself, they envision a world of emergent social progress, where seemingly intractable entanglements can be neatly resolved into morally tidy binaries. In effect, Wong's critics discuss her largely in terms that parallel her own, drawing lines to divide inside from outside, old from new, fake from real, and positioning themselves on one side or the other (usually, the other). An alternative to this proliferation of lines exists in Asian American literature.

13. Wong's visit to Asia, under the auspices of the State Department International Educational Exchange Service (IES), took place during the early months of 1953. The correspondence surrounding her trip is housed at the National Archives of the United States at College Park (NA) Archives II: 511.903/1-2353; 511.903/3-253; 511.903/3-1753; 511.903/3-2053; 511.903/4-253; 511.903/4-853.

Hisaye Yamamoto's "Wilshire Bus," written from the perspective of that omitted fellow Oriental in Wong's narrative, critically examines the very process of drawing dividing lines between people. Openly addressing the uneasy relation between Orientals, "Wilshire Bus" focuses not on what choices should be made, but on the difficulty and frustration of having to make them.

Published the same year as *Fifth Chinese Daughter*, "Wilshire Bus" opens with a description of Wilshire Boulevard that seems also to depict the smooth progress of assimilation: "Wilshire Boulevard begins somewhere near the heart of downtown Los Angeles and, except for a few digressions scarcely worth mentioning, goes straight out to the edge of the Pacific Ocean"(WB, 34). This unimpeded journey west down a "fairly fast" and modern-looking street is a familiar prospect to Esther Kuroiwa, who routinely rides the bus down this road each Wednesday to visit her husband in the soldiers' home. The western end of Wilshire Boulevard—"more pastoral, so that the university and the soldiers' home there give the appearance of being huge country estates" (WB, 34)—offers a picture of comfort, privilege, and belonging. Having fought for his country, Esther's husband has earned his bed in the soldiers' home, where he currently resides beause of a recurring, war-related back injury. Esther is socially at ease on Wilshire Boulevard: "She always enjoyed the long bus ride very much because her seat companions usually turned out to be amiable, and if they did not, she took vicarious pleasure in gazing out at the almost unmitigated elegance along the fabulous street" (WB, 34). Comfortable with her assimilated position in America, Esther converses amiably with her fellow passengers when possible or else cheerfully imagines herself sharing—with "vicarious pleasure"—in the prosperous surroundings.

One day as Esther is traveling this road, however, she has a disturbing experience, a lasting digression in the fable that is Wilshire Boulevard: "It was on one of these Wednesday trips that Esther committed a grave sin of omission which caused her later to burst into tears and which caused her acute discomfort for a long time afterwards whenever something reminded her of it" (WB, 34). What did Esther omit? The story's plot can be summarized briefly: a loud (presumably white) man gets on the bus, followed eventually by a Chinese couple, whom the man then proceeds to harass as Esther mutely sits by. When Esther finally reaches her husband's room in the hospital, she is so upset that she bursts into tears. Esther's "acute discomfort" may at first seem attributable to her failure to defend the Chinese couple. Yet on closer scrutiny, Esther's "grave sin of omission" describes not her failure to aid her fellow Orientals, so much as her inability to understand and to articulate why she failed to do so.

Esther begins her ride on the Wilshire bus that day feeling well disposed toward her fellow riders. When a man boards the bus, joking noisily with the driver, Esther is "somewhat amused" (WB, 34). She classifies him as an extrovert ("a somatotonic") and promptly disregards him—"she returned to looking out the window," no doubt resuming her vicarious pleasure in the scenes along the boulevard. When at the next stop, "an elderly Oriental man and his wife" climb on board, feelings of racial fellowship stir in Esther as she turns her head "to smile a greeting (well, here we are, Orientals together on a bus)" (WB, 35). But the woman, whom Esther presumes is Chinese, does not notice Esther's greeting. At this point, the somatotonic begins to speak in a loud voice, maligning the character of a famous athlete. "[H]e seemed to be addressing his seat companion," the narrator observes, "but this person was not heard to give a single answer" (WB, 35). The substance of the loud man's remarks is that an athlete who owns a good share of "the shining buildings" along the street is an exceedingly stingy man. Esther decides that the loud man must be drunk, but she nonetheless finds herself listening "with interest, wondering how much of this diatribe was true, because the public legend about the famous man was emphatic about his charity" (WB, 35). Fascinated that appearances might be so deceiving, Esther enjoys a quiet moral victory; the athlete who owns much property along the very street that she so admires is apparently not a paragon of virtue after all—his wealth and fame do not exempt him from a debasing moral weakness that is beneath even average, bus-riding citizens such as Esther and the loud man. The athlete now appears to have no superior moral claim to his holdings along the bus route. Esther's quiet identification with the loud man allows her to think favorably of herself in comparison to this American athletic hero, to see herself equally worthy of laying claim to the boulevard. Happily assimilated, Esther identifies with all her fellow passengers, regardless of race. Suddenly, the Chinese woman, who has taken a seat next to Esther in the front row, turns to see who is so loud, and the loud man, noticing her action, begins to accost her with racial slurs.

Like Esther, the loud man takes similar pleasure in self-approbation, though more overtly expressing his feelings of belonging as feelings of ownership. His harassment of the Chinese woman consists of denying the woman her right to share his space: "[w]hy don't you get off this bus, why don't you go back where you came from? Why don't you back to China?" He really begins to enjoy himself as he imagines the Chinese woman in environs quite different from those of the boulevard:

> Then, his voice growing jovial, as though he were certain of the support of the bus in this at least, he embroidered on this theme with a new eloquence, "Why don't you go back to China, where you can be coolies working in your bare feet out in the rice fields? You can let your pigtails grow and grow in China. Alla samee, mama, no tickee no shirtee. Ha, pretty good, no tickee no shirtee!"
>
> He chortled with delight and seemed to be looking around the bus for approval. (WB, 35–36)

Twice we are told that the man acts with what he thinks is the approbation of his fellow passengers; he acts "as though he were certain of the support of the bus" and then "seemed to be looking around the bus for approval." He expects his fellow passengers to identify with him, to affirm his feelings of superiority and entitlement—his belief that he belongs on the boulevard, whereas the Chinese woman does not. To disassociate her from the elegant prospects along the street, he taunts her with images of stereotypical Chinese backwardness: "you can be coolies working in your bare feet out in the rice fields." His delighted repetition of "no tickee no shirtee" mocks the attempts of Chinese immigrants (stereotypically imagined as laundry operators) to own property; what they hold (the shirt) does not belong to them, of course, for it already belongs to someone else. Throughout this humiliating harangue, the Chinese woman shows no readable reaction.

Esther, at this point, diligently ignores the incident, "pretending to look out the window." She can only "pretend" to look because her vicarious pleasure in the fabulous street has been wholly eclipsed by the happenings on the bus. The loud man's sudden, aggressive reminders of racial difference, prejudice, and unassimilability abruptly suspend her imaginative participation in the mainstream American culture represented by Wilshire Boulevard. And yet her feelings toward the event are ambivalent:

Esther herself, while believing herself properly annoyed with the speaker and sorry for the old couple, felt quite detached. She found herself wondering whether the man meant her in his exclusion order or whether she was identifiably Japanese. Of course, he was not sober enough to be interested in such fine distinctions, but it did not matter, she decided, because she was Japanese, not Chinese, and therefore in the present case immune. Then she was startled to realize that what she was actually doing was gloating over the fact that the drunken man had specified the Chinese as the unwanted. (WB, 36)

Although convinced that she is "properly annoyed with the speaker and sorry for the old couple," Esther's initial feelings of fellowship ("well, here we are, Orientals together on a bus") have been replaced with detachment and speculation as to whether she is "identifiably Japanese." Ready to follow the loud man's lead in essentializing racial identities—the very practice that led to her own internment during the war—Esther holds firmly to her sense of Japaneseness on the presumption that the man's "exclusion order" targets only the old couple: "she was Japanese, not Chinese, and therefore in the present case immune." The Chinese may be "alla samee," but the Japanese are not like them. Esther's realization that she is gloating over this unstable fiction needles her conscience, and her moral complacency begins to fade as she remembers, though perhaps not clearly or fully, her own buried feelings toward the racial prejudice she recently suffered—feelings of anger and hostility that she is able to direct only against fellow Orientals.

> Briefly, there bobbled on her memory the face of an elderly Oriental man whom she had once seen from a streetcar on her way home from work. (This was not long after she had returned to Los Angeles from the concentration camp in Arkansas and been lucky enough to get a clerical job with the Community Chest.) The old man was on a concrete island at Seventh and Broadway, waiting for his streetcar. She had looked down on him benignly as a fellow Oriental, from her seat by the window, then been suddenly thrown for a loop by the legend on a large lapel button on his jacket. *I AM KOREAN,* said the button.
> Heat suddenly rising to her throat, she had felt angry, then desolate and betrayed. (WB, 36)

Yamamoto's introduction of a Korean man here ingeniously frustrates expectations for an *"I AM CHINESE"* button, denying readers the opportunity to fall into a simplistic, binary understanding of identity. The Korean man, whom Esther at first looks upon "benignly as a fellow Oriental," becomes the focus for all her suppressed feelings of anger, desolation, and betrayal—feelings brought about by her treatment during the war. The narrative relates her internment in fairly neutral, even cheerful terms (she was "lucky enough" to get a job upon her return),[14] and does so only parenthetically. The parentheses—bracketing off the mention of Esther's camp experience[15]—underscore the suppressed, not fully recognized relation of the internment experience to what the rest of the passage describes: Esther's feelings toward the Korean man. Her resentment toward him seems to stem in part from the fact that she went to camp and he did not, but her exact feelings remain unclear. Does she blame him for waiting on an island, for trying to distinguish himself from Japanese people like her, for divorcing himself from her identity and thus abandoning—*betraying*—"a fellow Oriental"? Not quite, because "reason" returns shortly "to ask whether she might not, under the circumstances, have worn such a button herself" (WB, 36). Yet her anger does flare, and she wishes for "an *I AM JAPANESE* button, just to be able to call the man's attention to it, 'Look at me!'" (WB, 36). Ready at that moment to put herself in a window—to advertise her racial difference and exclusive identity—Esther immediately chastens herself by contemplating a list of circumstances that would mitigate the Korean man's offense: "perhaps he didn't even read English, perhaps he had been actually threatened, perhaps it was not his doing—his solicitous children perhaps had urged him to wear the badge" (WB, 36–37). Racial and ethnic identifications take on meaning only within specific contexts, Esther reasons, so perhaps this badge does not mean what it

14. Esther's ostensibly cheerful attitude toward the internment may be read as yet another sign of her desire to assimilate. To mainstream America, it was not unthinkable that the internees could delight in their new surroundings. *Life* describes the relocation as "spontaneous and cheerful," reassuring readers that the "reception center in which the internees found themselves proved a scenic spot of lonely loveliness. The Japs gasped when they saw Mt. Whitney, highest peak in the U.S., shrugging its white shoulder above lesser ranges just 15 miles away" (1942c, 15).

15. Yamamoto has at times referred to her own strong, suppressed feelings toward the camp experience: "Any extensive literary treatment of the Japanese in this country would be incomplete without some acknowledgment of the camp experience. . . . It is an episode in our collective life which wounded us more painfully than we realize. I didn't know myself what a lump it was in my subconscious until a few years ago when I watched one of the earlier television documentaries on the subject, narrated by the mellow voice of Walter Cronkite. To my surprise, I found the tears trickling down my cheeks and my voice squeaking out of control, as I tried to explain to my amazed husband and children why I was weeping" (qtd. in Cheung 1988, xi–xxv, xiii).

appears to mean. Perhaps the Korean man was not really identifying with white America in approval of Esther's own exclusion.[16]

Having thus recalled how pained she had felt at considering that "a fellow Oriental" would purposefully detach himself from her in a time of need, Esther turns to the Chinese woman sitting beside her and attempts "to make up for her moral shabbiness" (WB, 37). Esther smiles,

> shaking her head a little to get across her message (don't pay any attention to that stupid old drunk, he doesn't know what he's saying, let's take things like this in our stride). But the woman, in turn looking at her, presented such a face, so impassive yet cold, and eyes so expressionless yet hostile, that Esther's overture fell quite flat. Okay, okay, if that's the way you feel about it, she thought to herself. (WB, 37)

Esther's feelings of sympathy, moral generosity, and Oriental benevolence come to a chilly halt when the Chinese woman's cold and hostile eyes reject her overtures as effectively as would any "*I AM CHINESE*" button. Esther learns from her own reactions, as well as from those of the Korean man and Chinese woman, that Oriental solidarity, even when confronted by white hostility, cannot be presumed or relied on. Racial identifications, like the "*I AM*" buttons, affirm one Asian identity only in order to reject another.

Yet the ambivalence of identity and identification on the Wilshire bus is not limited only to Orientals. Caucasians also occupy perplexing and shifting roles. Esther's smile is not the first such overture to be sent in the Chinese woman's direction. Earlier, "a mild-looking man with thinning hair and glasses" had been "smiling at the woman and shaking his head mournfully in sympathy" (WB, 36), though, as was the case with Esther's initial "well, here we are smile," the woman had appeared not to notice. After the loud man's departure, the mild-looking man "stood up to go and made a clumsy speech to the Chinese couple and possibly to Esther":

> "I want you to know," he said, "that we aren't all like that man. We don't all feel the way he does. We believe in an America that is a melting pot of all sorts of people. I'm originally Scotch and French myself." With that, he came over and shook the hand of the Chinese man.

16. The meanings of the "I AM KOREAN" badge were even more politically complicated than Esther seems to suppose. Because Japan was occupying Korea at the outbreak of World War II, the U.S. government classified Koreans as subjects of Japan and sometimes required them to wear the identificatory badges (Takaki 1979, 363–67).

"And you, young lady," he said to the girl behind Esther, "you deserve a Purple Heart or something for having to put up with that man sitting beside you." (WB, 37).

Racial identities and sympathetic identifications once again become clouded in this awkward overture. The object of the mild-looking man's sympathies is the Chinese couple, and "possibly . . . Esther." Neither Esther nor the narrator can presume to know how specific the mild-looking man is, whether he recognizes Esther as "identifiably Japanese." He, on the other hand, shows great concern at the possibility that he might be mistakenly identified with the (white) drunk: "I want you to know . . . that we aren't all like that man." White people have their differences too, he apologizes: "I'm originally Scotch and French myself." A Scotch and French mixture in the "melting pot" hardly seems to require much melting, but perhaps to the mild-looking man (who possibly includes Esther in his apology), a Chinese and Japanese melting pot would require as little, or even less, melting. Then, as if to demonstrate the spirit of the melting pot, the mild man glibly subsumes the recent racist digression under the more general offense of boorish behavior: "And you, young lady," he says to the (racially unspecified and so presumably white) girl who had been the drunken man's seatmate, "you deserve a Purple Heart or something for having to put up with that man sitting beside you." Unfortunately, his forced gaiety, commending the girl's heroic sacrifice in the unified struggle of the well-behaved against the boorish, falls short if meant also to include Esther, for it only reemphasizes racial difference. Esther's husband, Buro, whom she travels to visit in the veterans' hospital, deserves "a Purple Heart or something" in reality, not just in metaphor. Yet this medal, which the mild man can automatically associate with virtue and heroism, may hold a much more conflicted, perhaps even reproachful meaning for Buro. As Roger Daniels has shown, the decision to enlist or resist was the source of much acrimonious feeling among interned Japanese Americans (1988, 257). For Buro, potentially, and certainly for both Esther and the mild-looking man, racial identifications and meanings—though alarming in their clarity—are even more disconcerting in their ambiguity.

The Chinese woman's impassivity underscores this ambiguity. How does the Chinese woman feel? Her sentiments remain largely unreadable throughout the story. One might infer that she is angry at and pained by the humiliating scene in which she finds herself. In the suppressed quality of her reactions, the Chinese woman most resembles Esther, who feels resentments keenly but quickly buries them. Throughout the loud man's insults, Esther "felt the tenseness in the body of the woman beside her. The only movement from her was the trembling of the chrysanthemums with the motion of the bus" (WB, 36). The "tenseness" Esther perceives suggests barely controlled anger, a reading at first supported by the trembling of the flowers but then immediately undercut by the mention of the bus motion. If the bus motion causes the trembling, perhaps the Chinese woman is not so angry after all. In fact, her responses could be understood without reference to the racial politics on the bus. There is no overt sign that the Chinese woman snubs Esther because of Esther's Japaneseness; the Chinese woman also ignores the mild-looking white man's sympathetic smile and shows no response to his clumsy speech. Possibly, as in the scenarios Esther imagines for the Korean man, the Chinese woman may not even understand the racialized meanings surrounding her; the Chinese woman's anxious concern about her husband's "faint English," which he had to repeat "several times before the driver could answer" (WB, 35), suggests her limited familiarity with the language. The loud man's remarks, whether about the sports star or about the undesirability of the Chinese, may have been unintelligible to the Chinese woman—all of it just obnoxiously loud talk on a bus. The Chinese woman's discomfort, in other words, may have been no greater than that of the loud man's (presumably white) seat companion. Racial identity, from the Chinese woman's point of view, may play no part in the unpleasant incident. Esther and the mild-looking man are perhaps sympathizing with feelings that the Chinese woman is not experiencing. If so, the proper objects of sympathy should be Esther (only "possibly" included in the mild-looking man's speech) and the mild-looking man himself, for both are bothered by this incident of prejudice, though neither is its direct target.

The confusing and mortifying events of the Wilshire bus ride shake Esther's faith in assimilation, replacing her equanimity and optimism with panic and despair at her inability to identify the sympathies of those around her. Is betrayal so pervasive after all? Can it hide so easily, like stinginess in an athlete famed for his generosity? Esther remains after the mild-looking man has departed, but the nature of the bus ride for her has altered drastically:

The rest of the ride was uneventful and Esther stared out the window with eyes that did not see. Getting off at last at the soldiers' home, she was aware of the Chinese couple getting off after her, but she avoided looking at them. Then, while she was walking towards Buro's hospital very quickly, there arose in her mind some words she had once read and let stick in her craw: People say, do not regard what he says, now he is in liquor. Perhaps it is the only time he ought to be regarded.

These words repeated themselves until her saving detachment was gone every bit and she was filled once again in her life with the infuriatingly helpless, insidiously sickening sensation of there being in the world nothing solid she could put her finger on, nothing solid she could come to grips with, nothing solid she could sink her teeth into, nothing solid. (WB, 37)

With racial and ethnic division now effectively—albeit confusingly—reinscribed, Esther can no longer enjoy her imaginative participation in Wilshire Boulevard; she can only stare out the window with eyes that do not see, her utter alienation from the Chinese couple expressed by her refusal to look at them as she leaves the bus. As Esther contemplates what has just occurred, she reacts in the same way as she had when confronted by the badge-wearing Korean man. She tries to dismiss the signs of racial hatred (the loud man's remarks) as not meaning what they appear to mean: "do not regard what he says, now he is in liquor." Extraordinary circumstances, such as drunkenness or war, must excuse other people's behavior. Immediately, however, another reading overwhelms Esther: "Perhaps it is the only time he ought to be regarded." As these words repeat in her mind, Esther's "saving detachment" from racism dissolves. Recognizing her reasonings to be rationalizations, she finds herself "filled once again in her life" with a sickening and helpless inability to identify ("put her finger on"), understand ("come to grips with"), and combat ("sink her teeth into") an enemy consisting of "nothing solid."

But why "once again"? In Stan Yogi's terms, the "buried plot" (1989, 170) here is that of Esther's internment experience—her pain, humiliation, and desolation at being specified as the unwanted during that digression on the road to assimilation. Normally firmly and cheerily suppressed, these feelings return with a vengeance as Esther tries to make sense of the incident on the bus. There is "nothing solid" in the world, nothing and no one to blame directly for her anguish, but most horrifyingly, nothing to distinguish even herself from the very people she might want to blame.

"[W]e aren't all like that man," the mild-looking man had pleaded, and Esther had wished to proclaim that not all Orientals are alike either, *"I AM JAPANESE . . .* 'Look at me!'" (WB, 36–37). The helpless sensation, however, is Esther's frustrating recognition that prejudice calls forth prejudice, and that corrective declarations of difference—"we aren't all like that," *"I AM KOREAN," "I AM JAPANESE . . .* 'Look at me!'"—are the problem before they are the solution.

Unlike *Fifth Chinese Daughter,* Yamamoto's story is not a progressive narrative of self-liberation through individual expression. It attends instead to the digressions. Self-identifications in "Wilshire Bus" are neither original nor empowering; at best they appear clumsy ("I'm originally Scotch and French myself"), at worst deliberately hurtful (*"I AM JAPANESE . . .* 'Look at me!'"). In general, they are clichéd, recycled, almost parodic: "I AM KOREAN," "I AM CHINESE," "I AM JAPANESE," "I'm originally Scotch and French myself." Esther's revelation on the Wilshire bus does not allow her to affirm herself, nor does it inspire her to conduct herself with new moral resolve. Instead, she runs to Buro's room and bursts into uncontrollable tears: "Buro was amazed because it was hardly her first visit and she had never shown such weakness before, but solving the mystery handily, he patted her head, looked around smugly at his roommates, and asked tenderly, 'What's the matter? You've been missing me a whole lot, huh?' And she, finally drying her eyes, sniffed and nodded and bravely smiled and answered him with the question, yes, weren't women silly?" (WB, 38). Esther clings to her old ways. Unwilling to embarrass Buro in front of his roommates, she once again buries her feelings and acquiesces to an identity imposed on her (lovesick woman). Esther experiences no liberation. Yet her decision to protect the solidity of Buro's world by dismissing her own experience as a digression scarcely worth mentioning cannot be regarded as entirely weak, wrong, or morally shabby. Identity politics in "Wilshire Bus" are not simple, and racism is not merely an outrageous obstacle to be overcome handily by indignant protagonists. Rather, the story attends to the complexity of racism and to the ambivalence of identity.

What then was Esther's "grave sin of omission"? Was it her failure to defend the Chinese woman in a loud and public way, to show stronger support for her—something more than just a sympathetic smile—despite the woman's apparent hostility? Was it her failure to speak honestly about the incident within the new social context of Buro's hospital room, her willingness to compound the offense by trivializing her reaction to it as mere female silliness? Was it her failure to remember and express, even to herself, her anger about the camps and her inability to do anything about this anger or its cause? Or was it just a euphemism for her own feelings of guilt and complicity in the racism that occurred that day on the bus? With nothing solid to secure Esther's identity, integrity, and moral universe, the story offers no definitive answer.

By placing *Fifth Chinese Daughter* and "Wilshire Bus" within their common historical context, the differences between their representational strategies become more meaningful. Both texts respond to a moment in history that forced Asian Americans to reconsider their relation to white Americans and to one another—to rethink the significance of race. *Fifth Chinese Daughter* does so by working within mainstream notions of "Chinese" and "American" culture, spotlighting those aspects of Jade Snow Wong that consolidate her identity as an expressive, unique, Chinese American. "Wilshire Bus," by contrast, focuses on the ways in which fictions of identity and integrity can easily crumble, leaving individuals feeling helpless yet culpable in a world in which nothing is solid. This striking contrast between Jade Snow Wong's exuberant individualism and Esther Kuroiwa's fragile balance may perhaps speak as much to Wong's and Yamamoto's differing temperaments as to the differences in the Chinese American and the Japanese American experiences of the war. Yet why has *Fifth Chinese Daughter* received so much recent negative critical attention, whereas "Wilshire Bus"—similar to it both in subject and in context—has gone virtually unremarked? The answer to this question, I suspect, lies in the kind of heterogeneity that "Wilshire Bus" brings with it as it undermines and complicates notions of personal integrity, heroic action, and political agency—the very concepts that, in simplified form, have fueled the debate over *Fifth Chinese Daughter*. Jade Snow Wong's autobiography may be "rather pathetic," but in a politically useful way. By creating dichotomies, *Fifth Chinese Daughter* and its critics force people to take action by compelling them to take sides. "Wilshire Bus" does not. Rather, it questions the very process of identifying such sides, while at the same time acknowledging the helplessness inherent in denying these identifications. One might say that "Wilshire Bus" describes the reasons for its own critical obscurity.

Passenger Side

Ted Wilson

It is the passenger side
                              of me
that makes me write
It is   the passenger side   of me
that   makes me write

That side   that is driven
by the racecar   race car   race—car
driving saxophonic musiccrazed
avante garde chauffeur who is
always in control   never
out of control

From sunup to sundown the interpretation
has been stated and restated
it's all be-bop   new old avante or
antique

Prayer is prayer   no matter how you
cut it   publicly   it is orating to
your friends   privately   true praying is
what is spoken between man and his creator

We've heard it all said before
musically ˙ on canvass   in a photo   poem
play or some other written oral
whatchamacallit   it's there

You see   we came here from Goree
but we left Goree for another planet
can you get to that   follow me closely
somewhere closer to the sun
when we got a word from Brother LeRoi
not a note but a space   carrying a coded
message

Contrary to popular opinion
and the ranking status of the learn ed
given a select few   we now know
indisputably   there is life on Mars
and those living organisms are not
by any stretch of the imagination called
martians   no more so than
People on earth calling themselves
earthlings or earthisms
even tho'   all systems of any note
presently are described as one ism or
another   albiet most die from some type of
orgasm in mickey d's or the like trying
to go to the toilet and it ain't happening
——coroner's report   death caused by a
catharsis of the bowels from a build up of
calcified pizza   smokey's bar-b-q
cuchifritos   fried chicken   cream cheese
and lox on a bagel with an egg roll

Additionally   that is   internationally if we
were to use   our supersonic electro-
magnetic laser penetrating futuristic
eavesdropping system and connect it to our
multinational   that is   universe wide
speakers   commonly called audio cable
we would not hear any such sounds imagined
as spee spee sppeee spee shwee schweee schwee
or other ant-like noises out of hollywood

sound lavatories   I mean laboratories
same crap   What we would hear is:
"am i blue   what am i going to do
cause you make my heart stand still   just
for a thrill"——WHIP WHAM   BING BAM
UP AGAINST THE WALL MF   THIS IS A STICKUP
i don't care if you are part of the war
resister's   league   whatever that is
this is mars and we don't deal in
candy bars   sugar will kill you
pull down your pants   bend over and show
us your true colors   no this is not a code
red the planet is red according to an
earthly definition of color   but that's
another story   it's red because it's hot
like the music in the east not like the
cool easy listening west coast CD 101.9
so assinine   didn't you know we sent
that is   created buddy bolden   kid ory
fats navarro satchmo and the rest   do you
think jimi hendrix thought all of that up
by himself   why would some one come to
earth with a name like yardbird who could
play and create be-bop unless he was sent
tensed for being off beat   i repeat and
what about monk do you think his parents
gave him that name because he had
at most SPHERE rounding midnite changes mysteriosely
then there was ALBERT AYLER and his
wailing dirges if that ain't celestial
your word i don't know   correction
you don't stand a ghost of a chance of
realizing survival
remember SUN RA he couldn't make it
any plainer   *space is the place   space is the place*
goin to chicago sorry but i

can't take you
anyway   you have been found guilty of
earthlike behavior and now you will be
inoculated with   the thing
which will eliminate your ability to enjoy
or enjoin the company of your peers while
observing the backwardness of civilized
earth behavior and you will not be able to
dig anything but Patrick Boone music from
the russian ozarks as you stand on the
corner the coroner with no place to
be somebody screaming   I AM SOME BODY   i
may only be a man or three fifths
whatever that is   the red planet being
too hot for you to handle because the only
place of any appreciable pigmentation will be
on your rear identifying you as not
totally alien but exiled for the duration
of your senseless aberation   can you get
to that   if you can't
grits are groceries and you know the rest—-
later on homes.

Meanwhile back on earth an old man sits on
the dock of the bay grinning
as the words slowly rise
smiling faces smiling faces tell lies
they don't tell the truth

RIDDLE: is this otis redding
                richard nixon
                ronald reagan boris
                yeltsin george bush
                manuel noriega
                bill clinton or all of the above

Answer: NONE OF THE ABOVE
      this a conversation between
      amiri baraka and sekou sundiata
      looking eastward up at the sky
      after larry neal made an
      appearance and hipped them to the
      real deal
      so now you see this is serious—
      be bop is was and will always
      *ACHE`

*Ache` means power in Youruba

Literary Blues and the Sacred Text

Arthur Flowers

I am Flowers of the delta clan Flowers and the line of O. Killens. Call myself a literary bluesman.

Old Robert Johnson say he went to the Crossroads and sold his soul to the Devil. This has been a consistent trope of the blues. Old school bluesmen claim that if you go to the Crossroads at midnight the Devil tune your guitar for you and cause you to be a great bluesman. The Crossroads an important part of Congo, Yoruba, and Fon theology. Where the mundane and the sacred meet. This world and the spiritworld. Where one crosses over. Moves through.

Officially repressed, Crossroads theology survived in southern mythology and folk knowledge and was recorded by the blues, a griotic code serving an illiterate people in danger of losing their souls. A cultural custodianship championing cultural imperatives pertinent to our survival under actively hostile conditions. A riff on Legba—as they call the trickster round these parts.

Old Legba, the Fon God of the Crossroads, pretty much the only African deity that made the trip across the Atlantic and survived the severe repression inflicted on African culture in the United States. The Western worldview translated the mischievous old Messenger as the Devil and that interp entered African American hoodoo folklore. Since the beginning, African cultural retentions been considered "bad." Since the beginning the African aspect of the uniquely Afroam voice has had to struggle to be heard.

There are, though, those of us in Afroam lit who feel that we are heirs to two literary traditions, the Western written tradition and the African (/American) oral tradition, and hope in the fusion to contribute to the evolution of both.

From Clarence Major *(Dirty Bird Blues)*, Gayl Jones *(Corrigedora/The*

Healing), Ishmael Reed *(Mumbo Jumbo),* and Alice Walker *(The Color Purple)* to the works of August Wilson, John Edgar Wideman, and Toni Morrison, some of the most important and innovative voices in African American fiction have done works with bluesbased characters, narratives, metaphysics, and sensibilities.

These writers have chosen bluesbased works as a more authentic expression of the African American literary sensibility and their own evolving artistic vision. They are consciously attempting to forge a uniquely African American narrative language based on the oral tradition and its musical notes, such as blues, jazz, and hiphop. They are attempting to litericize African American folk language and enhance its functionality as an instrument of emotional/cultural/literary expression and 21st century thought and development.

Consciously operating as cultural custodians attempting to develop a heightened narrative language that serves as both a literary and sacred language, as both text (personal and cultural expression) and Text (cultural guidance). Forging a narrative instrument worthy of 21st century nuance, an instrument of literary, political, and spiritual redemption. An attempt to ensure the 21st century viability of African American culture.

August Wilson recounts what he considers his moment of artistic revelation, when in the fall of 1965 he put on an old 78 rpm, "Nobody in Town Can Bake a Sweet Jellyroll Like Mine" by Bessie Smith, and says it was a "resurrection and a redemption," says the "universe stuttered and everything fell into a new place," says it was

> the beginning of my consciousness that I was representative of a culture and the carrier of some very valuable antecedents. . . . I saw the blues as a cultural response of a nonliterate people whose history and culture were rooted in the oral tradition. The response was to a world that was not of their making, in which the idea of themselves as a people of imminent worth that belied their recent history was constantly assaulted. It was a world that did not recognize their gods, their manners, their mores. It despised their ethos and refused to even recognize their humanity. In such an environment the blues was a flag bearer of definition . . . a spiritual conduit that gave spontaneous expression to the spirit that was locked in combat and devising new strategies for engaging life and enlarging itself. It was a true and articulate literature that was in the forefront of the development of both character and consciousness. I turned my ear, my heart and whatever analytical tools I possessed to embrace this world. I elevated it, rightly or wrongly, to biblical status. (1998, 564–65)

Based as much on music and oral tradition as on conventional literary forms, bluesbased fusionwork is a uniquely African American literary form befitting artists of an often conflicting dual heritage and sensibility. It is an organic conflict reflected in Chestnutt's halfformal halfdialect narratives, in the dispute between Zora Neale and Rich Wright over what he considered her minstrelsy, and in today's distance between "serious" literary works tending to a more African American narrative form and a growing body of more commercial works tending to conventional narrations and "proper" English.

"I was after all a bluesman," says August Wilson, "Never mind I couldn't play a guitar or carry a tune in a bucket. I was cut out of the same cloth" (1998, 566).

Afroam literary language differs from mere dialect work. Dialect work doesn't try to take the language somewhere else. Dialect work accepts limitation. Folk literary works like Toomer's *Cane*, Hurston's *Eyes*, Brown's *Road* tried to expand the boundaries of the language. As do contemporary works by folks like Jones, Wideman, and Morrison.

Its more than phonetic spelling. We talking phraseology here.

And something even deeper, searching for that little extra something that defines black literature and black art as fundamentally as it defines black music. Stuff like audience participation, orality, and functionality. Stuff like Magic.

What Toni Morrison refers to in "Rootedness" after explaining how she uses the earth as an afrocentric chorus responding to the action in *Tar Baby*:

> Those are ways in which I try to incorporate, into that traditional genre the novel, unorthodox novelistic characteristics—so that it is, in my view, Black, because it uses the characteristics of Black art. . . . I don't regard Black literature as simply books written by Black people, or simply as literature written about Black people, or simply as literature that uses a certain mode of language in which you just sort of drop g's. There is something very special and very identifiable about it and it is my struggle to find that elusive but identifiable style in my books. (1984, 343–44)

In addition to old faithfuls like Repetition and Call and Response, African American lit exploring narrative experiments like Incantation. Clarence Major does it in *Dirty Bird Blues*. Does it good. Real good. Gayl Jones call her redemption novel *The Healing*. In *The Healing* the bluesbased narration of *Corrigedora* has evolved into a mature and smoothly distinctive African American narrative form more fully reflecting the path she laid out in *Liberating Voices*.

The rather prosaic fundamental 3 line blueswork of *Corrigedora*

"I don't want a kind of woman that hurt you" he said.
"Then you don't want me."
"I don't want a kind of woman that hurt you."
"Then you don't want me."
"I don't want a kind of woman that hurt you."
"Then you don't want me." (Jones 1986, 185)

become the mature flexible bluesreps of *The Healing*. By extracting the quotation marks that distinguish dialogue from narration, Jones uses the resulting ambiguity with repetition and folkwork to preach without violating the demands of effective fictional narration.

"She really do some powerful healing, though. And she ain't a root doctor neither. She don't need no root to heal. Some people say that that is a superior form of healing when you don't need no root to heal. When you just healing people by knowing that they is healed" (Jones 1996, 15).

Because the narration is dialogue as narration—a told tale—once established the incantatory ambiguity works just as well to tame the overtly sacred: "I didn't even ask for the spirit gift, I begin softly. I wasn't prepared for the spirit gift. But it came, it came. I modulated my volume so my voice grow gradually loud. It came. The Lord good. Yes. What can you do but claim what the good Lord give" (Jones 1996, 33).

As it does to illuminate the mundane through the accretion of incantatory narrative power. "Now that's the truth. That the truth. You can tell all the turtle stories you want to tell but that's the truth" (Jones 1996, 135).

It was Beth Rosenberg, a student of mine, drew my attention to a significant effect Gayl Jones gets with incantatory narrative strategies: Gayl Jones narration—truly of the mind—depicts an extreme interiority. She practically transubstantiates the narrator; the distance between writer and reader is blurry.

Narrative form develops in order to allow a writer to express what has to be said. Form follows necessity and style is the personal mark of the artist. The struggle to find voice. The struggle to be heard. The fundamental struggle of any writer—to express your artistic vision as truly as humanly possible.

In *The Autobiography of LeRoi Jones,* Amiri say he had to dig deep and move through to write *The System of Dante's Hell:*

> I consciously wrote as deeply into my psyche as I could . . . tearing away the readymade, that imitating Creely (or Olson) provided. So I scrambled and roamed, sometimes blindly in my consciousness to come up with something more essential, more rooted in my deepest experience, I thought of music, I thought of myself as an improvising soloist . . . hacking deeper and deeper . . . until at the end of the piece I had come, found, my own voice or something beginning to approximate it. (Baraka 1998, 349)

African American writers have always had to be two-headed folk.

From the beginning of our sojourn in the West, assimilation of blacks in America has been predicated on devaluing their African nature and socializing them as submissive inferiors. Consequently "slavery" and "resistance to assimilation" were the big issues confronting the first African Americans and the literature that began to speak for them. This tension was reflected in the Slave Narratives and the First Works of Wheatley, Harmon, Horton, et al. Most First Works folk were published because what they wrote was comfortable to the powers that be. Even so, they generally signified to the best of their ability and inclination. This conflict been a pretty consistent condition in African American literature.

Although the early Afroam literary folk had to learn how to work within European formats, the folk tradition retained the African sensibility and afrospiritual practice thrived at the Crossroads. Reflecting our ongoing cultural tension between assimilation and selfexpression.

Caught in the double consciousness identified back in the day by DuBois. Bilingual and Biconscious. A two-headed conjure culture looking front and back. Samesame African American writers. Since the beginning been talking to two audiences, our folk and other folk. Problem is generally been other folk who decide whats real literature. Which has generally meant most classically correct. Anybody want to explore a more colored style was marginalized and unpaid. Or like Dunbar, one of the earliest voices subjected to the bipolar tension, only allowed to sing and dialect when what he really felt he had to say was that "The measure of our songs is our desires / we tinkle where old poets use to storm / we lack their substance tho' we keep their form / we strum our banjo-strings and call them lyres" (Dunbar 1962, 189).

Chestnutt felt like he had to show he could handle the conventional before he worked the dialect. In *The Negro Artist and the Racial Mountain,* Langston signified on Countee Cullen for his still classic "I'm just a writer not a black writer" bit, and when Toomer turned his back on the culture that gave him Cane, he lost his power, and Legba took away his voice.

Afroam literary writers and thinkers eventually make a conscious decision. If I devote my work, my lifework to the tradition and accept the marginalization, will it be worth it in the long run. I look at folk like DuBois, and I see where he could have been a straight up scholar specializing in Homer or something. You ask yourself, Do I really believe that black culture is a culture with a contribution to the human mosaic worthy of any other? Is it worth my time? My life? My work?

Those of us in Afroam lit who consider ourselves trained cultural custodians and masters of Nommo—a Dogon dogstar word, the ability to use the magic of words to forge reality—have consciously decided to contribute our lifeworks to the viability of that culture and to defend it against those who would destroy or cripple it. Within or without. To ensure that our culture will not disappear. That we are not erased as a people.

Language is the voice of a culture. The expression of its soul. To the extent that black English, "Ebonics" if I may be so bold, is functionally limited to that extent is our culture limited. To litericize the vernacular, to raise the folkloric language to literary language, is to give it more complexity and expand its functionality. The more viable we can make Afroam organic language, the more useful it is as an instrument of 21st century thought and development, the more liable our culture to survive the culture wars.

Not only our survival as a people and culture, but our evolution, our illumination, our prosperity—our Destiny. Our understanding is that strong works contribute to a strong culture. That strong works are healing spells and committed writers are a manifestation of the African American survival instinct.

As the folk language evolves as a viable instrument, it begins to travel. Do more duty. From early Black Arts Movement efforts like Sarah Fabio's "Tripping with Black Writing" in which she in 1971 has a particularly prophetic riff particularly dear to my own heart, "Killens. Killens' chilluns. On their jobs. Taking care of business. 'Deniggerizing' the world" (Fabio 1994, 228). To Craig Werner's piece on August Wilson's *Bluespoetic* in his book *Playing the Changes*—an otherwise conventional work in which he segues from the thick language necessary for academic respect (what Audre

Lorde called "the masters tools") to an attempt to reflect the African American literary dynamic on which he comments.

Down in the Delta the blues are a metaphysic. They are a Way. Redemption songs. Lotta folks don't really understand the blues. Think the blues about feeling bad. Au contrary. The blues about getting through the blues. About getting through life. Through trial and tribulation and the transformation of adversity into strength. The blues about finessing the hardtimes and celebrating the goodones. About living a life of harmonic grace and maintaining and nurturing the culture.

Blueswork encompasses the finesse of tribulation through personal and social transformation—the redemption component that drives Afroam culture at its best. A griotic format that maintained the culture through the lean years, it was the blues called from the beginning racemusic. It was the blues that carried the culture when it was against the law for black folk to read and write. It was the blues talking about rambling when most black folk was slavetied to their sharecrops. It was the blues talking about what couldn't otherwise be said.

Some writer once said when I want to give answers I write essays and when I want to ask questions I write novels.

When I want to move the congregation I sing the blues.

Griot. A French word for various types of African bards. Some folk object to it cause its French. Aint had no problems co-opting otherfolks stuff before. Works for me. Griots were storyteller/historians of African oral culture who kept the collective memory in order to provide communal guidance. Bringing through oral performance the understanding of the past to the issues of the day in order to shape community ethics, behavior, and decisions—the collective destiny. For every occasion the words appropriate to the moment. Words as sacred instruments.

Cultural guidance is a traditional function of literature. Consciously griotic, African American literature is passionately concerned with cultural custodianship. As the voice of a culture that has since its inception felt itself under mortal siege, African American literature is fundamentally shamanistic and vitally concerned with communal health and empowerment. Its most revered figures have all been culturally engaged. Creating the visions without which the people shall perish and serving in its mythic heart its age-old griotic function of keeping the culture alive and viable.

In *Figures in Black,* Gates makes the statement, "It is the black poet who bridges the gap in tradition, who modifies tradition when experience demands it, who translates experience into meaning and meaning into belief" (1989, 176). Course then he goes on to say that African American musicians have more effectively served this function. A shaky but fashionable claim reflecting the insecurity of literary folk before the music.

In *Corrigedora*, the slavemaster burns the records in order to erase the abuse of generations of Corrigedora women, but the women pass the truth on to the bluessinger narrator through the oral tradition in order to keep it alive. "They burned all the documents Ursula . . . like you burn out a wound. Except we got to keep what we need to bear witness" (Jones 1986, 72).

To understand the power of the word is to understand ideological power and the writer as ideological orchestrator.

Marcus Garvey was highly influenced by *Ethiopia Unbound* by Casely Hayford, from which he took, among others, the phrase, "One God! One Aim! One Destiny!" In turn Marcus Garvey influenced thousands and thousands of blackfolks, thereby influencing the historical dynamics of his times and our destiny for the foreseeable future.

This happens to some degree every time a reader (or, even better, another intellectual) is touched by your work. Literature opens minds and passes on ideas. Literature allows folk to see themselves and their lives in a new perspective and opens audiences to new possibilities. What Julie Dash calls "rupturing their reality."

Ideological orchestration: the ongoing efforts of ideologically inclined intellectuals to ensure the competitive viability of their particular ideology. Some works are designed to influence people or public opinion or both whereas longgame works are designed to influence the ideology (culture) you represent. Which will in turn shape more generations.

What we know in our heads, our children will know in their hearts, our generations in their souls.

It was Bob Law during an interview once asked me, How does it feel to be part of the mythopoetic tradition of the Delta? I had to think about it a moment, savor the concept, feels good I told him, feels real good.

I am of the literary hoodoo school of Afroam literature. Mystically inclined writers who have attempted to manifest hoodoo, the indigenous African American spiritual tradition, through their works and lives. It was Chestnutt with *The Conjure Woman* tales first start systematically using hoodoo as literary ground, Zora Neale that most facilitated hoodoo's evolution from a folk tradition to a literary one, and Ishmael "Just because you cant see d stones don't mean im not building" (Reed 1972, 59). Reed transformed hoodoo from a magical system to a functioning 20th century afrocentric ideology.

Literary hoodoo comes out of the griotic and hoodoo tropes in African American literature. In *Conjuring Culture,* Theophus Smith claim that African American culture is a "conjured culture" in which literature as conjuration has been a definitive force. The artist as shaman.

Every book a spell, every draft a divination.

A Sacred Literature: a primary tool of shaping the tribal soul and the tribal destiny. Works that record a culture's spiritual and social wisdom. Its lessons of Life. Its Way. That cultures understanding of the human condition. Its understanding of God and our relationship with God. Passing on its survival knowledge.

Working the tribal soul.

Rootwork:

Working the roots, the soul, the spirit, the essence of things.

The tribal soul—the consciousness of a people. Its group psyche. Its Way. The soul of a people as shaped and reflected in their culture and their literature. Their spiritual traditions. Their music and their art. Their folklore, myths, and legends. The lives its people live. The communities they build. Their way of being.

The black psyche manifested through culture.

The hoodoo premise is that you take care of the tribal soul and everything benefits. We call that Rootwork.

When the tribalsoul is healthy and vigorously evolving, its people live healthy, vigorous lives. Their culture produces works that enlighten the entire human race and become part of the Worldspirit. The hoodoo premise is that the health of the tribalsoul is the root of all blessings. If the cultural soul is healthy, our strategies are healthy, our lifestyles are healthy, our communities are healthy. If the soul is sick, everything else is dysfunctional—our lifestyles, our relationships, our communities, our vision.

African American culture has been as much dysfunctional as it is vibrant. All cultures are simultaneously dynamic and entropic, a constantly fluctuating blend of strengths and weaknesses. Which path shall it be.

Shall we survive and prosper as a people and culture, or shall we decline and wither.

One cares for the tribalsoul by monitoring it through its cultural products, contributing what it needs to balance out its weaknesses and emphasize its strengths. Minimizing the dysfunctional components and emphasizing the transformational. The battles over gangster rap and mercenary literature like *PUSH* are battles for the control of cultural traits. Of our destiny.

In my literary youth I felt that the will to power was the answer to blackfolks problems. I aspired to be a Machiavellian thinker who would forge blackfolks into a conquering horde and fling them into battle. Power was my field of study and people were just factors to be used. This was reflected in my work. One day John Killens pulled me aside and said, "Art, you a brilliant writer but with a little compassion you could be profound."

I didnt get it. "Brilliant" was all I heard. It wasn't until many years later that I realized he was trying to ensure that my artistic contribution to the tradition, my legacy as his student, would not be hard and cold but warm and loving—an old shaman trying to ensure the health of the tribal soul.

"Cast your vision young hoodoo as far as you can see. Determine the challenges the tribe will face. Prepare the tribal soul to meet them" (Rickydoc n.d.).

I claim for hoodoo the prophets way.

In his seminal exploration of "text" through a collage of text, subtext, intra and intertext, Ishmael Reed in *Mumbo Jumbo* challenges the notion of text as written document. Raised the question in my mind of oral (mythology and folklore) text as text and its relationship to text as cultural template.

Many sacred languages, such as the Catholic Church's Latin, are archaic forms of the contemporary language. The folk form of African American language serves it as a dynamic sacred text—a constantly evolving insider language and cultural statement. By the time the mainstream culture translates it, its moved on.

Word up.

Sacred text as a heightened language signifying the mythologic, the sacred, and the luminous.

Sacred text as a cultural template that shapes a cultures evolution and provides a cultural vision. An evolutionary inclination shaped by significant works of art and thought.

Literature as a primary instrument of cultural orchestration and retention, a culture's reflection and expression, its voice. The generations of the future shall base much of their lives on what our generation's literature says about us. We are their history, we are their roots.

Mumbo Jumbo claim that the movement Jes Grew is searching for its text and dies out when it is unable to find it. Unable to be "written down" so to speak. Kinda like W. C. Handy in *The Father of the Blues* talking about how he first really notice the blues waiting on a bus down in Tutwiler Mississippi about 2 o'clock in the morning, say he seen a country boy with a guitar repeating over and over that he going to where the Southern meets the Dog, where the Southern meets the Dog—say a lotta folk down that way had heard the blues, but he was the first one to write them down cause of a habit of "writing down ideas" he had gotten from his father.

In capturing folkthought, you define it. Working the root of the culture. As Zora did with the HighJohn the Conqueror myth. Her mythwork published back in 1943 shaped the tribal conception of HighJohn the Conqueror as archetypic cultural hero. A conjureman who helped blackfolks get out of slavery. A trickster whose spirit resides in the conquerroot to return whenever blackfolk need him. Because she wrote it so it is so.

As I define so shall it be. Be I then worthy of I gift.

Back in the day, slaves risked death and torture to learn how to read and write, instinctively understanding the word to be a magic that would literally free them from bondage. The first thing old Fred Douglass did with his new knowledge was write himself a pass out of Maryland.

According to fellow desperado Keith Gilyard, the primary trope of Afroam lit is and always shall be struggle. The ongoing struggle for survival and empowerment that blackfolks have waged since we came to this land and that has more than anything shaped us as a people.

It seems to move in pendulum swings of engagement and withdrawal. I speculate the generational pendulum bout to swing again and blackfolk bout to get busy. The Struggle is On. And far more complex than ever before. As shall be its literature.

Previous highpoints of African American lit were accompanied by political ferment. The Harlem Renaissance was the voice of the New Negro and the Great Migration that transformed a rural peasantry to an urban 20th century people. The Black Arts/Aesthetic movement was the voice of the Civil Rights movement and that of Black Power, in which black became if not yet truly beautiful at least viable.

The Black Arts movement significantly influenced my literary generation. We are both a continuation of and a reaction to. Its most salient legacy was turning away from primarily addressing white audiences to addressing black audiences and concerns. Houston Baker's study of intellectual generational shifts as call and response explains somewhat contemporary litcrit's propensity to elevate form over content. A response to Addison and the BAM folks elevation of content over form. An unnecessary dichotomy in any case. Who would deny that Toni, one of our most militant, is also one of our most artistic:

> If anything I do, in the way of writing novels (or whatever I write) isn't about the village or the community or about you, then it's not about anything . . . which is to say, yes, the work must be political. It must have that as its thrust. That's a pejorative term in critical circles now; if a work has any political influence in it, somehow it's tainted. My feeling is just the opposite; if it has none, it is tainted. The problem comes when you find harangue passing off as art. It seems to me the best art is political and you ought to be able to make it unquestionably political and irrevocably beautiful at the same time. (Morrison 1984, 344–45)

Or as John O used to tell us, "The more important that you have to say the more obligated you are to say it well."

Folks claim committed work fictionally challenged. The challenge for committed writers is how to make committed work sing. How to make committed work reflect the grace and complexity of great literature and not descend into preachy sociology.

Course the litcrit folk of our generation, so busy courting academic respect, tend to claim that content don't count no matter how well you sing it. Those critics. No sense of proportion. You'd think they think its all about them these days. Ought to be shamed, trying to usurp the primacy of the artist. Got Sister Joyce calling critics conjurors and Brother Gates claiming the critic as the House of Legba. Now far be it from me to deny a literary gateskeeper named Gates the spirit of Legba, but I do believe the boy confusing personal sponsorship with professional sponsorship. Studying the dance ain't quite the same as doing it.

What with affirmative action (GodBless AA) many of our primary voices, both artistic and litcrit, now in the Academy. This is both an opportunity and a problem. In order to prosper in academia, one learns to sing the company tune. No matter how bland or offkey it be. Intellectual hegemony is addressed in the multicultural wars—a tussle for the soul of a newly emergent multicultural America and the works of black intellectuals.

In a 1973 *New York Times* book review of *Sula,* Toni's first novel, the reviewer call herself warning Toni not to be too colored, said if Toni doesn't restrict herself to colored topics she might make something of herself one day. That she might then "transcend that early and unintentionally limiting classification 'black woman writer'" (Blackburn 1973, 3).

The problem of course is that we still don't control our cultural images. Our significant voices are too often chosen and shaped by instruments of cultural hegemony—publishing houses, TV, *NYT Book Review,* the *New Yorker*—folk like that, critical folk of the Information Society. In the current rightwing ascendancy, mercenary neocons like Crouch, Clarence, and Connorly flourish, Washingtonian interlocutors like Gates stride the stage, the dollar rules, commercial lit is valued over committed lit, and "Im just a writer not a black writer" will get you paid. So what else is new.

Well—Media and the Internet for one thing. The old rootdoctor notice that folk processing info differently these days. Doctorow recently identified some responses of contemporary fiction in the devaluation of expositional/transitional narration. Contemporary fiction tends to get to the point. My girl Doris Jean Austin used to say fiction best to finesse media if it wants to retain its cultural primacy. And sooner or later black writers gon have to approach the web as an artistic/ideological instrument instead of just using it for a marketing device like a bunch of civilians— selling books instead of ideas. Word to the Wise. Best not to wait until the hypertextual train leave the station. Marginalization in the 21st century probably worse than marginalization in the 20th.

Endgame

The judgment of any literary movement is the quality of the works (masterpieces) produced by it. The issues raised pertinent to its generations. The ideological instruments forged to finesse its challenges. Its influence on future literary work. Its legacy.

Afroam literature is working literature. It is conjurational, and at its best it is visionary. As such, it continues to address the critical issues that concern us as artists and as a people. Gender, Family, and Community. Marginalization, Multiculturalism, and Globalization. Empowerment both personal and communal. And most significantly—Destinic Vision—while Craft striving for a uniquely African American narrative voice and artistic sensibility. All translated of course through the personal vision of the artist. Mix in the growing Commercialization and Canonization of African American literature and bring to a boil.

I speculate the most significant challenge of the moment is that of Identity. Just what does it mean to be black and African American in an increasingly global, multicultural, and, dare I say it, cablinasian world. Just what future do we see for blackfolk. Not just what's most likely, but what do we want. Shall we thrive and evolve as one of the respected peoples of the planet (and eventually the cosmos), or shall we eventually fade away as a distinct people and culture.

African American culture has a serious survival instinct. Plenty historical examples of cultures that were defeated politically yet triumphed culturally and Afroam culture is one of the more influential cultures of both America and the World. Witness the HipHop Nation.

I consequently speculate the attempt to develop a uniquely African American literary text will be one of the definitive components of 21st century literature and thought. A sacred text and Text of our ongoing struggle to survive and prosper as a people and a culture. Our Destiny. Our Fa.

Ultimately the struggle shall be one of grace—which is the better Way. Or as Ishmael Reed wrote in *Conjure,* "May the best church win, shake hands now and come out conjuring" (Reed 1972, 19).

Or in the words of bluesman Keb' Mo':
I been to the crossroads
and aint no devil down there. (1988)

That is all.
It is done.
I am Rickydoc.

Prayer For Cora

Kathy Engel

1. Turning Over

it is the eve of a new year
in the land of potatoes and tractors
in the country where young men and women
put on their best faces for dying far from home
when we know they should stay home

it is the eve of a new day
in the land of back hoes and seeds
where we pray, yes get down on our hands and knees
and pray that our children will be safe
that they will read and write and a booster shot
will be the only way a needle finds its way to their
soft behinds and sturdy young arms
the only shot that silently enters them

it is the eve of a new era
in the land of waves and sand and dirt
where people still live separately
where a young black woman marries a young white man
braving history
braving cruelty
braving the tides

and they sing together
in the woman's church

and the black woman's mother
and the black woman's father
lay a brick with the young lovers
cut a curtain with them
dig a row in their earth
bless them
finally, yes, bless them
turning over and over
the black and white and bloody traveled land
and break ground
kiss the soil with their ancient hands
and pray

2. God Whispers To You In The Dark

For no reason except one God whispers to you in the dark
when you are alone with your silences
a man is killed in a car
back in the south of the country
back home, going back home

a good man every friend and relative calls him
a decent man
your partner
the father of your grown children
the father of your growing-up grandchild
the father of the kids in the neighborhood who needed one
a decent good man
he knew how to make things grow.
And he took the boys' hands
and gave them a chance.
He knew how to help them grow.

The Baptist Church on the country road
where one side of the earth lives

overflows with grievers, and missers, overflows
with every kind of person who might be touched by an honest man.

The organ overflows
with the man's soul
pumped out by his daughters
who play for him
play for him
in the house of God he built
in the house of growing he built
with you

in the song house
you built together
shingle by shingle
cement slab and brick
in the rise before dawn house
in the work many jobs house
in the cleaning other people's houses house
in the work for yourself house
in the dignity house

you belt it out
the voices of your daughters
your grown daughters
their eyes
in your eyes, hold you
the gaze between you
mother and daughters
fixes the air.

They stand
as you taught them
unflinching.
You carry your pierced heart
upward to the sky
as if looking to him on his journey

about to speak to him
plainly and loud
the way you always speak

laughing not at a joke
but a laugh that pulls you forward
that says: I'm not stopping here.

Your tears turn back into your own private sea.
The discipline of years-long love
shows its full power
grown and proud and beautiful.
It is true
from belly to heart
organ to piano
the children have reaped your vigilant sewing

and so you sing together
for what you built
and for what they will build

and so you sing

In the Spaces Between the Words

An Interpretation and Performance of Identity

Dominique Parker

> *"The kind of work I have always wanted to do requires me to learn how to ma-*
> *neuver ways to free up language from its sinister, frequently lazy, almost always*
> *predictable employment of racially informed and determined chains."*
> —*Toni Morrison, playing in the dark*[1]

I am an invented variety of American, having assumed myself into existence. I
have always concerned myself with my "African-American-ness" (if there is such
a thing). In college, a friend accused me of shifting between identities, home-
grown national African-American and a more foreign identity, African-
Caribbean, or, even more specifically, Haitian-American. The movement is fluid
though not necessarily comfortable. The movement is most often conscious. I
have used the possibility of multiple representations of my identity as a way to
confound others' expectations. I shift to be first one permutation of American,
then another to prevent my convenient "pigeonholing" by anyone trying to decide
where I "belong."

This is the external movement. A kind of cultural allusiveness I climb into
and out of like a skin. The internal movement is a more difficult fragmentary ne-
gotiation. I am aware of a kind of duplication of identities. The problem lies in
the sense of a necessary choice that remains unmade. I have gotten into the habit
of thinking of the different parts of my identity as separate self-contained frag-
ments. As if each word, each identifier, is at once who I am and merely a part of
who I am. So I am Haitian-American and African-American. I can say that more
of me is something called American or -American. What, though, is required to

---

1. I take my notion of interpretation and performance from Toni Morrison. She says,
"Readers and writers both struggle to interpret and perform within a common language share-
able imaginative worlds" (1990, xii).

create a hyphenated American identity? Can I be more than one kind of American simultaneously, or can I only be a shape shifter now referenced here, then there?

The problem of creating myself as an American was always one of intimate familial context. My mother spoke French to us—my sister and me. We learned to speak English on the block with the other kids in the neighborhood. Quickly, we became aware of differences. My mother spoke with an accent and for years never spoke English at home. She cooked food my friends didn't recognize and listened to a music different from that I heard at my friends' houses.

My mother raised my sister and me. Yet, my father, whom I never met and who was never mentioned, is my concrete link to my American-ness. In a pragmatic sense my father is where my American identity begins. Legally, my claim of citizenship is based on my father's status as an American. Though I was born in Haiti and my mother was not, at that time, an American citizen, I claim citizenship through my father. The difficulty in creating an identity based on my father's American-ness is considerable. For years, my father's very existence was not spoken of. He was the absence around which was sealed an almost impenetrable silence. I came to understand that there were secrets associated with the silence.

The world as I discovered it
1. There was me. There was my mother and my sister.
2. There was no father.
3. The Father is dead.
4. There are no pictures of the Father.

I never knew my father. He died when my mother was expecting me, when my sister was a baby. He was light-skinned and good-looking. He was killed by a car as he was crossing the street. As I got older, I'd say he was hit by a truck. He was in school. He was going to be a lawyer. When he died, my mother was pregnant and sad—early 1960s dark-brown woman with a baby girl and another on the way. In the South, in the States, dark woman alone and sad, speaking English slowly. My mother went home to her family. I was born in Haiti. My sister is American. She was born in the states in the South. I am American. I was born. My mother was sad. My father was dead and American.

As I discovered it
1. There was me. There was my mother, my sister, and my aunt.
2. There was no Father.
3. The Father's name was Charlie Parker.
4. The Father is gone.
5. There are no pictures.
6. There are divorce papers.

I discovered my mother's secret
at the public library
during a field trip
I found my father, Charlie Parker
Bird—it said across the bottom of the poster
I recognized him right away,
curly hair, like mine
the way his eyebrows sweated
down across his eyes like tears,
the way mine do in the summer
The horn in his hand was made of gold
He looked sad
Probably he's missing me . . .
I understood why mother hid papers
that said divorce, couldn't bear to hear
music she couldn't call classic.
I showed her pictures from books
so she could know
I'd brought my father home for dinner
He grinned slyly from the pages, happy at last
while my mother cooked. Between chicken and beans
I asked about Jazz
but she pretended not to know.

I discovered
1. They married quickly.
2. The Father beat the mother.
3. The mother escaped.
4. There are no pictures.

Three months after he smiled at her
showing all his teeth, she forgot the words
she knew of caution, married him.
They were strangers in each others' languages,
and she was shy, even with familiar
words, huddled down between the spaces
of sounds. The first time he slapped her,
open-palmed across her mouth, it was almost accidental, the way
he drew blood, split her lip, cut her.

There must have been words to conjure
his belief, he wanted to control
allocate silence, tell her
she would not be allowed to speak out of turn.
his fists loosened her teeth for teaching

their baby an unknown language
to speak against him. She struggled
to grow a tongue, less sluggish, to curl
around his language of privilege.
Sometimes he squeezed her face

pain sounds from her mouth.
He cursed her. She believed her words
too blunted, unable to cut the net
of silence. Her mouth would open,
echoing the sound of skin breaking
skin. Still she did not speak
when she discovered they'd soon have another child
or when he told her he'd unmake *this* mistake.
Instead, she left him in silence.

The World I am uncovering
1. There are no pictures.
2. Once, my sister told a story about half-siblings.
     I was drunk and don't remember much.

My mother said she thinks my father may have died in Vietnam. I suppose someone notified her. I never asked. I've managed to avoid any kind of specific knowing. I've gotten within one hundred yards of the wall (the Vietnam Memorial) and turned back.

Claiming my identity as an African-American was self-conscious. There were, a priori, limitations in the choices of hyphenated identities available to me. I could not have, even had I wanted to, chosen to be Jewish-American or Italian-American. From the beginning I understood how much race figured into any invention of identity. The specific local context in which I tried to make myself into an American was Queens, New York. Even before I would have been able to articulate it, I understood how the idea of the person I was creating for myself required the participation of others. In order for me to be an American in the context of my world, my block, the people around me had to agree to accept my representation of myself.

My mother seemed aware of the need to equip us to be "real" Americans. She made sure she was informed about African-American culture, and she passed that knowledge on to me, to us, as best she could. When we were very young, my mother bought us two extra sets of encyclopedias. One was called the Negro History Library and the other was the Ebony Success Library. I read and even enjoyed them, but with my friends I listened to the music and learned the vocabularies I needed to know.

South Ozone Park. 134th Street from 115th Avenue to the Richmond Hill line. That's geography. It was where we lived. On the block. Next door Aunt Myrna, Uncle Bob, Serena 'n Eric. We didn't count the boys, they were mostly grown; Bobby always with some girl; Michael, crazy, was plain dangerous. Everybody said he got dropped on his head as a baby. Serena 'n Eric got to do things we didn't. Run the streets, stay out late. Aunt Myrna did some sewing on the side. When she got busy, she threw everyone out. Sometimes coming home from a night shift or a double, Mom'd find Serena outside even as far as the bus stop where we were mugged but were too surprised to scream even though we'd practiced. Uncle Bob worked out at Kennedy. We knew he had the eye, cheated on Aunt Myrna.

We lived across the street from Hawkeye, Miss Suzy. She sat up in her big front window all day, seemed like, even all night. If Miss Suzy didn't know your business it was cause you didn't have any worth knowing. You could ask, "Miss Suzy, you seen CeeBee or Robin?" She always knew where people were heading off to, when they were likely to be coming back. When we first moved in, she was the first to alert everyone—families and marriages at risk—two young women, a couple kids, and no men buying the house in the middle of the block. The danger passed. The women (Mom and my aunt) went to work, were strict with their kids, minded their business, kept their eyes off other women's men, went to church. It didn't even matter after a while about the accents. Enough folks had people from the islands in their families. It helped Michelle Barnes's mother was Jamaican and snotty, thought she was better than regular black folks. My mom was different, but everyone agreed she had no attitude.

We hated bigheadWanda and her whole family. Hating them confirmed that we were better somehow. It's not that they were poorer. none of us had as much as we bragged about. It wasn't that they got extra help, a check. One summer CeeBee's mother signed practically the whole block up for some kind of nasty free lunch. What we hated was something ugly. How Wand's daddy had this black car he loved more than anything, would spend hours washing then waxing it. Never let his kids ride in it, and once beat his youngest Littleman for putting fingerprints on it. Most times Wand's mom had to drag the laundry and three kids out to the place near Key Food, pulling on a shopping cart. Hating them was how they fit in. They were the things we weren't and feared being or becoming.

Thomas lived on the other side of bigheadWanda. Weekends he'd go down to Jamaica Avenue, deep-brown skin set off by a white-blond wig, bright makeup, high heels, a dress. He'd strut the length of the street in front of Big Daddy's pizza, flirting with the good-looking men who caught his eye. Waiting for the Q9 one day we saw a black and white pull up beside him, heard the white police officer's smiling voice drift out the open window, "Hey, baby." We laughed thinking that cop didn't know, had believed the illusion; she was a fine woman. Other days he was ordinary. Dressed in work clothes like our parents. Skipper called him crazy once. No one else seemed concerned. Coming in, going out, we'd watch him. Sometimes we could see a hint of Saturday wriggle in his walk, and we'd say softly my back is achin', my belt's too tight, my boodie's shaking from left to right . . .

How to define myself as American? I was born on a tropical island vastly different from the landscape in which I was raised. Perhaps the notion of the diaspora is what connects us, disparate groups of hyphenated black Americans living in the United States. Perhaps we are connected by commonalities in the political, social, and legal dimensions of our American identities; in how the world sees us, talks about us, and deals with us.

Blancs pauvres c'est noirs. Noirs riches c'est blancs.

Conventional wisdom (Haitian version)

Translation: I am a problem. What to call me? The current language is no longer adequate to classify me. As Americans our cultural inability to understand, confront, and transform racial history means differences can be discussed only in oppositional, polarized, or essentialist terms. Black means not only not white; it has assigned to it characteristics, traits, beliefs, norms, and even ways of being.

In the world I inhabit now, I am viewed as a variety of displaced, misplaced person. I am conversant, even fluent, in other dialects and familiar with other customs. I do not forget though that I am a visitor. I have acquired the tools of another tribe. Yet those tools do not enable me to accurately re-create the experience of displacement. Socioeconomic and sociopolitical theories regarding cultural capital, the relative insignificance of race, and the importance of class can never entirely capture the reality of how I move in the world, always with caution, often without peers, too often imagined rather than seen.

How to express in a poetry workshop what I bring, what I strive to bring to this craft?

I bring in a poem about Susan Smith. I am told it is not universal. Aren't I as much the universe as you? I am told my speakers don't "sound black enough," that their speech patterns are too complex. Listen to my voice. Do you hear Queens where we stand on line, eat iceys, and spend summers down south? Bwai, do you know what it's like after you finish your daywet in the factory, the hospital, the sound you make when you eat your food hot with pickles? You ask what it means to be redbone, ashy-legged, peasyheaded, a mess. Can you hear the block as I almost suck my teeth? Do you recognize the language of critical race theory I add to your discussion of the dangers of identity politics? Do you understand what I mean about beauty when I write about Romare Bearden? Listen to the inflections in my voice. Do you hear the layerings of accents, education, geography, and experiences? Do you hear "just another political angry black poet?"

I can say I am the product of the post–Civil Rights expansion of opportunity and access that laid the foundation for the expansion of the black middle class. I can say I am part of the second wave of beneficiaries of affirmative action. I can lay claim to familiarity with the workings and language of power.

I am no longer surprised by the inability (or slowness) of structures to adapt in any significant way to my presence. I am a veteran of institutions that in some instances failed to accommodate me and in others were hostile to my existence. I am an alum of a large public high school (academically tracked), a small liberal arts college (Seven Sisters), and a national law school (prestigious). I can take pride in my very American capacity to adjust as needed. Instead I worry. I believe in theory and in fact that my presence has and does change the places where I live and work. I worry though about how those places act and have acted on me. about How I am changed.

At a family reunion
a woman seems to speak
a language no one else understands;
thinks she's becoming white.
Though the change is almost subatomic,
she can feel herself turn in space,
respond, to the pull of unseen waves.
She doesn't want the change. Can't figure out how to stop.
She calls a friend, tells her she's afraid.
The friend laughs. *It's happening to you too.*
The friend is unhappy. Has her own fears,
the usual desire not to think about them.
They exchange a lot of words
stuffed with great speed into their phones:
race . . . bilingual . . . alone.
The argument goes round,
the woman decides to end it. Convincing
her friend they are diseased has made her forget
the unwanted way her cells are shifting.

She calls the sickness—anomie—
how what they knew who
they were was breaking down.
The friend didn't disagree, only added
mainly she thought they were lonely.

In Ellison's *Invisible Man,*
the man ends up in a hole.
Invisibility—
sounds like such a poetic problem.
Walking along, a blink, you disappear;
a second before you were occupied space.
Sometimes, a lingering sense of distortion;
a snagged thread in the weave of the air.
This is not the woman's problem.
she has moved up to the next level:
She lacks protective covering,
is easily marked by the predatory eye.
The one most likely to be eaten.
Maybe she is evolving,
like the amphibian ancestor who bumbled
out of the slop primordial
to discover it was possible
to live, gasping, on land.

Education, economics, circumstances, and, yes, even choice have put me today in a mostly white environment. I am a graduate student and teach at a large university with a population that is about 10 percent African-American (with a larger percentage of people of color). Yet, in my program of study, I am the only black student; I am one of thirty-four (in college we were twelve of about three hundred, and in law school we were twenty or so of more than three hundred). Often I feel exposed. Sometimes I think how my visibility keeps me safe. Other times I do a lot of second guessing of myself and others. In a class discussion on James Baldwin and race I choose not to speak. I decide it is better to be silent than to be taken as the "race representative." Better to be silent than to have my thoughts taken as "what African-Americans think."

In a classroom discussion, an Anglo woman asked, "Why have we as Americans chosen a rational form of perception?"

I suppose, many outside of my community would describe me as paranoid. Inside my group I am ordinary. My best friend says, like Audre Lorde, "we were not meant to survive." Exaggeration? Where I live it feels like reality. In a Sherman Alexie story, a woman is sterilized. I know this story. For many years under the auspices of the U.S. government Department of Health, Education, and Welfare, African-American, Native-American, and Latina (particularly Puerto Rican) women were involuntarily sterilized by the thousands. Sometimes the women were not informed, sometimes they were lied to, sometimes the sterilization was the "price" they paid for medical care during a pregnancy. See "Racism, Birth Control, and Reproductive Rights," in Women, Race, and Class *by Angela Davis (1981). Writing this I am cautious. I don't want to expose how sometimes my perceptions are so at odds with those of the world I move in. If I say or write something too different, I make sure to cite a source.*

I grew up knowing that at Albert Schweitzer, the American Hospital in Haiti, white students were allowed to practice on a grateful black population with impunity. I grew up knowing that medicine, the church, and the government did not have my best interests at heart. I knew not to take my well-being for granted. My rational perception of the world includes the knowledge of the Tuskeegee syphilis experiments; dozens of stories, growing up, of black and brown bodies beaten by the police. I grew up knowing why the Haitian revolution—defeat of the white invader—wasn't taught at any of my schools. That if you lived in certain neighborhoods and you wanted help, you called "fire" and not for the police. That if you ever wanted the police, you should tell them that an officer (a white officer) was being beaten up. That you had to be better, smarter, cleaner, work harder to get half the chance. I learned how to tell if the news is about white or black people, and what it means to be told, with surprise, that I am articulate. That when unsure where to "place" you, some white people assume "up," assume you are part of their group.

Sometimes I have moments of disjunction, and it becomes almost impossible to bridge a gap of understanding, assumption, language, belief, or comfort. Sometimes I get scared. These are the kinds of perceptual differences that usually don't get discussed across race lines. I know where I live and have lived colors my version of American rational perception.

The problem of the mutable American identity is similar to the problem associated with any created text. Once you create the text and put it out into the world you lose control over its interpretation. I am still surprised when I am told, "I think of you as more _____ rather than _____. Problems with the interpretation or acceptance of an American identity can surface at any time and from anywhere.

Once, when I was little, my older cousin Reggie told me all the bad names he knew a black person could be called. The way he said them, chanting, made it seem like a song: tar baby, sambo, spear chucker, jungle bunny, jigaboo, bubblelip, big bertha, aunt jemima, zulu, nigger, coon. I asked about *oreo* and he told me it was different. How *oreo* was a *must* fight. Like having someone say, "ya mamma." A signal that it was for real, not the game we played among ourselves. One of the few insults you couldn't let slide, you couldn't turn with a smile or a joke or a phrase. With any of the words from the song, you could stop, make it a badge, a medal you wore pinned to your soldier's uniform. Say "too black, too proud" and laugh.

Oreo was a challenge you couldn't let go unanswered. It said: traitor, outsider, stranger. It said: outside you pretend to be one of us, inside you are one of them, not to be trusted. Being light-skinned I felt I had to be more vigilant. Couldn't let anyone confuse my color with my loyalties. I knew the names of kingdoms and warriors. Could tell stories of white slave owners massacred, former slaves victorious. I had to prove I was chocolate all the way through—no cream filling. I was ready to fight.

Coconut surprised me the first time I heard it. An unexpected weapon in someone else's arsenal. Before I analyzed what it could mean, I knew enough to fight. I could tell the seriousness of the insult from the tone and the reaction of others around me. Afterward I understood it was another way to be cast out. A way to say, even within the group there is a special category for people like you—foreign, different. You are not even an oreo, the old word, the old wound. You are outside. Even the old insults must be changed to measure the distance between us.

Perhaps the answer lies in creating an identity or group that is unexpected and therefore temporarily unclassifiable. A woman I know was having lunch in a

Cuban restaurant in New York City. The woman is striking, attractive, clearly African-American. After a while the server asked her, "What are you?" She replied, "An African in exile in America."

I have gotten into the habit of thinking of my work in binary terms. Either my work is part of my Haitian strand and expresses an immigrant, an island sensibility, or it is part of my African-American strand and expresses a native sensibility. I like to say that what I write is dependent on which part of my brain I use. It is only with great difficulty that I recognize elements in my work that spring from my whole brain.

White

Safiya Henderson-Holmes

1.

The language of illness and disease is foreign to many,
and for the many who speak it, our tongues often knot
around each letter of the day and, if not knotted,
perhaps try too hard to give sound to the syllables
which have bought us to this far and foreign place,
where visitors sometimes stand and wave shores away.
And those visitors who dare with their love and or fear
to venture closer to our island of frail and uncertain
human bodies, dare to touch our now unknown skin, still
with theirs. We have all traveled such a long way to
get here.

2.

Ever since I've been black and female, I've been
"other," the space beyond the pointed finger and the
awkward stare or glare. Ever since my hair's been
coarse and nappy and the dry grayness my mama calls
"ash" always creeping back to my knees and elbows, I
knew that whoever really, really touched me would have
to, touch me. Would have to walk through that space
beyond the pointed finger, that wide and narrow stare
or glare that often named me and whatever I owned in a
blink, in a roll of an eye, in the suck of teeth. I
knew and know difference like air—familiar, invisible,
sometimes not enough, desperately trying to breathe in
such a space. Far too many days I've been breathless in
this skin. Gagging on difference, and the indifference

it made. Ever since that first day, when I looked in
the mirror and saw my new breasts bloom in their soft,
quiet darkness and stole my daddy's secret magazines
which grew in his closet right above his good sunday
clothes, magazines with pictures of all the women who
didn't look like me or my mama. Yet I knew their
bodies, their breasts, their thighs, knew they were what
I wanted to be. Woman. Touched. Loved. How I slept
with those pictures and those women, looked at my daddy
across the dinner table, graced and blessed my plate
with prayers for my skin and hair to change into the
women in his magazines, thinking he'd love me more, and
difference would be gone from me forever and ever.
Amen.

3.

In a stark, white hospital, my black female body between
its sheets, sutured and gauzed, pierced with tubing,
squares of small plastic bags above and below. I am
another "other." The pointed finger is pulled into the
suggestion of "illness," the awkward stare is lowered to
read statistics, my name is written in a loose-leaf
binder and placed in a metal box clipped to the foot of
my bed. I am "the

4.

one" near the window.

5.

As a sister with three brothers, living in the Soundview
projects in the Bronx, I wanted my own room, my own bed
near the ruffled curtained window. I wanted to kick my
younger brother out, smother his snores, tear his
baseball heroes from my walls, fumigate his scent from
my closet, put flowers and candles in each corner and
lay on my back in the dark and pray to god to keep my
room just this way.

6.

To drift on an island of my own choosing.

7.

I pray for my brothers to fill this foreign space, bring
a chorus of snores, crowd the walls with their smells
and all their heroes, to junk up this narrow hospital
closet with their shoes and pants, make a mess of the
night table, scatter the pills and the kidney-shaped
bowl.

shout sport scores, belch, fart, and cheer for their
winners, chew and spit out their losers.

8.

Patient.

9.

Patience.

10.

I slept with my younger brother when he was five and I
was eight. Before sleeping we'd make shadow hand puppets
on the wall: duck, dog, and rabbit silhouettes which
talked and grazed on the walls long after our hands
tucked under our sheets. And my brother and I slept
back to back. Our small, round buns touching ever so
slightly, our elbows, restless wings of rare and clumsy
birds, trying to take flight from either side of the bed
of our twin bed. And sometimes in the morning, I'd wake
before my brother and find his head and snores on my
heart and I'd hold him and them there, gently. My
brother and I.

11.

A new inhabitant is brought to this island today, an
elder woman, white, her arms quietly crossing her chest.

Her breasts once full, fuller than my mama's breasts,
now kneel in her armpits. Though different, she is the
same to me, her scars nearly visible through the gauze.
We're dressed in the cloth and colors of this foreign
country, an entourage of I.V. poles and plastic
attendants, the quiet, familiar hum of pumped oxygen and
an aria of squeaking wheels announce her arrival. I
watch as she is lifted by six hands from stretcher to
bed, centered and tucked, the blanket carried over her
stomach. Her sleep appears easy, restful. The demerol
bag half full. I listen for any other familiar sounds:
the beep on the I.V. monitor, a foot rubbing against a
crisp sheet, the turning of a breath, and then I hear
her snore, loud and long, like my brother. Enough to
wake inhabitants on other islands, enough to wake the
dead. Thank god!

12.
And I sleep in the lull of my neighbor's roar.
Oh, how I sleep in the sweet lull of my neighbor's
roar.

13.
There are others like me.

Conversation Two

Safiya Henderson-Holmes and Ellen J. Goldner

S.H. I often think we are nowhere near shared community. Even when we come together in our mixed neighborhoods, we don't speak the same language. I want to talk about the language of racism that operates without words. How is the language of racism expressed even when no one says a word?

E.G. In gestures. In body language. In facial expressions.

S.H. In dress codes. In hair styles. In what corner you're going to stand on, in what train you're going to ride. In what stores you're going to shop in. In what stores you're *allowed* to shop in. I read an article about some kids who come from another neighborhood and go to school on the Upper West Side on Seventy-second Street. There are a lot of public schools in that area, and so a lot of kids come from the Bronx, come from other neighborhoods downtown. There's a store that won't allow a bunch of black kids to come in at the same time. They'll allow *one* black child to go into the store at a time.

E.G. They'll allow as many white kids in the store as want to come?

S.H. As many white kids, and as many adults, men and women.

E.G. And that's something a kid only has to see to know its meanings.

S.H. Exactly. But when they decide to talk about it, how do they talk about it? What words do they use? How do they fuel that racism with more words? More attitude? And the white folks that are going in the store, how do they express their ability to go into the store? Do they say it out loud, verbally? Do they just look at the black kids when they come out? The black kids got a lot of words for it. So, then, when those two communities encounter each other, for eight hours of the day they're in the same community, speaking a totally different language because of racism. You know, they could shop for the same soda, but they can't shop with the same voice, the same attitude, with the same words.

E.G. We're speaking out of different experiences right now. You're saying three or four things about the ways racism is tangled up in our lives, and I need to stop just to absorb them all. You're talking about the ways that racism shapes our senses of self differently—against one another. Are you also talking about the ways communities on different sides of the divisions work with the racism to extend it, or undercut it, and how we end up with different languages in the process?

S.H. I'm saying all those things.

E.G. One way that white communities work racism without saying a word is in the taboo against naming it—against acknowledging racism. I think that for many of us European Americans there's a powerful psychological need to deny that there is any racism. I say this because we are repeatedly shocked at evidence of racism. And I include myself here. People expressed shock at the videotaped beating of Rodney King. But, afterward, the news media and most European Americans seemed to forget about it, so that when brutality became terribly visible again, when Amadou Diallo was killed with forty-one bullets, we were shocked again. And we were shocked again at the brutality against Abner Louima, the Haitian who was tortured by police, or at the admission of New Jersey officials that their police really *do* profile suspects by race. There's a repeated forgetting that allows us to be shocked each time. I think that the political effects of racism are underwritten by this powerful psychological need to deny it. Then, of course, we can practice it with impunity. I think that for many European Americans, evidence of racism disturbs our belief in the United States as a democratic nation, and therefore it threatens our sense of ourselves as "Americans."

S.H. Our sense of ourselves as good.

E.G. Yes.

S.H. But, as Richard Pryor said, *I'm* never going to forget it. Within the denial of the physical aspects of racism—the things that you outlined, the beatings, the shootings—there's also a denial of any psychological ramifications for me. "Why are you angry? Why should black people be angry? Why don't you all just get over it?" You know, "Slavery's over. You have civil rights. You have a job. Why are you all so angry?"

E.G. Why did the movie based on Toni Morrison's *Beloved* lose money at the box office? How is it that this remarkably acted and directed movie was not even nominated for major academy awards?

S.H. The point about *Beloved* is a good one because the whole metaphor of the ghost, Beloved, is about such anger.

E.G. Anger and pain that can't be separated.

S.H. And pain. For one thing, it's based on a true story—this mother who would rather kill her children than allow them to be captured again. Now, what happened? What is worse? Death at her own hands is better than death at the slave master's.

E.G. *Beloved* is also about events that occurred *after slavery* and *in the North.* And I think that is very threatening for many European Americans. It implies that there's a legacy of slavery that cannot neatly be contained in the past.

S.H. And the ramifications—psychological, social—unseen ramifications of racism that we're all still trying to live with. How do they affect us emotionally, across the board, for whites, blacks, Asians, everybody? This returns us to the essence of this book. Who are we when we look at each other? Who are we when we're talking about each other? We're talking through this history, whether we deny it or not. It's the same for Jews and the Holocaust. When you do see it, we're still talking through it. In Germany, when you talk to a German, you're still walking through that. Well, how are you prepared emotionally, psychologically, to walk through that?

E.G. I think for most people in the dominant culture the denial is there so we *won't have to* walk through it, and I think that that goes on to feed into more of the same racism. For example, if we return to the movie *Beloved,* Thandie Newton's performance in the role of Beloved and Jonathan Demme's direction were remarkably powerful and very unusual. Normally such unique work would attract some kind of notice—a nomination for an award. *Beloved* was nominated for one award.

S.H. Costumes.

E.G. Yeah, costumes, but not for supporting actress, not for direction. I think that the box office showings indicate that many European Americans hear of a movie whose characters are almost all African American and decide it's not of interest to them. The half-conscious logic of ideology then uses the denial of racism as fuel. It says: "Given that we harbor no racism"—that's the assumption—"and that we find this movie of no interest to us, then it follows that this movie is of no interest. Period. It deserves no awards."

S.H. And Beloved's spirit, the spirit of the ex-slave, remains angry. Angry and uneasy.

E.G. And I felt uneasy when I went to visit you last week, because I still carry the resonance of all the stories I've heard and in some way believed, of all the images I've taken in from TV since I was a teenager, about black people, about black people in groups, about black people in inner-city neighborhoods as hostile and dangerous—stories and images that warned me Harlem was not a place to get lost in. Walking to the train from Malcolm X Boulevard, on the hot summer evening past people sitting on their front steps, I could feel myself wrestling with the echoes of those stories, breathing as deeply as I could, walking with as much ease as I could. I wanted to deny the racism, to deny its power over me, but also to deny its continuing presence within me, in the residue of all those stories.

I found myself wondering if I was unwelcome, an intruder in someone else's neighborhood. To be in a mixed neighborhood is to be comfortable. But to be the only white person on the street, in the summer weather with so many people on their stoops, I felt that mesh of race relations grab hold of me. So the racism spoke inside of me and the tangled race relations spoke around me. To walk through all that is suffocating.

S.H. I think in America there's been this great assumption: unless there's a war or unless there's a riot, everything's fine. And everybody understands everybody, and everyone's getting along.

E.G. I think it's also assumed that everyone understands everyone else *in the dominant language.*

S.H. And we know that's not true. As a student and a professor in an English Department, where I am the only black female, I don't care how well I articulate, enunciate, and speak clearly, and don't talk inner-city slang, I may not be heard today. I feel conscious of that. And I remember other black women feeling voiceless in the classroom, too—not voiceless in the sense that we don't speak, but that we are not heard. And that our language is not enough. That our words and the length and breadth of our discourse is not enough, or it is too much, or all we have to do is show up, and therefore we are discussed because "the other" is present. If you're talking about a text and there are black characters in the text, then there's the black character in the classroom, and therefore the black character in the classroom can now give validity to the black character in the text, and we can talk about them. Then I get defensive, and I say I'm not going to talk about the black character in the text just because I'm the black character in the classroom. If you all don't have anything to say about the black character in the text, I don't have anything to say about the black character in the text either. And, therefore, just because I'm the black character in this classroom, I'll be voiceless again. We're in the same community, and we speak the same language, but at the same time, we're not in the same community, and we don't speak the same language. Are we, on both sides, conscious of that? I think our book asks that question—because you cannot be conscious like that all the time.

E.G. You speak of the classroom. I teach mostly working-class students, many of them European Americans, but some of them immigrants—from the Caribbean, from Asia, from South Asia, from eastern Europe. In the classroom when we talk about racism, we do it reluctantly, sometimes with no African American students in the room and sometimes with a few African American students. If there are a few, I think they are automatically sitting in your position, as are the two or three other people of color in the room.

One student—a young man from Barbados who had been a very vocal and a very interesting student in a class of mine a year earlier—came up to me after a demonstration over the killing of Amadou Diallo. He said, "You know, last year when we read the ending of *Uncle Tom's Cabin* in class, the scene where Tom is beaten to death? It was a very upsetting for me to read that." We'd talked about the politics of Stowe's not letting Tom lift a hand in his own defense. And then he said, *"Why didn't you prepare me for that?"* And I felt the ground shift under me. He was asking this question from an angle different from any question I knew how to answer. In one sense, he was raising the issue of what it means for the culture to watch scenes in which a black man is killed. And I had thought of exactly the same scene, in the same novel, during the playing and replaying of the videotape of Rodney King's beating. But I did not know how to answer this young man, who was relatively new to the United States and who had seen an image of brutal racism that was just replayed in New York City. *"You should have prepared me,"* he said. What does that mean? I still circle round and round his question but cannot meet it. I've got my pedagogic response: next time, I'll bring his comment into class discussion and prepare the whole class for this brutality. But I know that's not what he was asking me. He spoke so urgently, as if his meaning was perfectly clear. *"Why didn't you prepare me for that?"* But for me, the question still needs translating. There is clearly a gap between us. We are not speaking the same language. If the possibility of community rests on our acknowledging one another's humanity, as it's forged in our different experiences, how do we acknowledge each other across that divide? How do I acknowledge this student across that divide? Those of us who find it easy to forget racism—who find it easy to ignore that we're walking through it—need reminders. This young man reminded me.

S.H. But what about those of us who can't forget? I wonder, is there something within the denial of racism that you were talking about that is supposed to work *for* us? You know, if I go around being as conscious as I am of the historical and psychological ramifications of racism, of how painful it has been. How painful it continues to be for so many of us in this country and in this world. How a black man can't get a taxi, regardless. How black men are still charged with that rape of that white woman or that killing of that white child. And how Amadou Diallo can still get shot forty-one times. I can't every day think that way or feel at that level. So what do I do? What do I do to have friends like you, to have friends like Kathy, to work at Syracuse University? What do I do to maintain my human being self? One of the things James Baldwin said was the first thing they took from the African in order to enslave him was his ability to be a human being.

E.G. I don't know an answer. Safe places? Time out? Maybe the time we need in our own communities?

(Silence.)

E.G. So the racism continues?

S.H. So the racism continues, but we don't want the racism to continue.

(Silence.)

E.G. Are there times where you feel people have been coming together in some kind of community without racism between them?

S.H. I'm not sure. I saw it come together in the demonstrations over the shooting of Amadou Diallo.

E.G. Do you think that happens often? The bridges I know of are built amid the mesh of racism. When I came to see you last week, carrying my racialized uneasiness about Harlem, a stranger broke through all the static I carried, and I appreciated it very much. I had to take the C Train. And to get off at your station I had to be in the first or second car. So I was waiting all the way up at the front of the station when there was an announcement that bounced off all of the tile walls, as announcements do in New York subway stations. I couldn't understand anything the announcer said except "the C train." Maybe my feeling out of place was visible or my attempt to shut up my voices that said "Don't get lost in Harlem," but a man came up to me, an African American man, and asked if I was waiting for the C train. He repeated the announcement. A complete stranger broke through the stereotypes I still carried about how I, as a European American woman, could *be* or *be received*—in Harlem. A stranger cleared away the static, and I was very grateful.

S.H. If I can presume to imagine the psychic space of that black male, at that time, in giving those directions, I can imagine he was grateful for that moment of humanity, too.

E.G. I think that small gestures that give the slip to racism happen both ways. More than once I've held open a door at a shopping mall for the person behind me and looked up to see a very surprised African American woman. It makes me wonder whether a gesture like this *speaks,* even if only for a moment, because it cuts against the long history of assumptions about who's supposed to be serving whom in this country.

S.H. I agree. We have to ask how do we build because the psychological ramifications of racism are on all sides. Racism has affected and continues to affect everyone. In this way, all of us are getting back to our human consciousness, our selves. Common courtesy and respect and dignity that we all know about, just in knowing how we feel and in wanting to be treated in a particular way. Common "good mornings" and "good nights" from everyone. Not feeling that you're being patronized or condescending, but that you're genuinely involved in giving as you wish to receive. I think that on an average daily basis there's a general attitude of contempt for our fellow human beings. Period. If I don't know you, I'm just not interested.

E.G. I wonder if some of the problem, if some of our not being genuinely involved, is related to time in this economy. Even when we are in a mixed neighborhood with our neighbors, we need time for things to happen—for people to connect or disconnect in moments that are not at all planned. There can't be any positive connections if there's no time to spend on the same ground, even if in different languages. In Syracuse, where I still spend my summers, summer evenings are the only times that people from different communities who live in the same neighborhoods even cross each other's paths. That's partly because the winters are so hard, but it's also because of current modes of capitalism, because of the economy. After all the economic downsizing, many people in the middle class—blacks, Latinas, Asian Americans, whites—experience what working-class people have often experienced. We're expected to fill up almost all our time with work, and the little bit left over is all people have left for their families. Capitalism is an active force working against the creation of communities across differences when it actively squeezes out all the time that might make possible our meetings across groups and cultures and languages. It actively squeezes out anything other than "private interests," which are defined either as money-making activities or as relations within the groups we're already part of.

S.H. I think the contempt is a capitalist thing and an American thing. You know, I've traveled to other countries where foreigners often say that Americans are really rude. So I come back to the States and say, "Let me think about this," because I'm from New York and people always say that New Yorkers are uptight. I think different cultures and different classes instigate or initiate different responses, so that within different classes and cultures and genders, you're going to get different considerations. If you are the female walking in your middle-class neighborhood that you've lived in for twenty years, and the grocer knows you and greets you warmly, that's one thing—as opposed to the woman who is African American, working class, but who is totally new to the neighborhood, and so won't get the door held or won't get a hello. "We don't know you." Because we're dealing with human nature, I don't think the lines are as clear all the time as other influences. The particular pervasiveness and pervertedness of racism—we can look at that as a historical current that's fluid, that adapts to various relations of class or gender. There are too many incidents where African Americans of the upper middle class have the money to live wherever they want, but cannot go to that neighborhood. They cannot go to that school. They cannot be buried in that cemetery. They cannot shop in that store. So the pervertedness of racism crosses those shifting grounds of culture, gender, and class. It's like a disease, you know.

E.G. But disease ought to be a proof of our common humanity. That's why we can to give it to one another.

S.H. Exactly. But racism is a disease that crosses class, crosses gender, and counters our common humanity.

E.G. In this conversation we've talked about the ways our experiences amid racism differ, about the ways our languages, forged in those differences, produce gaps between us that are hard to bridge, about the small resistances in our daily lives that might undermine racism, but we end here still talking about the persistence of racism. Are there places where you see hope?

S.H. Definitely. I'd like to close this dialogue by talking about the youth today. But before we do that, is there anything you want to say?

E.G. Yeah. In the face of the anger, the pain, and the losses to racism that we've grappled with in this dialogue, this project has given me moments of real joy in working with you and in coming to know others in this community of voices. All this makes me feel that, although racism remains, there are breakthroughs and ways of forming bonds that are as subtle or as subconscious or as complex as the routes of racism. For me, as an academic and speaker of the dominant language, the opportunity to be one voice among many voices is liberating, even when voices are strained and tense. To speak as one speaker among many speakers is a release from the kind of competition that insists there are very few slots for voices that can be heard. I guess I'm saying that the pre*dominant* mode of speaking can be a tyranny to those who speak it. What I see us as trying to do is to bring together as many voices as we can.

S.H. Like a chorus.

E.G. Yes, but a chorus in tension. And to figure out what the textures of voices are that prevent us from hearing each other, as well the things that enable us to speak to each other and to hear each other. The aim is refreshing.

S.H. I would like to talk about today's youth. You know, the future. What do we see within the movies or music or culture of our youth that is erasing the problem or racing toward the problem, maybe blurring the edges.

E.G. Sometimes I'm unsure that what looks like blurring the edges is actually accomplishing that—for example the enormous popularity of rap music among white suburban youth. That may just be appropriating the machismo of the other.

S.H. Right, because they wouldn't be able to come and eat dinner with you. But among the junior high and high school kids, I think there's more interracial dating. I don't think that's ungenuine. There are genuine relationships forming and general tolerance of a particular type of difference.

E.G. Since I don't have children, your finger is much more on the pulse of youth than mine. By tolerance, I assume you mean something active and positive, something different than the tolerance of the rude city where we don't have to deal with others we don't know.

S.H. Right. Right. *Essence* magazine had an article last month about black women dating white men, and what stares still occur, and what type of relationships are formed. What's the attraction for this black woman? And what's the attraction of this black woman for this white man? I think that with younger people, with junior high and high school kids, it's an attraction. It's the cute girl. The nice guy.

E.G. It's not just what Spike Lee portrayed in *Jungle Fever.*

S.H. I don't think so. I'm not talking like these kids are innocent. They're fully aware of the cultural and racial aspects of the relationships they're getting involved in, but I think they're still innocent enough in their love quest. You know, when you genuinely like somebody. And then as they get older, the experience becomes more risky in terms of extending it into the rest of their world, beyond their clique at school, as they go to college or join the workforce or a community. Or they want to live somewhere, or they want to go into that church, and they're the only odd couple. Then I think, as adults, they start looking at things. But that's still part of the dialogue. What's still going on? I mean, what are we as adults allowing to go on for our children in terms of racism? What are we responsible for in continuing our own racist attitudes—things they can't get out of because *we* haven't gotten out of them?

E.G. And it goes back generations and generations. We need to keep asking the questions.

Works Cited
Index

Works Cited

Abrahams, Roger D. 1983. *After Africa.* New Haven: Yale Univ. Press.

Allen, William Francis, Charles Pickard Ware, and Lucy McKim Garrison. 1867. *Slave Songs of the United States.* New York: A. Simpson.

Anderson, Benedict. 1991. *Imagined Communities: Reflections on the Origins and Spread of Nationalism.* London: Verso.

Andrews, William L. 1987. "Introduction to the 1987 Edition." In *My Bondage, My Freedom,* by Frederick Douglass. Urbana: Univ. of Illinois Press, xi–xxvii.

———. 1990. "The Novelization of Voice in Early African American Narrative." *PMLA* 105: 23–34.

———. 1991. "*My Bondage and My Freedom* and the American Literary Renaissance of the 1850s." In *Critical Essays on Frederick Douglass,* edited by William L. Andrews, 133–47. Boston: G. K. Hall.

Aptheker, Herbert. 1973. "Maroons Within the Present Limits of the United States." In *Maroon Societies,* edited by Richard Price, 151–67. New York: Doubleday.

Armstrong, M. F. 1971. *Hampton and Its Students.* New York: Books for Libraries.

Armstrong, Nancy, and Leonard Tennenhouse. 1989. "Representing Violence, or 'How the West Was Won,'" In *The Violence of Representation,* edited by Nancy Armstrong and Leonard Tennenhouse, 1–26. London: Routledge.

Baker, Houston A. 1971. *Black Studies, Rap, and the Academy.* Chicago: Univ. of Chicago Press.

Baldwin, James. 1985. *The Price of the Ticket.* New York: St. Martin's, Merek.

Ball, Charles. 1970. *Fifty Years in Chains.* New York: Dover.

Baraka, Amiri. 1998. "The Autobiography of LeRoi Jones." In *The Jazz Cadence of American Culture,* edited by Robert G. O'Meally, 349–68. New York: Columbia Univ. Press.

Barnes, Sandra, ed. 1989. *Africa's Ogun: Old World and New.* Bloomington: Indiana Univ. Press.

Bascom, William. 1969. *Ifa Divination: Communication Between Gods and Men in West Africa.* Bloomington: Indiana Univ. Press.

Bastide, Roger. 1971. *African Civilizations in the New World.* Translated by Peter Green. New York: Harper.

Blackburn, Sara. 1973. "You Still Can't Go Home Again." Review of *Sula* by Toni Morrison. The *New York Times Book Review,* 30 Dec., 3.

Blackwell, Louise, and Frances Clay. 1971. *Lillian Smith.* New York: Twayne.

Blassingame, John W., ed. 1982. *The Frederick Douglass Papers, Series One: Speeches, Debates, and Interviews.* Vol. 2 of 5 vols. New Haven: Yale Univ. Press.

Blight, David, W. 1989. *Frederick Douglass' Civil War: Keeping Faith in Jubilee.* Baton Rouge: Louisiana State Univ. Press.

Blumenfeld, Laura. 1994. "Mideast Side Story." *Washington Post,* 30 June, C1, C2.

Bontemps, Arna. 1969. *Great Slave Narratives.* Boston: Beacon.

Burkholder, Steve. 1989. "The Lawrence Eagle-Tribune and the Willie Horton Story." *Washington Journalism Review* 11, no. 4: 14–16.

Butler, Judith. 1994. *Bodies That Matter: On the Discursive Limits of "Sex."* New York: Routledge.

———. 1997. *The Psychic Life of Power.* Stanford: Stanford Univ. Press.

Cain, Joy Duckett. 1992. "The Source of Our Magic." *Essence* (May): 66.

Carby, Hazel. 1985. "On the Threshold of Woman's Era: Lynching, Empire, and Sexuality in Black Feminist Theory." *Critical Inquiry* 12: 262–77.

———. 1987. *Reconstructing Womanhood: The Emergence of the Afro-American Woman Novelist.* New York: Oxford Univ. Press.

Caruth, Cathy. 1996. *Unclaimed Experience: Trauma, Narrative, and History.* Baltimore: Johns Hopkins Univ. Press.

Cash, W. J. 1960. *The Mind of the South.* New York: Vintage.

Chan, Jeffery Paul, et al. 1991. *The Big Aiiieeeee! An Anthology of Chinese American and Japanese American Literature.* New York: Meridian.

Chappell, Louis. 1933. *John Henry, a Folklore Study.* Jena: Walter Biedermann.

Chesnutt, Charles W. 1981. "Dave's Neckliss." In *The Short Fiction of Charles Chesnutt,* edited by Sylvia Lyons Render, 132–41. Washington, D.C.: Howard Univ. Press.

Cheung, King-Kok. 1988. Introduction to *Seventeen Syllables and Other Stories,* by Hisaye Yamamoto, xi–xxv. Latham, N.Y.: Kitchen Table.

———. 1990. "The Woman Warrior versus the Chinaman Pacific: Must a Chinese American Critic Choose Between Feminism and Heroism?" In *Conflicts in Feminism,* edited by Marianne Hirsch and Evelyn Fox Keller, 234–51. New York: Routledge.

———. 1994. "Interview with Hisaye Yamamoto." In *"Seventeen Syllables": Hisaye Yamamoto,* edited by King-Kok Cheung, 71–86. New Brunswick, N.J.: Rutgers Univ. Press.

Chin, Frank, et al., eds. 1983. *Aiiieeeee! An Anthology of Asian-American Writers.* 1974. Reprint. Washington, D.C.: Howard Univ. Press.

Cliff, Michelle, ed. 1978. *The Winner Names the Age: A Collection of Writings by Lillian Smith.* New York: Norton.

Clinton, Catherine. 1982. *The Plantation Mistress: Woman's World in the Old South.* New York: Pantheon.

Cobb, Nora. 1988. "Food As an Expression of Cultural Identity in Jade Snow Wong and *Songs for Jadina."* *Hawaii Review* 12: 12–16.

Cooke, Patrick. 1991. "They Cried until They Could Not See." *New York Times,* 23 June, sec. 1, 24–5.

Coombe, Rosemary J. 1992. "The Celebrity Image and Cultural Identity: Public Rights and the Subaltern Politics of Gender." *Discourse* 14, no. 3: 59–88.

Courlander, Harold. 1963. *Negro Folk Music U.S.A.* New York: Columbia Univ. Press.

Curtin, Philip, ed. 1976. *Africa Remembered: Narratives by West Africans.* Madison: Univ. of Wisconsin Press.

Daniels, Roger. 1988. *Asian America: Chinese and Japanese in the United States since 1850.* Seattle: Univ. of Washington Press.

Deren, Maya. 1953. *Divine Horsemen: The Living Gods of Haiti.* Kingston, N.Y.: Mcpherson.

Dillard, John. 1972. *Black English.* New York: Random House.

Dixon, Melvin. 1987. *Ride Out the Wilderness: Geography and Identity in Afro American Literature.* Chicago: Univ. of Chicago Press.

Douglass, Frederick. 1987a. *My Bondage and My Freedom.* Edited by William L. Andrews. Urbana: Univ. of Illinois Press.

———. 1987b. *Narrative of the Life of Frederick Douglass, an American Slave.* In *The Classic Slave Narratives,* edited by Henry Louis Gates Jr., 243–331. New York: Mentor-Penguin.

———. 1990. *The Heroic Slave.* In *Three African-American Novels,* edited by William L. Andrews, 23–69. New York: Mentor-Penguin.

DuBois. W. E. B. 1944. "Searing Novel of the South." Review of *Strange Fruit,* by Lillian Smith. *New York Times Book Review,* 5 Mar., 1, 20.

———. 1969. *The Souls of Black Folk.* New York: Penguin.

———. 1973. *The Philadelphia Negro.* New York: Kraus Thomson.

Dunbar, Paul. 1962. *The Complete Poems of Paul Lawrence Dunbar.* New York: Dodd, Mead.

Ellison, Ralph. 1964. *Shadow and Act.* New York: Vintage.

———. 1972. *Invisible Man.* New York: Vintage.

Equiano, Olaudah. 1987. *The Interesting Narrative of the Life of Olaudah Equiano or Gustavus Vassa the African Written by Himself.* 1814. Reprinted in *The Classic Slave Narratives,* edited by Henry Lewis Gates Jr., 1–182. New York: Mentor-Penguin.

Espiritu, Yen Le. 1992. *Asian American Panethnicity: Bridging Institutions and Identities.* Philadelphia: Temple Univ. Press.

Fabio, Sarah Webster. 1994. "Tripping with Black Writing." In *Within the Circle,* edited by Angelyn Mitchell, 224–31. Durham, N.C.: Duke Univ. Press.

Faulkner, William. 1948. *Intruder in the Dust.* New York: Random House.

———. 1956. "Letter to the North," *Life,* Mar. 5, 51–52.

Feinstein, Sascha, and Yusef Komunyaka, eds. 1991. *The Jazz Poetry Anthology.* Bloomington: Indiana Univ. Press.

Felman, Shoshana. 1993. *The Literary Speech Act.* Translated by Catherine Porter. Ithaca: Cornell Univ. Press.

Fisher, Miles Mark. 1953. *Negro Slave Songs in the United States.* New York: Citadel.

Fisher Fishkin, Shelley, and Carla L. Peterson. 1990. "We Hold These Truths to Be Self-Evident: The Rhetoric of Frederick Douglass's Journalism." In *Frederick Douglass: New Literary and Historical Essays,* edited by Eric J. Sundquist, 189–204. Cambridge: Cambridge Univ. Press.

Fisk University. 1945. *God Struck Me Dead,* vol. 1 of *Unwritten History of Slavery.* Nashville: Fisk Univ. Social Science Dept.

Foner, Philip. 1978–1985. *The Black Worker: A Documentary History from Colonial Times to the Present.* Philadelphia: Temple Univ. Press.

Franchot, Jenny. 1990. "The Punishment of Esther: Frederick Douglass and the Construction of the Feminine." In *Frederick Douglass: New Literary and Historical Essays,* edited by Eric J. Sundquist, 141–65. Cambridge: Cambridge Univ. Press.

Gabler, Neil. 1995. *Gossip, Power, and the Culture of Celebrity.* New York: Knopf.

Gates, Henry Louis, Jr., ed. 1986. *"Race," Writing, and Difference.* Chicago: Univ. of Chicago Press.

Works Cited

———. 1988. *Signifying Monkey: A Theory of Afro-American Literary Criticism.* New York: Oxford Univ. Press.

———. 1989. *Figures in Black.* New York: Oxford Univ. Press.

———. 1991. "Binary Opposition in Chapter One of *Narrative of the Life of Frederick Douglass an American Slave Written by Himself.*" In *Critical Essays on Frederick Douglass,* edited by William L. Andrews, 79–93. Boston: G. K. Hall.

Giddings, Paula. 1984. *Where and When I Enter: The Impact of Black Women on Race and Sex in America.* New York: Bantam.

Gilman, Sander L. 1985. "Black Bodies, White Bodies: Toward an Iconography of Female Sexuality in Late Nineteenth-Century Art, Medicine, and Literature." In *"Race," Writing, and Difference,* edited by Henry Louis Gates Jr., 223–61. Chicago: Univ. of Chicago Press.

Gilroy, Paul. 1992. "It's a Family Affair." In *Black Popular Culture,* edited by Gina Dent, 303–16. Seattle: Bay.

Gilyard, Keith. 1993. "Disappointed with Dr. Irish." *Carib News,* 9 June, 19.

Gladney, Margaret Rose. 1993. *How Am I to Be Heard? The Letters of Lillian Smith.* Chapel Hill: Univ. of North Carolina Press.

Gould, Stephen Jay. 1981. *The Mismeasure of Man.* New York: Norton.

Green, Mildred. 1983. *Black Women Composers.* Cambridge, Mass.: G. K. Hall.

Greene, Lorenzo. 1930. *The Negro Wage Earner.* Washington D. C.: Association for Study of Negro Life and History.

Gutman, Herbert G. 1987. "Schools for Freedom: The Post-Emancipation Origins of Afro-American Education." In *Power and Culture: Essays on the American Working Class,* edited by Ira Berlin, 260–97. New York: Pantheon.

Hall, Stuart. 1991. "Ethnicity, Identity, and Difference." *Radical America* (June): 10–16.

Hartman, Saidiya V. 1967. *Dahomey: An Ancient West African Kingdom.* Evanston, Ill.: Northwestern Univ. Press.

———. 1997. *Scenes of Subjection: Terror, Slavery, and Self-Making in Nineteenth-Century America.* New York: Oxford Univ. Press.

Hill, Errol, ed. 1980. *The Theater of Black Americans.* Englewood Cliffs, N.J.: Prentice Hall.

Hoberman, John. 1997. *Darwin's Athlete.* Boston: Houghton.

Holloway, Joseph, and Winifred Vass. 1993. *The African Heritage of American English.* Bloomington: Indiana Univ. Press.

Holm, John A. 1988. *Pidgins and Creoles: Theory and Structure.* Cambridge: Cambridge Univ. Press.

———. 1999. *Pidgins and Creoles: Reference Survey.* Cambridge: Cambridge Univ. Press.

Holt, Thomas. 1990. "'Knowledge Is Power': The Black Struggle for Literacy." In *The Right to Literacy,* edited by Andrea A. Lunsford, Helene Moglen, and James Slevin, 91–102. New York: Modern Language Association, 1990.

Honey, Maureen. 1984. *Creating Rosie the Riveter: Class, Gender, and Propaganda During World War II.* Amherst: Univ. of Massachusetts Press.

hooks, bell. 1990. *Yearning: Race, Gender, and Cultural Politics.* Boston: South End.

hooks, bell, and Cornell West. 1991. *Breaking Bread: Insurgent Black Intellectual Life.* Boston: South End.

Hornby, Richard. 1993. "Regional Theater Comes of Age." *Hudson Review* 46, no. 3: 529–36.

Houston, Jeanne Wakatsuki and James D. Houston. 1974. *Farewell to Manzanar.* New York: Bantam.

Hughes, Langston, and Arna Bontemps. 1958. *Book of Negro Folklore.* New York: Dodd, Mead.

Hurston, Zora Neale. 1935. *Mules and Men.* Bloomington: Indiana Univ. Press.

———. 1958. "High John De Conquer." In *Book of Negro Folklore,* edited by Langston Hughes and Arna Bontemps, 93–101. New York: Dodd, Mead.

———. 1981. *The Sanctified Church.* Berkeley: Turtle Island.

———. 1983. *Tell My Horse.* Berkeley: Turtle Island.

Hutchinson, Earl Ofari. 1994. *The Assassination of the Black Male Image.* Los Angeles: Middle Passage.

Ien, Seymour. 1993. "American English Experts Respond!" *Carib News,* 2 Feb., 6.

Inada, Lawson Fusao. 1971. *Before the War: Poems As They Happened.* New York: William Morrow.

———. 1992. *Legends from Camp.* Minneapolis: Coffee House Press.

Irish, George. 1993. "Caribbean English Specialists Respond." *Carib News,* 16 Feb., 38.

Jahn, Janheinz. 1968. *Neo-African Literature: A History of Black Writing.* New York: Grove.

Jarrett, Michael. 1999. *Drifting on a Read: Jazz as a Model for Writing.* Albany: SUNY Press.

Jay, Gregory S. 1990. "American Literature and the New Historicism: The Example of Frederick Douglass." *Boundary 2* 17: 211–42.

Jespersen, T. Christopher. 1996. *American Images of China 1931–1949.* Stanford: Stanford Univ. Press.

Johnson, Guy. 1929. *John Henry: Tracking Down a Negro Legend.* Chapel Hill: Univ. of North Carolina Press.

Johnson, James Weldon. 1969. "O Black and Unknown Bards." In *The Book of American Negro Poetry,* edited by James Weldon Johnson, 123–24. New York: Harcourt Brace.

Johnson, James Weldon, and J. Rosamond Johnson. 1985. *American Negro Spirituals.* New York: DeCapo.

Jones, Gayl. 1986. *Corregidora.* Boston: Beacon.

———. 1996. *The Healing.* Boston: Beacon.

Jones, Howard. 1975. "The Peculiar Institution and National Honor: The Case of the Creole Slave Revolt." *Civil War History* 21: 28–50.

Jones, Leroi. 1963. *Blues People: Negro Music in White America.* New York: Morrow Quill.

Jordan, Winthrop. 1968. *White over Black: American Attitudes Towards the Negro 1550–1812.* Chapel Hill: Univ. of North Carolina Press.

Kaufman, Joanne. 1993. "Anna Deavere Smith: Passion Plays." *Washington Post,* 25 Apr., G1, G11.

Keb' Mo', "Muddy Water." 1988. Liner notes for *Slow Down.* New York: Sony.

Keneally, Thomas. 1994. "Holocaust Was Archetype of Race Hate Everywhere." *Daily Progress,* 27 Feb., A7.

Kim, Elaine. 1982. *Asian American Literature: An Introduction to the Writings and Their Social Context*. Philadelphia: Temple Univ. Press.

———. 1990. "'Such Opposite Creatures': Men and Women in Asian American Literature." *Michigan Quarterly Review* 29: 68–93.

King, Richard H. 1980. *A Southern Renaissance*. New York: Oxford Univ. Press.

Lahr, John. 1993. "Under the Skin." *New Yorker* (28 June): 90–93.

Landeck, Beatrice. 1961. *Echoes of Africa*. New York: Van Rees.

Laris, Katie. 1993. "Fires in the Mirror: Crown Heights, Brooklyn, and Other Identities." *Theatre Journal* 45 (Mar.): 117–19.

Levine, Lawrence. 1977. *Black Culture and Black Consciousness*. New York: Oxford Univ. Press.

Lewis, Barbara. 1993. "The Circle of Confusion: A Conversation with Anna Deavere Smith." *Kenyon Review* 15, no. 4: 54–64.

Life. 1941a. "A Chinese Town: Little Market Towns Make China Unconquerable." 24 Nov., 85.

———. 1941b. "How to Tell Japs from the Chinese: Angry Citizens Victimize Allies with Emotional Outburst at Enemy." 22 Dec., 81.

———. 1941c. "*Life* Goes to a Wedding in the Soong Family: The Youngest of China's Great Family Takes a Wife in San Francisco Episcopal Cathedral." 12 Jan., 87.

———. 1941d. "Life in Chinese Town Fixed in Ancient Forms." 24 Nov., 86–87.

———. 1941e. "Modern Industrial Japan Needs Steel, Oil, and Machine Tools." 8 Dec., 36.

———. 1941f. "The Story of Christ in Chinese Art: Scholars at Peking Make a Christmas Portfolio for *Life*." 22 Dec., 40.

———. 1942a. "Army Trainees Learn Jujitsu: Loyal U.S. Japs Teach Them." 9 Feb., 70.

———. 1942b. "Chinese Pilots: At Arizona's Thunderbird Field They Are Taught Lessons of Aerial Combat." 4 May, 59.

———. 1942c. "Coast Japs Are Interned in Mountain Camp." 6 Apr., 15.

———. 1942d. "The First Japanese Mission to America." 23 Feb., 80.

———. 1942e. "Go: Japs Play Their National Game the Way They Fight Their Wars." 18 May, 92.

———. 1942f. "The Homestead: A Great Hotel Entertains Jap Diplomats as Patriotic Duty." 16 Feb., 68–69.

Lim, Shirley Geok-Lin. 1992a. "Assaying the Gold: Or Contesting the Ground of Asian American Literature." *New Literary History* 24: 147–69.

———. 1992b. "The Tradition of Chinese American Women's Life Stories: Thematics of Race and Gender in Jade Snow Wong's *Fifth Chinese Daughter* and Maxine Hong Kingston's *The Woman Warrior*." In *American Women's Autobiography: Fea(s)ts of Memory*, edited by Margo Culley, 252–67. Madison: Univ. of Wisconsin Press.

Lomax, Alan. 1960. *Folk Songs of North America*. New York: Doubleday.

Lomax, John, and Alan Lomax. 1947. *Folk Song U.S.A.* New York: Meredith.

Loveland, Anne C. 1986. *Lillian Smith: A Southerner Confronting the South*. Baton Rouge: Louisiana State Univ. Press.

Lovell, John. 1972. *Black Song: The Forge and the Flame*. New York: Macmillan.

Lowe, Lisa. 1991. "Heterogeneity, Hybridity, Multiplicity: Marking Asian American Differences." *Diaspora* 1: 24–44.

Maddox, Melvin. 1979. Liner notes for *Billie Holiday*. Giants of Jazz Series. Alexandria, Va.: Time Life.

Major, Clarence, ed. 1970. *Juba to Jive*. New York: Penguin.

Martin, Carol. 1993. "Anna Deavere Smith: The Word Becomes You." *Drama Review* 37, no. 4: 45–62.

Martin, Waldo E., Jr. 1984. *The Mind of Frederick Douglass*. Chapel Hill: Univ. of North Carolina Press.

———. 1990. "Images of Frederick Douglass in the Afro-American Mind: The Recent Black Freedom Struggle." In *Frederick Douglass: New Literary and Historical Essays*, edited by Eric J. Sundquist, 271–86. Cambridge: Cambridge Univ. Press.

Mbiti, John. 1975. *African Religions*. London: Heinemann.

Mehrez, Samia. 1991. "The Subversive Poetics of Radical Bilingualism: Postcolonial Francophone North African Literature." In *The Bounds of Race: Hegemony and Resistance*, edited by Dominick LaCapra, 255–77. Ithaca: Cornell Univ. Press.

Mitchell, Juliet, and Jacqueline Rose. 1982. "Introduction II." In *Feminine Sexuality: Jacques Lacan and the Ecole Freudienne*, edited by Juliet Mitchell and Jacqueline Rose, translated by Jacqueline Rose, 27–57. New York: Norton.

Monson, Ingrid. 1994. "Doubleness and Jazz Improvisation: Irony, Parody, and Ethnomusicology." *Critical Inquiry* 20, no. 2: 283–313.

Morgan, Edmund. 1975. *American Slavery, American Freedom*. New York: Knopf.

Morrison, Toni. 1972. *The Bluest Eye*. New York: Washington Square.

———. 1984. "Rootedness: The Ancestor as Foundation." In *Black Woman Writers (1950–1980)*, edited by Mari Evans, 341–46. New York: Anchor, Doubleday.

———. 1987. *Beloved*. New York: Knopf.

———. 1990. *playing in the dark: whiteness and the literary imagination*. Cambridge, Mass.: Harvard Univ. Press.

———, ed. 1992. *Race-ing Justice, En-Gendering Power: Essays on Anita Hill, Clarence Thomas, and the Construction of Social Reality*. New York: Pantheon.

Moy, James S. 1993. *Marginal Sights: Staging the Chinese in America*. Iowa City: Univ. of Iowa Press.

Newbury, Michael. 1994. "Eaten Alive: Slavery and Celebrity in Antebellum America." *ELH* 61: 159–88.

Newsweek. 1941. "No Mistake, Please." 22 Dec., 67.

Odum, Howard and Guy B. Johnson. 1926. *Negro Workaday Songs*. Chapel Hill: Univ. of North Carolina Press.

Oliver, Paul. 1970. *Savannah Syncopators: African Retentions in the Blues*. New York: Stein and Day.

Park, Mungo. 1800. *Travels in the Interior Districts of Africa*. New York: n.p.

Parrish, Lydia. 1965. *Slave Songs of the Georgia Sea Islands*. Hatsboro, Penn.: Folklore Associates.

Pease, Donald. 1994. *National Identities and Post-Americanist Narratives*. Durham, N.C.: Duke Univ. Press.

Quarles, Benjamin. 1964. *The Negro in the Making of America*. New York: Macmillan.

Ramsey, Frederic. 1960. *Been Here and Gone*. New Brunswick, N.J.: Rutgers Univ. Press.

Works Cited

———. 1977. *The American Slave*. Supplement Series 1. 12 vols. Westport, Conn.: Greenwood.

Reed, Ishmael. 1972. *Conjure*. Boston: Univ. of Massachusetts Press.

Reynolds, David S. 1996. *Walt Whitman's America: A Cultural Biography*. New York: Vintage-Random.

Rickydoc. n.d. "The Hoodoo Book of Flowers." Unpublished oral text, made available compliments of the author.

Rose, Tricia. 1994. *Black Noise: Rap Music and Black Culture in Contemporary America*. Hanover: Wesleyan Univ. Press.

Said, Edward. 1983. *The World, the Text, and the Critic*. Cambridge, Mass.: Harvard Univ. Press.

Sau-ling, Cynthia Wong. 1992. "Autobiography as Guided Chinatown Tour? Maxine Hong Kingston's *The Woman Warrior* and the Chinese-American Autobiographical Controversy." In *Multicultural Autobiography: American Lives*, edited by James Robert Payne, 248–79. Knoxville: Univ. of Tennessee Press.

Scarborough, Dorothy. 1925. *On the Trail of Negro Folk Songs*. Cambridge, Mass.: Harvard Univ. Press.

Schechner, Richard. 1993. "Anna Deavere Smith: Acting as Incorporation." *Drama Review* 37, no. 4: 63–64.

Sekora, John. 1994. "'Mr. Editor, If You Please': Frederick Douglass, *My Bondage and My Freedom*, and the End of the Abolitionist Imprint." *Callaloo* 17: 608–26.

Silverman, Jerry. 1968. *Folk Blues*. New York: Oak.

Simon, Dawne E. V. 1992. "29 Characters in Search of Community." *Ms.* 3 (Sept.–Oct.): 67.

Smith, Anna Deavere. 1993. *Fires in the Mirror: Crown Heights, Brooklyn, and Other Identities*. New York: Anchor.

———. 1994. *Twilight: Los Angeles, 1992*. New York: Anchor.

Smith, Lillian. 1943. "Two Men and a Bargain." *South Today* 7, no. 1: 6–10.

———. 1944. *Strange Fruit*. New York: Reynal and Hitchcock.

———. 1961. *Killers of the Dream*. 1949. Reprint. New York: Norton.

Smith, Theophus H. 1994. *Conjuring Culture*. New York: Oxford Univ. Press.

Snead, James. 1984. "Repetition as a Figure of Black Culture." In *Black Literature and Literary Theory*, edited by Henry Louis Gates Jr., 59–80. New York: Routledge.

———. 1994. *White Screens: Black Images*. New York: Routledge.

Sone, Monica. 1979. *Nisei Daughter*. Seattle: Univ. of Washington Press.

Sontag, Deborah. 1992. "Caribbean Pupils' English Seems Barrier, Not Bridge." *New York Times,* 28 Nov., 1, 22.

Sosna, Morton. 1977. *In Search of Silent South*. New York: Columbia Univ. Press.

Southern, Eileen. 1965. *Readings in Black American Music*. New York: Norton.

———. 1971. *The Music of Black Americans*. New York: Norton.

Spillers, Hortense. 1987. "Mama's Baby, Papa's Maybe: An American Grammar Book." *Diacritics* 17, no. 2: 65–81.

Stanislavski, Constantin. 1958. *Stanislavski's Legacy: A Collection of Comments on a Variety of Aspects of an Actor's Art and Life*. Edited and translated by Elizabeth Reynolds Hapgood. New York: Theater Arts.

Stepto, Robert B. 1986. "Sharing the Thunder: The Literary Exchanges of Harriet Beecher Stowe, Henry Bibb, and Frederick Douglass." In *New Essays on Uncle Tom's Cabin*, edited by Eric Sundquist, 135–53. Cambridge: Cambridge Univ. Press.

————. 1991. "Storytelling in Early Afro-American Fiction: Frederick Douglass's *The Heroic Slave.*" In *Critical Essays on Frederick Douglass,* edited by William L. Andrews, 108–19. Boston: G. K. Hall.

Stuckey, Sterling. 1987. *Slave Culture.* New York: Oxford Univ. Press.

Sundquist, Eric J. 1991. "Fredrick Douglass: Literacy and Paternity." In *Critical Essays on Fredrick Douglass,* edited by William L. Andrews, 120–32. Boston: G. K. Hall.

Swee, Kathleen Loh, and Kristoffer F. Paulson. 1982. "The Divided Voice of Chinese-American Narration: Jade Snow Wong's *Fifth Chinese Daughter.*" *MELUS* 9: 53–59.

Takaki, Ronald T. 1979. *Iron Cages: Race and Culture in Nineteenth-Century America.* New York: Knopf.

————. 1990. *Strangers from a Different Shore: A History of Asian Americans.* New York: Penguin.

Thompson, Robert Farris. 1974. *African Art in Motion.* Berkeley: Univ. of California Press.

————. 1980. "An Aesthetic of Cool: West African Dance." In *The Theater of Black Americans,* edited by Errol Hill, 99–112. Englewood Cliffs, N.J.: Prentice Hall.

————. 1983. *Flash of the Spirit: Afro-American Arts and Philosophy.* New York: Random House.

Time. 1941. "How to Tell Your Friends from the Japs." 22 Dec., 33.

Trilling, Diana. 1944. "Fiction in Review." *The Nation,* 18 March, 342.

Trudgill, Peter. 1974. *Sociolinguistics: An Introduction.* Harmondsworth: Penguin.

Turner, Lorenzo. 1949. *Africanisms in the Gullah Dialect.* Chicago: Univ. of Chicago Press.

Turner, Patricia A. 1993. *I Heard It Through the Grapevine: Rumor in African-American Culture.* Berkeley: Univ. of California Press.

Turner, Victor. 1974. *Dramas, Fields, and Metaphors: Symbolic Action in Human Society.* Ithaca: Cornell Univ. Press.

U.S. Senate. 1842. 27 Cong., 2d sess., 19 Jan. II, no. 51, 1–46.

Van Leer, David. 1990. "The Anxiety of Ethnicity in Douglass's *Narrative.*" In *Frederick Douglass: New Literary and Historical Essays,* edited by Eric J. Sundquist, 118–40. Cambridge: Cambridge Univ. Press.

Wald, Gayle. 1994. "Anna Deavere Smith's Voices at Twilight." *Postmodern Culture* 2: 1–17.

Walker, Peter F. 1978. *Moral Choices: Memory, Desire and Imagination in Nineteenth-Century American Abolition.* Baton Rouge: Louisiana State Univ. Press.

Washington Post. 1995. "The Delany Sisters, Having Their Day." 14 May: G1, G4.

White, John. 1987. *Billie Holliday: Her Life and Times.* London: Omnibus.

Williams, John A. 1985. *The Man Who Cried I Am.* 1967. Reprint. New York: Thunder's Mouth.

Wilson, August. 1998. "Preface to Three Plays." In *The Jazz Cadence of American Culture,* edited by Robert G. O'Meally, 562–69. New York: Columbia Univ. Press.

Wilson, Harriet E. 1983. *Our Nig; or, Sketches from the Life of a Free Black.* New York: Random House.

Wilson, William Julius. 1996. "Work." *New York Times Magazine,* 18 Aug., 26+.

Winks, Robin. 1969. General Introduction to *Four Fugitive Slave Narratives.* Edited by Robin Winks. Reading, Mass.: Addison Wesley.

Works Cited

Wong, Jade Snow. 1989. *Fifth Chinese Daughter.* 1950. Reprint. Seattle: Univ. of Washington Press.

Wood, Peter. 1974. *Black Majority.* New York: Knopf.

Work, John. *American Negro Song.* New York: Crown, 1940.

Wright, Richard. 1940. *Native Son.* New York: Harper.

Yamamoto, Hisaye. 1988. "Wilshire Bus." 1950. Reprinted in *Seventeen Syllables and Other Stories.* Latham, N.Y.: Kitchen Table.

Yarborough, Richard. 1990. "Race, Violence, and Manhood: The Masculine Ideal in Frederick Douglass's *The Heroic Slave.*" In *Frederick Douglass: New Literary and Historical Essays,* edited by Eric J. Sundquist, 166–88. Cambridge: Cambridge Univ. Press.

Yogi, Stan. 1989. "Legacies Revealed: Uncovering Buried Plots in the Stories of Hisaye Yamamoto." *Studies in American Fiction* 17: 169–81.

Ziolkowski, Thad. 1991. "Antitheses: The Dialectic of Violence and Literacy in Frederick Douglass's *Narrative* of 1845." In *Critical Essays on Frederick Douglass,* edited by William L. Andrews, 148–65. Boston: G. K. Hall.

Žižek, Slavoj. 1997. *The Žižek Reader.* Edited by Elizabeth Wright and Edmond Wright. Oxford: Blackwell.

Index

affirmative action, 88

African American culture, 6–10, 175; double consciousness in, 180, 238–40, 242–44; expression of voice in, 198–206, 239–43; and literacy,198–99, 203–6; and western culture, 238–39. *See also* African American literature; African American oral tradition

African American labor: on railroads, 6–7, 57–62, 70; and deaths, 61, 64–71; and U.S. economy, 62

African American literature: art and politics in, 195–202, 238–44, 248–51; and blues-based tradition, 238–51; and cultural custodianship, 239, 243–51; as resistance, 198–202, 238–51. *See also* African American oral tradition; Smith, Anna Deavere

African American manhood, 54, 60–62, 68, 70, 73–76. *See also* African American labor

African American oral tradition: call and response in, 8, 58–59, 64, 152, 178, 240; and cultural memory, 63–72, 74, 238; incantation in, 240; liminality in, 64, 66–71, 74–75, 238–40, 241; mobility and, 70–72; as resistance, 9, 71–74, 242–45; rhythms in, 64, 65, 64n., 65n.; rhythms and politics in, 134–38, 152; and the sacred, 67–69, 178–80, 238–39, 241, 244–48; and U.S. history, 63–65, 68, 241, 242–48, 250–51. *See also* African American literature; blues; jazz; performativity

African American womanhood, 72–73

African American work songs, 6–7, 59n., 60n. *See also* John Henry

African diasporic cultures, 7, 66–71, 74–76, 63n., 64n., 65n., 66n., 67n., 68n.; the griot in, 244; and language, 204–5. Legba in, 61n., 238, 248; music in, 139n. *See also* African American oral tradition

Aiiieeeee!, 135, 207, 211

Allen, Lewis, 99n. *See also* "Strange Fruit"

Amistad, 196

Armstrong, Lewis, 137

Asian American identities: and gender, 80–83; differences within, 211–12, 224–29; 214n.

Asian American literature, 127, 129, 132–33, 134–36; debates about, 207, 232; and gender, 127; narratives of assimilation in, 149, 209–11, 222–24, 227–28, 229–31, 226n.;

Asian Americans: and racial identifications, 211–14, 224–28; and resistance, 134–36, 140–42, 149–52. *See also* Inada, Lawson; racist discourse;

Asian identities: differences within, 128, 129, 131–32; and gender, 80–83, 207, 209–11, 221

Astorga, Nora, 85

Baker, Houston, 202

Baldwin, James, 16, 85, 277

Baraka, Amiri (LeRoi Jones), 137, 234, 242

Bernstein, A. M., 167

Big Mo, 171

bilingualism, 205

Black Arts movement, 249

black English, 204–6, 243

black nationalism, 71

Black Power movement, 249

blues, 10, 57, 62, 64n., 239, 244, 248; *See also* African American oral tradition; African American literature

Buck, Paul, 105

Caribbean American identities, 256–67

Carby Hazel, 114, 118

Cato, Carmel, 173–74

Cato, Gavin, 164, 169

Chesnutt, Charles, 9, works by: *The Conjure Woman*, 240, 242, 245; "Dave's Neckliss," 198–99

Civil Rights movement, 5, 249

Clinton, Catherine, 115

Coltrane, John, 152

cross racial communities, 2–4, 84–92,

Index

50–53, 109–12, 116–17, 121, 142, 179. *See also* racism.
rap music, 170–71, 201–2, 247
Reed, Ishmael, 239, 246, 251–54
resistance (to racism), 2, 6–7; blues-based traditions as, 10, 238–40, 242–43, 245–51; conversations as, 1–3, 196; counternarratives as, 9, 195–206; in daily life, 277–79; and difference, 2, 88–89, 91–92; and European Americans, 85–91, and feminism, 7, 84–92; international, 85–86, 91–92; jazz aesthetics as, 8, 134–52; and language, 2–4, 10–11; liberation theater and, 8–9, 158–63, 165–77; and political action, 3–4, 7, 86–89, 91, 277–78; and multiracial institutions, 86, 88; poetry as, 134–54; rumor as, 196–200; self-definition as, 195–96, 200, and work songs, 71–74
Rose, Jacqueline, 109, 112–13
Rose, Tricia, 202
Rosenbaum, Yankel, 164, 169

Said, Edward, 177–78
segregation, 106–8, 116–17, 121–22
Shange, Ntozake, 169–70
slave narratives, 35, 50–51
slave revolts, 45–47, 71, 74
slavery: and cultural memory, 63; and identity construction, 165, 171, 173; and ideology, 5; and language, 195–96; Northern complicity with, 43–46; resistance to, 40–42, 45–47, 50, 72; and song, 70
slave trade, 45–46, 70
Smith, Anna Deavere: American character in, 165, 168; and audience, 160, 161–62, 175–76, 178–81; biography of, 161; and communitas, 163, 178; and ethnic identities, 164–65, 169–73; performativity in, 161–63, 165–67, 169, 175–79; and respect for difference, 167–69, 175–76, 179, 181; social drama in, 158–59, 161–74; spoken language in,160, 166–67, 169–70, 172–75; theory and method of theater in, 159–63, 165–69, 171–72; and transformation, 161, 178–79, 182; works by: *Fires in the Mirror*, 163–65, 167, *On The Road*, 160–62, Twilight, 161. *See also* African American oral tradition; cultural borderlands
Smith, Bessie, 239

Smith, Lillian, 7, 99–123; and Congress of Racial Equality, 106; and desegregation, 104–5n.; as lesbian, 103; and postmodernism, 108; on psychology of racism, 103–5; and *South Today*, 101, 106; works by: *Julia*, 101n.; *Killers of the Dream*, 108, 113, 115, 116, 119, 121; *Strange Fruit*, 100–104, 107, 110–21; "Two Men and a Bargain," 101. *See also* racist discourse
Snelling Paula, 101, 106
"Strange Fruit," 99–101, 100n. *See also* Holiday, Billie; Allen, Lewis

2 Live Crew, 202
Terkel, Studs, 161
Time magazine and orientalism, 214–16
Toomer, Jean, 240, 243
Trilling, Diana, 100
Turner, Victor, 163, 165

U.S. nationalism (WWII): and Asian American identity formations, 222, 226–27; and Asian identity formations, 215–17; and individualism, 108–9; and Japanese American internment, 134–36, 140–41, 143, 149–52; jazz aesthetics as response to, 134, 136–37, 147, 152–54

Walker, Alice, 238
Waring, J. Waties, 106
Washington, Madison, 44–45
West, Cornell, 3, 92, 182
whiteness. *See* racist discourse
Wideman, John Edgar, 239
Williams, John A., 197
Wilmot Proviso, 34
Wilson, August, 239–40, 243
Wilson, Harriet, 9, 198
Wong, Jade Snow: and Asian racial identity formations, 211–14; critical debates about, 207–9, 220–22, and *Fifth Chinese Daughter*, 207–14, 219–21, 232; treatment of race and gender in, 220–22
Woods, Donald Walter, 85
Wright, Richard, 122n., 121

Yamamoto, Hisaye, works by: "17 Syllables," 127, 129, 132; "Wilshire Bus," 9, 208–9, 222–32, 213n., 226n.
Yone, Wendy Law, 127
Young, Lester, 134, 137

Acknowledgments

This work was supported in part by a grant from The City University of New York, College of Staten Island Research Stipend Award.

Permission to quote or to reprint in whole or in part from the following publishers and authors' estates is gratefully acknowledged.

"Blindsided": Reprinted from *Volatile* © 1999 by Kimiko Hahn by permission of Hanging Loose Press. "Revolutions": Reprinted from *Earshot* © 1992 by Kimiko Hahn, by permission of Hanging Loose Press.

Lillian Smith's letter to Frank Taylor, June, 1944. Harcourt Brace, publisher. From Margaret Rose Gladney. *How Am I to Be Heard? Letters of Lillian Smith.* 1993. University of North Carolina Press. Quoted in McKay Jenkins, "Metaphors of Race and Psychological Damage in the 1940s American South: The Writings of Lillian Smith."

HarperCollins: "Trackworker's Lining Song" from *Mules and Men* by Zora Neale Hurston. Copyright © 1935 by Zora Neale Hurston. Copyright © renewed 1963 by John C. Hurston and Joel Hurston. Reprinted by permission of HarperCollins Publishers, Inc. Reprinted in Gale Patricia Jackson, "'If He Asks You Was I Running You Tell Him I Was Flying, If He Asks You Was I Laughing You Tell Him I Was Crying': Reading John Henry as American History 1870."

"Strange Fruit"—Lewis Allan © 1939 (renewed) by Music Sales Corporation. All rights outside the United States controlled by Edward B. Marks Music Company. Used by permission. All rights reserved. Reprinted in McKay Jenkins, "Metaphors of Race and Psychological Damage in the 1940s American South: The Writings of Lillian Smith."

The New Yorker: Quotations from "Under the Skin" by John Lahr. Originally published in *The New Yorker,* 28 June, 1993: 90–93. Quoted in Kimberly Rae Connor. "Negotiating the Differences: Anna Deavere Smith and Liberation Theater."

New York Times: Quotations from "They Cried until They Could Not See," by Patrick Cooke, © 1991 by the *New York Times* Co. Reprinted by permission. Quoted in Kimiko Hahn, "Blindsided."

Quotations excerpted from Carol Martin, "Interview with Anna Deavere Smith: The Word Becomes You," TDR/The Drama Review, 37:4 (T140) Winter, 1993, pp. 45, 46, 48, 50–53, 55–57, 59. Copyright © 1993 by New York University and the Massachusetts Institute of Technology. Quoted in Kimberly Rae Connor. "Negotiating the Differences: Anna Deavere Smith and Liberation Theater."

Persea Press "White" by Henderson-Holmes originally appeared as part of the poem "'C'ing in Colors," in *Living on the Margins: Women Writers on Breast Cancer,* edited by Hilda Raz. Copyright © 1999 by Safiya Henderson-Holmes. Reprinted by permission of Persea Books, Inc., New York.

Racing and (E)Racing Language: Living with the Color of Our Words was designed and composed in 9/14 Stone Serif by Kachergis Book Design of Pittsboro, North Carolina; printed by offset on 55-pound Glatfelter Supple Opaque by Thomson-Shore of Dexter, Michigan; published by Syracuse University Press, Syracuse, New York 13244-5160.